NATIONAL GEOGRAPHIC
TRAVELER
London

NATIONAL GEOGRAPHIC

TRAVELER
London

Louise Nicholson

Contents

How to use this guide 6–7 About the author 8
London areas 45–218 Excursions 219–234 Travelwise 235–64
Index 265–69 Illustrations credits 270

Page 1: Tower Bridge
Pages 2–3: St. Paul's
Cathedral and the
Embankment at night
Left: The Household
Cavalry band in
state dress

How to use this guide

See back flap for keys to text and map symbols

The *National Geographic Traveler* brings you the best of London in text, pictures, and maps. Divided into three sections, the guide begins with an overview of history and culture. Following are 12 area chapters with featured sites chosen by the author for their particular interest and treated in depth. Each chapter opens with its own contents list for easy reference. A final chapter suggests possible excursions from London.

A pictorial map introduces each area of the city, highlighting the featured sites and locating other places of interest. Walks, plotted on their own maps, suggest routes for discovering the most about an area. Features and sidebars offer intriguing detail on history, culture, or contemporary life.

The final section, Travelwise, lists essential information for the traveler—pre-trip planning, getting around, communications, money matters, and emergencies—plus a selection of hotels and restaurants arranged by area, shops, and entertainment possibilities.

To the best of our knowledge, site information is accurate as of the press date. However, it is advisable to call ahead or visit the website whenever possible.

Color coding

58

Each area of the city is color coded for easy reference. Find the area you want on the map on the front flap, and look for the color flash at the top of the pages of the relevant chapter. Information in **Travelwise** is also color coded to each area.

Museum of London

🅰 Map p. 56

✉ London Wall, EC2

☎ 7600 3699.
Information: 7600 0807

www.museumof london.org.uk

🚇 Tube: Barbican, St. Paul's, Moorgate, Bank

Visitor information

Practical information is given in the side column by each major site (see key to symbols on back flap). The map reference gives the page number where the site is shown on a map. Further details include the site's address, telephone number, website, days closed, entrance fee (if any) ranging from $ (under $4) to $$$$$ (over $25), and the nearest tube stop. Visitor information for smaller sites is listed in parentheses within the text.

TRAVELWISE

Color-coded area name
Category name
Hotel name & price range
Address, telephone & fax numbers, website
Brief description of hotel
Hotel facilities & credit card details
Category name
Restaurant name & price range
Address & telephone number
Brief description of restaurant
Restaurant facilities & credit card details

Hotel & restaurant prices

An explanation of the price ranges used in entries is given in the Hotels & Restaurants section beginning on p. 241.

AREA MAPS

- A locator map accompanies each area map and shows the location of that area in the city.

Important featured sites

Point of interest

WALKING TOURS

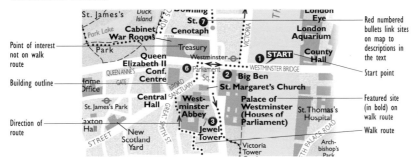

Point of interest not on walk route

Building outline

Direction of route

Red numbered bullets link sites on map to descriptions in the text

Start point

Featured site (in bold) on walk route

Walk route

- An information box gives the starting and ending points, time and length of walk, and places not to miss along the route.
- Where two walks are marked on the map, the second route is shown in orange.

EXCURSION MAPS

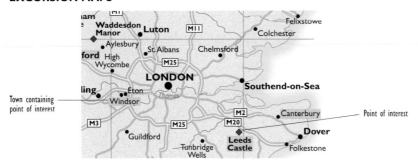

Town containing point of interest

Point of interest

- Towns and cities described in the Excursions chapter (pp. 219–34) are highlighted in yellow on the map. Other suggested places to visit are also highlighted and are shown with a red diamond symbol.

NATIONAL GEOGRAPHIC

TRAVELER

London

About the author

Louise Nicholson lived in London for 25 years and continues to find it the world's most diverse and exciting city, with always something new to discover. A trained art historian, she has worked in conservation, campaigning for London buildings; in the art market, at the auctioneers Christie's; and since 1985 has combined journalism with writing 25 books, eight of them about London. Her awards include the London Tourist Board's for the best book about London published in the 1980s. Since 2001 she has lived in New York, gaining useful insights into her home city on regular return visits.

History
& culture

Guard at Whitehall

London today

LONDON IS A LIVING AND CONSTANTLY CHANGING CITY. SOME CITIES depend on impressive historic buildings for their greatness, others on being the center of government or culture or finance; still others are exciting because they are new. What makes London unique is that it is all of these in one. It is simply the most culturally rich, stimulating, and dynamic city in the world.

There is, delightfully, always too much to do, to see, to visit, and to explore. First-time visitors almost always return to revisit favorite haunts or to explore a little bit more. Each time they discover London is richer than they had realized. So they come again and again and again. In fact, about 30 million people visit each year.

London's 7 million residents find this great city just as exciting. More than 30 percent were born elsewhere. Of the remainder, many are only second- or third-generation immigrants. Where have they come from? Some have merely fulfilled a childhood dream of moving from another part of Britain to the capital. Some have come from much farther afield, choosing to leave homelands such as India, Pakistan, and the Caribbean when the British Empire ended after World War II. Others have arrived fleeing political unrest in China, Cyprus, Italy, Kenya, or Uganda. Still others fled religious persecution—100,000 Jews arrived in London after the pogroms in Russia and Europe at the end of the 19th century, and more came during World War II. Thus, London is truly cosmopolitan. Almost 200 languages are spoken. English may be predominant, but you might hear Chinese dialects, Gujarati, Urdu, Punjabi, Bengali, Turkish, Arabic, Italian, and Spanish on any street corner.

Arriving in this pulsating mass for the first time takes one's breath away. Nowhere else offers such quality in such quantity. Take one example, art. Most people know in advance that they want to visit the British Museum or the Victoria & Albert Museum, but few are aware that there are some 300 other museums to choose from—plus myriad commercial art galleries that make London the world center of the art trade. Take another example, the theater. London's theater is legendary, and visitors naturally want to sample it. But they are often surprised, even baffled, that they have to choose between more than 100 theaters staging plays or musicals at any one time; and some of the best shows may be in theaters well away from the main theater district, the West End.

The museums and theaters are often superb buildings themselves, each telling a tiny part of London's history. Indeed, the quality of London's historic buildings may not surprise the visitor, but the quantity—almost 17,000 protected buildings tucked into every corner of this huge, sprawling city—most certainly does. For instance, Buckingham Palace is not the only royal palace; you can visit six others including the palaces of Westminster, Hampton Court, and Kensington.

These palaces are spread out right across the huge expanse of London, so that Hampton Court Palace in the west is about 18 miles from Greenwich Palace in the east. Even in the center, Big Ben is 2.5 miles, or 20 minutes on the Tube, from St. Paul's Cathedral.

Grasping an idea of the general layout of this vast city is the first challenge for any visitor. The core of London is spread along the north bank of the twisting Thames River, the capital's backbone. The oldest part, confusingly known as the City, is the tightly packed financial hub, where until recently international merchants looked out over the great port that stretched downstream from here eastward. The City's sleek buildings, soaring around the dome of St. Paul's and 100 other City churches, are the destination for many of the million or so sharp-suited commuters who, from Monday to Friday, flood into London by train or car. Other City workers

The soldiers who symbolically protect the Queen and the royal palaces are selected from the seven Guards regiments.

cross the capital on the Tube (as the Underground train system is commonly called) or squeeze into red double-decker buses.

Outside the City's east wall stand the riverside Tower of London and Tower Bridge. Behind stretches the East End, where the story of London's immigrants and dockworkers unfolds in the streets of Whitechapel and Spitalfields—French Huguenot silk-weavers' fine houses, Jewish synagogues, the Cockney traders of Petticoat Lane market, and the spice-scented streets where many Bengalis have recently moved in. Here, too, lives Europe's greatest concentration of artists, designers, and musicians, many using old warehouses as studios. East of the Tower, 11 miles of docks left silent when the port moved to Tilbury have been revived. Known as the Docklands, the area has its own elevated Docklands Light Railway, some daring new buildings, and extensive sports facilities. From here it is easy to reach two interesting areas on

The London Eye—the world's largest observation wheel—opened in 2000 to mark the millennium.

the South Bank: ancient Greenwich Palace and its surrounding town, and newly revived Greenwich Peninsula with its landmark Millennium Dome.

Hard by the City's north wall lies Clerkenwell with its monastic remains, rising to Islington with its elegant houses, thriving fringe theaters, and a plethora of restaurants.

West of the City lies Westminster, London's political and royal center. Here, north of Westminster Bridge, stand the Houses of Parliament, Westminster Abbey, and the government's sprawling Whitehall offices. Buckingham Palace and St. James's Palace are nearby, surrounded by St. James's and Green Parks. This is where smart residential London first grew up, and the area has retained its status—St. James's and Mayfair contain some

of London's most stylish shops, art galleries, and restaurants, as well as gentlemen's clubs, both Christie's and Sotheby's auction houses, and deluxe hotels such as the Ritz. London continues westward into the elegant residential and shopping districts of Belgravia, Knightsbridge, and Chelsea. Still farther west lie Kensington, Holland Park, and South Kensington, home to the Science, Natural History, and Victoria & Albert Museums. In these areas look for building facades that often have decorated doorways,

Street entertainers perform outside St. Paul's Church in Covent Garden Piazza, a pedestrian square lined with cafés, shops, and museums.

terra-cotta friezes, or blue plaques noting that a person of historical importance lived at that address. Farther west lie former aristocrats' country mansions, now swallowed up by the suburbs: Osterley, Syon House, Kew Palace and Gardens, and finally Hampton Court Palace.

The part of London between the City and Westminster has a distinct character. On the north bank of the Thames, the old lanes and squares of Holborn, Bloomsbury, Covent Garden, and Soho contain the West End theaters and a rich concentration of museums and restaurants. Meanwhile, along the south bank of the Thames, a strip of entertainment centers running from Tower to Westminster Bridges includes the Royal National Theatre and Tate Modern.

London's legal Inns of Court extend through Holborn from Gray's Inn to riverside Inner and Middle Temple. Leafy Bloomsbury squares are the setting for the British Museum, much of University of London, and a string of specialist museums stretching down to Covent Garden, a center for theaters, restaurants, shops, and street entertainment. To the west of Covent Garden there is Trafalgar Square, where the National Gallery looks down over the fountains and the pigeons to Whitehall

Trafalgar Square retains its central place in visitors' London.

and St. James's. A few minutes' walk north from Trafalgar Square, Leicester Square—a focal point on the night scene—marks the start of Soho. Its southern part is London's Chinatown; its northern part is a mixture of bars, restaurants, and Continental food shops. Theater-lined Shaftesbury Avenue slashes through Soho to Piccadilly Circus. Regent Street, lined with upmarket shops, sweeps elegantly north from here, along Mayfair's eastern edge and up toward Regent's Park. Beyond lie the residential areas of St. John's Wood, hilltop Hampstead, and Highgate.

So, each area of London has its own special character, its own history, its own rhythm. Despite this variety, Londoners and visitors need to find peace. While the financial markets buzz, there are many ways to relax.

Since the food revolution, London can claim to have become the world's food capital. With almost 6,000 restaurants to choose from, you can see if this is true. The 5,000 or so pubs and bars, many in old buildings or in pretty locations along the river, also serve food and some have music and even theaters.

If relaxation means shopping, try Oxford Street, the longest retail street in Europe. London's two greatest department stores are Selfridges, on Oxford Street, and Harrods in Knightsbridge. Some 350 street markets include Portobello Road's antiques shops and stalls. If relaxation means a walk in a park, make the most of London's parkland. If it means music, you can enjoy the sweet notes of more than 1,000 concerts a week taking place in concert halls, music colleges, churches, and museums.

Despite this banquet of choice, visitors to London can sometimes find themselves choked by crowds of other visitors, unable to taste the essence of the city they have come to visit. If this happens, it is best to leave the lines at Madame Tussaud's or the Tower of London behind, and hop on a bus or take the Underground to one of London's more colorful areas. Try Soho or Islington, or take a walk along the south bank of the Thames from Westminster to Tower Bridge.

THE MAKING OF LONDON

The twisting, slow-flowing Thames, Britain's longest river, was for centuries London's nerve center. Roman London stood on its north bank, alongside its vital port. Later, under the Tudors, the river, busy with the comings and goings of merchant and naval ships, would deliver international power to London. Vast wealth flowed in, and London became the rich capital of what would grow to be a world-encircling empire. A thousand years after the Romans arrived, Edward the Confessor established his new riverside palace and monastery upstream to the west, on the marshes of Westminster, and so London's second city was born. William the Conqueror consolidated Westminster's position as the royal, political, and religious capital of his new land, while later sovereigns enjoyed a string of palaces built on the banks of the Thames from Hampton Court to Greenwich.

London grew fast. By 1700 its population was 575,000, making it the largest and fastest-growing city in Western Europe. Soon London was 20 times the size of the next biggest English city and contained one-tenth of England's population. The city expanded westward, northward, and, in the 19th century, southward over new river bridges, and eastward around the docks. By the 1930s, its population peaked at 10 million.

Until comparatively recently, it was up the Thames that most immigrants arrived, seeking their fortune or a refuge from persecution. Today, despite the port's move to Tilbury, the river is still a key factor in London's development. Docklands has been the largest urban renewal site in Europe, and historic riverside buildings such as the Tower of London and the Houses of Parliament are joined by new ones, including Embankment Place, and the world's largest dome at Greenwich Peninsula.

PARKS

Londoners seeking escape on weekends do not need to leave their city. Parks of all kinds spangle the capital, about 1,700 in all. They range from the walled Chelsea Physic Garden (see p. 169) and the handkerchief-size City churchyards (see p. 58) to the great expanses of Richmond Park (see p. 178) and the formal Royal Botanic Gardens (see p. 180). Indeed, nearly 11 percent of Greater London is parkland, a total of 70 square miles.

It was the monarchs who first protected large open spaces for their hunting. Greedy developers had to work around these personal, royal possessions. Today, these hunting grounds survive as the magnificent royal parks (see p. 89). Hyde Park, formerly considered the fashionable center of London, has fine landscaping and plenty of activity available. The childhood serenity of neighboring Kensington Park, with its palace backdrop, is quite different. Regent's Park retains the grandeur of its original aristocratic country estate plan. St. James's Park, close to Buckingham Palace, is the one for pageantry, and nearby Green Park offers tranquility and shady trees. In the far west of London, Richmond, the largest royal park, has wonderful views from its hills, while Bushy Park, with its grand chestnut avenue and deer, shares its history with Hampton Court Palace. In the east, Greenwich Park sweeps up from gleaming Queen's House to provide the finest panoramic viewpoint of London.

London's other green spaces have evolved in different ways. Hampstead Heath (see p. 142) was once common grazing ground. Victoria Park and Battersea Park, opened in 1846 and 1858 respectively, were created to improve local conditions. The City of London Corporation's land includes Highgate Wood, to be kept open in perpetuity for the benefit of City dwellers. Peace and quiet can be found in cemeteries and churchyards—St. Dunstan-in-the-East (see p. 64), a secret garden within a ruined church, is especially magical. And that London peculiarity, the garden square, makes many lush oases in the city hubbub.

WILDLIFE & NATURE

London not only supports a population of around 7 million people, it is a nature sanctuary

whose diversity and importance are unrivaled by those of any other capital. London bees produce a good honey, and Richmond Park's 200 species of beetle have helped make it a Site of Special Scientific Interest.

Great, thick forests once encircled London, before they were pushed back for agriculture and grazing. Vestiges include the spinneys of Highgate Woods and Holland Park, and some of the ancient oaks of Richmond Park. As London grew, so the royal parks took on a new importance for wildlife. The 18th-century Enlightenment and Picturesque movements awakened Londoners to nature's beauties, both tamed and untamed. It was at this time that Kew's Royal Botanic Gardens (see p. 180) were planted.

In the 19th century, the Victorians replaced many traditional limes, elms, and chestnuts with plane trees, which can thrive in polluted air and self-clean by shedding their bark. They also controlled their parkland vistas by

Londoners relax, picnic, and play in St. James's Park, just one of London's many green spaces.

introducing evergreen oaks, copper beeches, false acacias, arbutus, and trees of heaven.

This may be nature directed by man, but there are other parts of London that are truly wild, notably neglected cemeteries where hedgehogs, weasels, frogs, and foxes have resettled. And birds—redstarts, kestrels, and herons—are returning to London, to join the pigeons, sparrows, and seagulls.

Take a look at three corners of London. In St. James's Park weeping willows, fig trees, and London planes line the banks of the lake near Duck Island. In Berkeley Square, the massive plane trees were planted in 1780. In Regent's Park's Queen Mary's Rose Garden, which was laid out in 1938, the roses, azaleas, and pond-side irises and flags create a perfumed heaven, seemingly far from the city. ∎

History of London

IT IS PEOPLE WHO HAVE, OVER THE CENTURIES, SHAPED THE LONDON WE know today. Some have left a tangible legacy: The Romans left their Temple of Mithras, Samuel Pepys his vivid diary, and William Hogarth his caricatures of 18th-century life. Heroes are commemorated with statues: Sir Winston Churchill stands in Parliament Square. Some Londoners are household names: Sir Christopher Wren, Dr. Johnson. Others deserve to be better known, such as Joseph Bazalgette, the engineer whose land reclamation scheme transformed 19th-century London. However, the star players have been those in control of the capital's two cities: In the financial City of London they include Thomas Gresham, founder of the Royal Exchange; in the royal and political City of Westminster they range from Edward the Confessor to Margaret Thatcher. London today is the city created by all those who have taken part in its 2,000-year history.

ROMAN LONDON

London might have been born in 54 B.C. when Julius Caesar and his Roman army attacked the Catuvellauni forces who held two hills beside the Thames, at the point where it stopped being tidal and could easily be forded. But Caesar returned to Gaul (France). It was under Emperor Claudius, in A.D. 43, that the Romans came back and founded Londinium port on the same spot. They built the first London Bridge, linking their ports on the southeast coast (now Kent) to Camulodunum (Colchester), capital of their British province.

After a revolt of the British tribes, led by Queen Boudicca of the Iceni, who burned the city down in A.D. 61, the Romans made Londinium their capital. A tall, thick wall protected its 30,000 to 60,000 inhabitants. Public buildings included baths, temples, gardens, a basilica, and a forum. But in 410, mirroring Rome's decline, Roman troops left London.

SAXONS & VIKINGS

After the Romans left, London dwindled. However, its location ensured that trade continued—and its wealth attracted invaders. Over the next three centuries, Angles and Saxons from northwest Germany gradually established small kingdoms in England—Kent, Mercia, Wessex, and others. Saxon London, called Lundenwic, was sited along the Strand. Through the sixth and seventh centuries it prospered with international trade.

In 604, King Aethelbert of Kent (R.560–616) built a small, wooden church dedicated to St. Paul on Ludgate Hill for Mellitus, a monk from Rome who was ordained Bishop of London, although the seat of the Primate of England would be at Canterbury.

But there were other eyes on London. Viking longships left Norway, Sweden, and Denmark to raid England. In 842 and 851, Danish Vikings stormed London, and in 872 they made it their headquarters. It was Alfred (R.871–99), the Christian king of an enlarged Wessex, who recaptured the city in 886 and made peace with the Danes. Although Winchester was the royal capital, Alfred made Lundenwic the power base. He moved the earlier Saxon settlement from the Strand, where enemy longships could easily beach, back inside the walls and renamed it Lundenburh. He repaired the defenses and invigorated international trade, while keeping tight control over coinage, devising a countrywide code of law and a system of taxation, and instituting military service. He also promoted scholarship, translated texts into the vernacular, and founded monasteries. When the Danish Vikings returned in 980, the state was strong enough to hold firm, even if hefty "Danegeld" tribute money was needed to buy off war.

The last Danegeld payment was to the young Viking Dane, Cnut (R.1016–1035). London, not Winchester, was his chosen capital—a position it would never again lose. Cnut brought prosperity to the country and patronized the Church. London was the heartbeat for

St. Edward's Crown, placed on the Sovereign's head in the Coronation ceremony; see it in the Tower of London.

Cnut's England, notable for its peace, laws, and formidable taxes (which were higher in real terms than any until the 17th century).

MEDIEVAL LONDON

Behind the events of the years 1042 to 1485, Westminster was established as the seat of the monarchy, while the City's merchants exercised more and more control over their city and their kings.

When Edward the Confessor (R.1042–1066) dared not make his pilgrimage to Rome (he feared a coup if he left the country), Pope Leo permitted him to restore the modest Westminster Abbey instead. Thus began one of London's greatest building projects: the monastery, abbey church, and royal palace of Westminster. But it was Edward's cousin, William (R.1066–1087), Duke of Normandy, who established Westminster as the seat of royal and state power. Invading England in 1066, he crushed Edward's successor, Harold, at the Battle of Hastings. Norman rule, with imported administrators and soldiers, replaced Anglo-Saxon; and, to keep watch over the City merchants, William built the Tower of London.

William's great tax survey of England, the Domesday Book, reveals an ordered society that would thrive under Norman and Plantagenet rule. This was a period of Crusades abroad and monastic building at home. Between 1077 and 1136, 13 monasteries and 126 churches were built in and around London wall's, including St. Bartholomew's Church and Hospital. At Westminster, Henry III (R.1216–1272) began the Gothic rebuilding of the Abbey in 1245.

In the City, the merchants won the right to be self-governing in 1191. Soon after, Henry FitzAilwin became their first lord mayor, and Richard I (R.1189–1199) gave up the lucrative Thames management rights in return for City funding for his crusades. In 1215 King John (R.1199–1216) put his seal to the Magna Carta, which curbed his powers. By 1295, the Model Parliament of Edward I (R.1272–1307), government was by consent, not rule.

The next century witnessed the Black Death (1348–1350) epidemic, when half of London's population died; the Peasants' Revolt, which Richard II (R.1377–1399) quelled at Smithfield; and the Wars of the Roses (1455–1485) inheri-

tance dispute. On a happier note, in 1477 William Caxton produced the first book printed in England on his Westminster press.

TUDOR LONDON

When Henry VII (R.1485–1509) came to the throne, ushering in Tudor rule (1485–1603), London's prosperity and status surged forward, out of the medieval world into the Renaissance and onto the international stage.

War-torn England recovered under strong rulers, and the benefit was felt most in London. Commerce expanded. Wharves lined the riverfront. In 1566, Thomas Gresham built the Royal Exchange to enable London financiers and merchants to compete with Antwerp. London's population leaped from 75,000 to 200,000, making it the fastest-growing European city, and equal in size to Paris and Milan.

Trade boomed as merchant-adventurers opened up new trading routes, to Asia for silks and spices, to America for tobacco and sugar. At Deptford and Woolwich, a navy was built up that would quash Philip II's Spanish Armada in 1588, and enable Francis Drake, Walter Raleigh, John Hawkins, and others to explore new trade routes, laying the foundation for the British Empire.

The Church, however, was turbulent. Henry VIII (R.1509–1547), lacking a male heir, instructed his lord chancellor, Cardinal Wolsey, to win permission from the Pope to divorce Catherine of Aragon. When he failed, the king dismissed him, took over his palatial homes at Hampton Court and Whitehall, and in 1532–34 broke with Rome to become Supreme Head of the English Church. The Reformation began. It promoted Protestant ideas, English-language Bibles and, most radical of all, the Dissolution of the Monasteries (1536–1540). About 800 religious houses were closed, 20 of them in and around London. The capital's atmosphere and character were profoundly altered as secular power replaced the religious influence.

Henry was succeeded by his son, the boy-king Edward VI (R.1547–53), his daughter Mary I (R.1553–58), and then his younger daughter, Elizabeth I (R.1558–1603). With her heady mix of intelligence, charm, and arrogance, and a shrewd use of iconlike propaganda portraits, she gave her name to an age: the

Plan of London from *Civitates Orbis Terrarum*, ca 1580, showing London Bridge (the only bridge) and the Tower of London.

Elizabethan Renaissance. This was the age of the first custom-built theaters (where Shakespeare's plays were performed), of committed art patrons, and of grand court and City pageantry.

STUARTS & REVOLUTION

Londoners greeted James VI of Scotland as their James I of England (*R.*1603–1625) with eight triumphal arches. But Stuart rule (1603–1714, except for 1649–1660, the period of the Republic) failed to unite Catholics and Protestants.

Parliament turned against the extravagant, well-meaning monarchs. Protestants left for the New World—the Pilgrim Fathers sailed on the *Mayflower* from Rotherhithe in 1620. Papists threatened the king's life—Catholic conspirators tried to blow up the royal family and Parliament in 1605. Finally, after Charles I (*R.*1625–1649) was executed for treason, Oliver Cromwell and his Puritan followers formed the Commonwealth (1649–1653), and then the Protectorate (1653–59).

Their Puritan London did not last. Soon after Cromwell's death, the monarchy was restored and Charles II (*R.*1660–1685) took the throne. This marked the start of the Restoration, where dramatist John Dryden, composer Henry Purcell, scientist Isaac Newton, painter William Hogarth, and architect Christopher Wren were key figures in a creative outburst. But Parliament's attempts to restrict royal power soon broke down.

When Charles's Catholic successor James II (*R.*1685–88) fled to France, the bloodless Glorious Revolution witnessed Parliament inviting the Dutch Prince William of Orange (*R.*1689–1702) and his wife, Mary (*R.*1689–1694), both Protestants, to take the throne. They signed the Bill of Rights (1689), defining

and limiting the monarch's power and excluding Catholics from the throne. In Parliament, modern elements of government evolved such as political parties, cabinet government, and the limited parliamentary term. Later, under Queen Anne (R.1702–1714), Scotland and England signed the Act of Union (1707).

Meanwhile, Londoners had suffered the Great Plague, which killed some 110,000 in 1665, then the Great Fire of London, which raged for four days in 1666 and destroyed four-fifths of the wood-built City. Afterward, the wealthy moved westward and Wren's St. Paul's Cathedral and churches gave new character to the City. A financial explosion stimulated by William Paterson's new Bank of England (1694) generated ideas that would produce the Stock Exchange, the Baltic Exchange, and Lloyd's.

GEORGIAN LONDON

When Queen Anne died without a direct heir, the crown went to the great-grandson of

Londoners watch from boats as flames engulf St. Paul's Cathedral in the Great Fire of 1666, by Lieve Verschuier (1630–1686).

James I, the German-speaking Elector of Hanover named George. Thus began the Hanoverian line that continues today, called Windsor since 1917.

Under the Georges—George I (*R.*1714–1727), George II (*R.*1727–1760), George III (*R.*1760–1820), and George IV (Prince Regent 1811–1820, king 1820–1830)—London prospered as never before. Trade and the arts flourished, and the population doubled to one million. London became Europe's largest city.

This huge metropolis needed houses. The wealthy moved westward again, first toward the Court at St. James's and then over the Bloomsbury fields, and northward up to Islington, Hampstead, and Highgate. Inspired by Inigo Jones's Covent Garden

Piazza of 1631 and Henry Jermyn's lucrative development of St. James's Square in the 1660s, developers coated aristocrats' London estates with terraces and squares to create Mayfair, Mary-lebone, and later Belgravia— the Grosvenor family's vast estate accounted for much of Mayfair and all of Belgravia. London also expanded southward:

The splendor of the Prince Regent's Carlton House (now demolished) matched his vision for the replanning of London.

Westminster Bridge opened in 1750, and others followed. Northward, the flamboyant Prince Regent and his architect, John Nash, laid out Regent Street and Regent's Park and Canal in 1811–1828.

Grand private mansions were also built, such as Apsley House, Kenwood, Syon, and Osterley, where the Scottish architect Robert Adam introduced his delicate neoclassicism. Indeed, classicism and intellectual inquiry were fundamental to the 18th-century Enlightenment movement. In London it found expression in Dr. Johnson's dictionary (1755), David Garrick's classical theater, Lord Burlington's Palladian villa at Chiswick, and in the establishment of learned and artistic societies such as the Royal Society of Arts (1754) and the Royal Academy (1768).

London's wealth rested on trade. The industrial revolution and the expansion of the empire made London the world's largest port in 1800—up to 8,000 ships might be on the Thames at any time. To thwart pilferers and speed up the unloading of cargo, the merchants built walled, enclosed docks, a 13-mile-long system completed in 1921.

VICTORIAN LONDON

In 1837 the young Victoria ascended the throne, to reign for 63 years. She gave her name to an age of change, invention, growth, and contrast, particularly in her capital—now the center of an empire that stretched across the world. Colonialism became Imperialism; in 1877, Victoria became queen-empress of India.

During the 19th century, London's population exploded from one million to more than six million people. Despite London's wealth, the problems of transport, water supply, sewerage, and slums posed huge challenges. Nevertheless, entrepreneurs, philanthropists, and entertainers prevented the city from grinding to a standstill.

London was now too big to walk through, too widespread to be served by the Thames ferries. In 1829, London's first regular public bus service started: George Shillibeer's horse-drawn buses pulled 22 passengers each, from Paddington to Islington, and on to the City. Later, in 1856, the London General Omnibus Company was formed. Electric trams followed in 1901, motor buses in 1905.

London's first railway opened in 1836. Two years later, Euston terminus was built; there were a dozen more by 1899, making the capital easy to visit. From 1851, the North London Link brought workers from outlying London villages to the docks. The railway companies' need to issue precise timetables resulted in the establishment of British Standard Time in 1884, and it was soon adopted around the world. The world's first underground railway had opened in 1863; the first deep-dug lines for electric trains followed in 1890, soon known as the Tube.

Sir George Gilbert Scott's St. Pancras Station and his Grand Midland Hotel, painted by John O'Connor (1830–1889), are still landmarks today.

People migrated from the countryside in droves. There were also waves of immigrants. Following the Irish potato famine of 1845–48, 100,000 Irish arrived, cramming into speculators' tenement housing, which, lacking drainage and running water, quickly became slums. Later, in the 1880s, more than 100,000 Jews arrived, fleeing anti-Semitic

Bombing in World War II brought chaos all over London, especially in the City and docklands, but London kept on regardless.

pogroms in Russia and Eastern Europe. Many settled in Whitechapel in the East End.

London had been seriously overpopulated since the 1830s, and its hygiene infrastructure collapsed. More than 400 sewers emptied into the Thames. Typhus, smallpox, and cholera were rampant, and the life expectancy for a working-class man was only 22 years. After the 1848–49 cholera epidemic and the Great Stink of 1858, the engineer Joseph Bazalgette designed London's first sewage system. He then created the Embankments, built between 1864 and 1874, reclaiming land from the Thames to house a trunk sewer, an underground railway, gas mains, and a water conduit, with a road and public gardens above.

Meanwhile, the philanthropists came to the forefront. Among them, the 7th Earl of

Shaftesbury fought for factory improvements and better housing for the poor; medical missionary Dr. Thomas John Barnardo founded his first home for destitute children in 1867; and revivalist preacher William Booth founded the Salvation Army in 1878.

Prince Albert, Queen Victoria's Consort, realized his grand plan for promoting learning and trade. On May 1, 1851, his Great Exhibition opened, displaying "the Works of Industry of all Nations" in a great glass hall in Hyde Park, designed by a gardener, Joseph Paxton. Six million people visited it, a third of the British population. Afterward, Albert was the vision behind a permanent showcase of science and the arts in South Kensington. Beginning with the Victoria & Albert Museum in 1855, museums, colleges, and institutions soon covered an area fondly known as Albertopolis.

Londoners needed lighter entertainment, too. In Leicester Square, Queen Victoria watched the circus at the Alhambra, opened in 1858. More halls were built nearby, and along Shaftesbury Avenue. By the 1890s, London had 38 West End theaters and was the theater capital of the world. In the East End, Marie Lloyd was one of the stars who sang in more than 30 music halls, each seating up to 1,400. Meanwhile, countless heroes of empire, science, and the arts were honored with public statues, most notably Admiral Lord Nelson in Trafalgar Square, named for the battle in which he died defeating the French.

TWENTIETH-CENTURY LONDON

Under Edward VII (R.1901–1910), Victorian grandeur acquired a certain extravagance and decadence that was halted by World War I. George V (R.1910–1936) saw his capital suffer zeppelins, unemployment, overcrowding, and an influx of refugees. George VI (R.1936–1952) witnessed the World War II bombs of the Blitz, the arrival of Polish refugees, the dissolution of the Empire, and, in 1948, the creation of the Commonwealth. Since 1952, his daughter Elizabeth II has reigned over a truly multicultural London, whose cosmopolitan outlook continues to enable waves of cultural innovation to influence the rest of the world.

The 20th century has seen mainly physical

change in London. It began when Aston Webb laid out a royal processional route from Buckingham Palace, along The Mall to Admiralty Arch. After World War II, bomb sites such as the Barbican were rebuilt as high-rise housing, while ruthless developers took advantage of the property slump—most of Mayfair's palatial mansions were destroyed at this time. This gave energy to the burgeoning conservation movement, whose advocates fought to save Covent Garden, Islington, and other areas from demolition.

When London Port was moved to Tilbury, the docklands began to close down. Then, in 1981, the world's largest urban renewal program began, heavily backed by the government. The "Big Bang" in 1986 led the City to rebuild half of its office space; the following year saw Rupert Murdoch's revolution in newspaper production silence London's home of printing, Fleet Street.

London's people changed, too. When the population of Greater London peaked at ten million in the 1930s, housing was short, the smog was unhygienic, and one million worked on the docks. Political refugees were also arriving by the thousands: Jews went to the East End, then to northern areas such as Golders Green, Edgware, and Stamford Hill; Turkish Cypriots settled in Haringey and Stoke Newington, and the Italians to Clerkenwell. After World War II, more than one million Londoners left for the verdant suburbs. Their houses were often divided up for the thousands of immigrants coming from the Commonwealth—Jamaicans went to Brixton and Stockwell, Trinidadians and Barbadians to Notting Hill, Asians to Southall, Greek Cypriots to Camden, and Hong Kong Chinese to Soho.

Amid these crises and upheavals, London witnessed many landmark events—the first radio broadcast in 1922, all women over 21 winning the vote in 1928, the first television broadcast in 1936, and in 1951, the Festival of Britain. Held on the south bank of the Thames to raise Londoners' morale after postwar austerity, the festival marked a release of new creative energy. The South Bank is now one of Europe's largest arts complexes.

The Swinging Sixties followed, and then an outpouring of innovative music, art, archi-tecture, and fashion. Terence Conran, Andrew Lloyd Webber, Norman Foster, Vivienne Westwood, and many more lifted London's status. The city was once again a fashionable and exciting place to live and work in, with good entertainment and quality restaurants that reflected its rich variety of cultures.

Beatles-inspired fashion for Swinging Sixties' young Londoners on the West End's Carnaby Street

THE MILLENNIUM
The run up to the millennium was particularly exciting for London. Eurostar's trains began running from Waterloo to Paris via the Channel Tunnel in 1994. The revitalization of the Docklands reawakened the London riverscape for public buildings, such as Tate Modern at Bankside, and for residential warehouse conver-sions. When Labour won the General Election in 1997, Prime Minister Tony Blair confirmed the Tories' proposal for a government-backed Millennium Experience at Greenwich, whose centerpiece is the world's largest dome. Other millennium projects included the British Museum's Great Court, the Science Museum's Wellcome Wing, and Millennium Bridge link-ing St. Paul's Cathedral in the City to Tate Modern on the South Bank. ■

The arts

LONDON IS REMARKABLE NOT FOR ITS CULTURAL COHESION BUT FOR ITS cultural diversity. Almost everything you might ever want is here—it is merely a question of finding it. A thousand years of architecture, painting stretching back to early Gothic delights, statues from the Romans onward, and music and theater of every description. If you are looking for a good fort, go to the Tower of London, Britain's best medieval example. If you seek baroque painting, hurry to the Banqueting House, where Sir Peter Paul Rubens painted the huge ceiling. If you want to see urban renewal today, take a spin on the Docklands Light Railway, or walk along the Thames's South Bank. London's museums, galleries, churches, and open houses can be overpoweringly rich. If the Victoria & Albert Museum is too exhausting to contemplate, try the smaller Courtauld Galleries or the Whitechapel Art Gallery instead. There are private palaces to visit, such as Osterley House, and intimate museum-homes, such as the writer Thomas Carlyle's house.

Art is unavoidable. Commercial galleries and auction houses show art on the move. Sculptures spangle London's streets and parks. Both private houses and impressive public buildings may be decorated with fine ironwork or terra-cotta friezes—you have only to lift your eyes above street level to see them.

As for lifestyle, there is a world of it in London—literally. In August, Clerkenwell's Italians stage a daylong *festa* in honor of the Virgin Mary. Brixton's Caribbean community has its own lively market, while Southall's silk sari shops, spice-sellers, Bombay film music, and restaurants transport you into a subcontinental dreamworld. Modern international design, with its cafés, restaurants, and fashion-conscious people, is found in Knightsbridge and less central areas such as Islington.

ARCHITECTURE

London has superb examples of virtually every British architectural style. Westminster's story leads through grand public buildings, such as Westminster Abbey, the royal palaces and parks, and the aristocrats' mansions and amusements. In the City the remains are a rich mix of livery halls, offices, dealing rooms, and markets that culminate in Broadgate and other recent developments.

Pre-Norman remains

Evidence of occupation in the London area goes back to about 500,000 B.C., but the most substantial pre-Norman remains are Roman. Archaeologists have located the forum, basilica, amphitheater, governor's palace, and public bath sites. The Museum of London possesses some fine mosaic floors and a wall-painting from Southwark. In the City, there are thick chunks of Roman wall at Trinity Square and on Tower Hill.

Norman castles & churches

The houses of London's Saxon, Norman, and medieval merchants and craftsmen were built of wood and plaster, so they did not last. Just before the Norman Conquest, the Saxon King Edward the Confessor built Westminster Abbey (consecrated 1065), inspired by buildings at Jumièges and Caen in France. The Romanesque style he adopted, with its chunky piers, rounded arches, galleries, and open timber roof, was so widely used by the Normans that in Britain it is known as Norman style.

William I built a ring of castles, including Windsor, around his capital, and his White Tower (1078–1097), kernel of the Tower of London, is an important example of Norman military architecture. Built of Caen stone, the walls are 12 feet thick, and the square plan contains three rooms on each floor; the cupolas on the corner towers are 14th-century additions.

In London the best surviving Norman church is St. Bartholomew-the-Great, built in 1123 as part of the priory and hospital, and now the City's only surviving 12th-century

Andrew Lloyd Webber's *Cats* closed in 2002 after 21 years—making it London's longest-running musical.

monastic church. Another masterpiece of Norman ecclesiastical architecture is St. John's Chapel in the White Tower: tiny, simple, and with two massive arches.

Medieval architecture

Medieval London's walls, with towers and seven double gateways, are still identifiable by street names such as Aldersgate, Aldgate, and Bishopsgate. They surrounded a city made up of flimsy wooden houses, livery company halls, and about 140 churches. The circular Temple Church, begun in 1160 and enlarged in 1220, is one of London's earliest buildings constructed in the Gothic style, seen in the pointed arcade arches and the (later) chancel piers, capitals and lancet windows.

Surviving secular medieval buildings include the labyrinth of Inner and Middle Temples dating from 1350 and Lincoln's Inn from 1400. Richard II's Westminster Hall, with its spectacular hammerbeam roof, was started

From the air, you see the Thames curve downstream under bridge after bridge from Westminster to the City.

in 1394, while City merchants built their Guildhall between 1411 and 1440. Archbishop Morton built the redbrick gatehouse of his Lambeth Palace around 1495.

The most impressive of the 20 medieval religious houses in London was Westminster Abbey, the royal abbey church of St. Peter, together with its monks' cloisters. In 1245, Henry III demolished it and began building a lavish Gothic church. Four monastic houses stood just north of the City: St. Bartholomew's Priory, Charterhouse Monastery, St. John of Jerusalem's Priory, and Clerkenwell Nunnery. St. John's great gateway evokes their grandeur.

Tudor buildings
Some of the most romantic and glorious buildings seen in London today were built as

expressions of the capital's growing world status under the Tudor sovereigns, who ruled from 1485 to 1603. Henry VII added his soaring, lacelike chapel to Westminster Abbey in 1503 to 1512. The fine fan-vaulting and large windows typical of this period give it a spiritually uplifting airiness. A rare, surviving domestic building, Charterhouse Priory's heavy Washhouse court, built between 1500 and 1535, contrasts sharply.

A major catalyst for this growth was Henry VIII's Dissolution of the Monasteries (1536–1540), which released large swaths of land for building by royals, aristocrats, and developers. While the monarchs concentrated on their palaces and parks, aristocrats and bishops built along the Strand, which was the riverfront between the City and Westminster. These buildings survive only in street names—Bridewell, Savoy, Northumberland.

The Old Hall of Lincoln's Inn, built in 1492 as the living room of the lawyers who resided there, gives an idea of how most of Tudor London must have looked. There is also Staple Inn, built in 1586, a group of 16th-century domestic houses: The half-timbering, horizontal strips of windows, high gables, and overhanging upper floors are typical of the period, although brick houses with chimneys and glass windows were growing in number.

The Tudor monarchs realized the importance of an outward show of power. Henry VII began the royal wave of secular building with Richmond Palace and Baynard's Castle at Blackfriars, both completed in 1501. When Henry VIII came to the throne in 1509, he inherited these palaces, plus the Tower of London, Eltham Palace, and others—a total of 16 residences within a day's ride of the capital.

At Greenwich, Henry built tennis courts, a tiltyard (medieval knights' competition area), and a large royal armory that could compete with Continental products. With the fall of Cardinal Wolsey, he seized Whitehall Palace and added entertainment areas and riverside State apartments, painting the brickwork red, white, and black. At Wolsey's already vast Hampton Court Palace, he built a great hall, chapel, kitchens, and service courts. Henry also seized the former leper hospital of St. James's. It is in these last two that Tudor palace-building can best be seen today.

While advances were made in domestic housing, overpopulation in the City led to multiple occupancy of houses, poor hygiene, more fires, poverty, and an increase in fatal illnesses—smallpox, tuberculosis, and bubonic plague. A royal proclamation in 1580 forbade the building of any new houses or the subdivision of any existing ones.

There was plenty of wealth in the City, even if there are almost no surviving Tudor buildings to show it. This wealth was mostly controlled by the guilds and the mayor's officers at Guildhall. To protect their jobs and standards of workmanship the medieval craftsmen and merchants formed guilds, which later became monopolies, limiting numbers and ensuring jobs for Londoners. Guild members wore a special livery, or uniform, hence Liverymen; the guilds were called livery companies. It was these men who governed the City. Dick Whittington, a mercer who died in 1423, was Mayor of London three times.

Stuart & Georgian London

Inigo Jones gave Stuart London its first Palladian buildings—Queen's House at Greenwich, built in 1616, Banqueting House at Whitehall in 1619, Queen's Chapel by St. James's Palace in 1623–27, St. Paul's Covent Garden in 1631–38, and London's first square, Covent Garden Piazza, in 1631.

The Great Fire of 1666 provided the impetus for further change. In 1667 the first Building Act was passed: All structural walls were to be of brick or stone, and the only projections allowed were balconies. There were also rules governing foundations, timbers being near chimneys, house heights, street widths, and other requirements. The aim was to raise building and safety standards, and to control town planning. The result was that plain, flat-fronted terraces and squares would be built over the fields as London expanded, creating the classic character of residential Georgian London.

The post-Fire architectural hero was Sir Christopher Wren. He rebuilt St. Paul's Cathedral, beginning in 1675, designed 51 churches to surround it, and worked for the King and Queen at Kensington and Hampton Court Palaces, and at both Chelsea and Greenwich Hospitals.

Massive Norman piers surround the choir of St. Bartholomew-the-Great.

The 18th-century Enlightenment attracted a plethora of fine classical architects to London. Nicholas Hawksmoor's Christ Church, Spitalfields, completed in 1714, and James Gibbs's St. Martin-in-the-Fields, of 1721, were two of many new churches. Impressive public buildings included William Kent's Treasury of 1733, William Chambers's Somerset House of 1776, and Robert Smirke's British Museum of 1823. Meanwhile, Lord Burlington's Chiswick House of 1725, and Robert Adam's remodeling of Syon, Osterley, and Kenwood mansions in the 1760s, introduced new lightness and elegance to classical buildings. Finally, the Prince Regent employed John Nash from 1816 to 1828 to create the great sweep of Regent Street and Regent's Park, all coated in gleaming, white stucco.

Victorian & Edwardian architecture

As the London of Queen Victoria transformed itself into the huge capital of an empire, sweeping changes took place in many spheres. In architecture, classicism was challenged by a Gothic revival, and by a return to a redbrick, vernacular style inspired by Christopher Wren.

Nineteenth-century developers followed the lead of Georgian builders, whose planning centered on garden squares. Thomas Cubitt's Belgravia by Buckingham Palace was the grandest. Other developments included the Cadogan and Ladbroke estates, and the Islington squares. Bedford Park, begun in 1875, and Hampstead Garden Suburb, begun in 1906, broke new ground in suburbia.

There was a proliferation of public buildings aimed at bringing education to the general public, among them William Wilkins's National Gallery of 1832, and the glasshouses of Kew. The South Kensington buildings stimulated by the Great Exhibition of 1851 included Alfred Waterhouse's Natural History Museum and Richard Norman Shaw's Royal Geographical Society, both of 1873, and Sir Aston Webb's Victoria & Albert Museum of 1899. Other public buildings included hotels such as Arthur Davies's Ritz, and market buildings such as Smithfield built in 1866. Westminster changed radically: The Houses of Parliament suffered a disastrous fire in 1834 and A. W. N. Pugin and Charles Barry designed the new Houses of Parliament in elaborate Victorian neo-Gothic.

London's vastly increased size necessitated improvements in its infrastructure. Joseph Bazalgette's engineering work along the reclaimed river embankment included a trunk sewer, while G. E. Street's Royal Courts of Justice, completed in 1882, served the newly centralized courts. New communications demanded new types of building: Sir George Gilbert Scott designed the Gothic St. Pancras railway station and adjacent hotel of 1868–1874. Wide Shaftesbury Avenue was one of several new roads that sliced through slums, serving the increasing volume of road traffic.

Twentieth-century London

London's population today is about the same as it was in 1900 when, at around 7 million, it was the world's most populated city—New York had 4 million people, Paris 2.7 million.

In the 1920s and '30s, crowding, smog, and dirt generated a middle-class exodus to the suburbs, hastened after World War II. Garden suburbs were seen as the idyllic solution to the ills of city life. Nevertheless, the city's population and boundaries continued to grow, and in the 1930s peaked at 10 million.

In central London, Bethold Lubetkin's Penguin Pool for the London Zoo, of 1934, introduced modern Continental ideas. British-designed buildings included Sir Giles Gilbert Scott's monumental Battersea and Bankside power stations of 1929–1935 and 1955, as well as his Waterloo Bridge of 1939 and Owen William's *Daily Express* building of 1932.

After World War II damage, postwar construction focused on much-needed housing, including the City's large Barbican Estate, begun in 1959. In the public sector, Robert Matthew's Royal Festival Hall was built for the 1951 Festival of Britain, and marked the start of the South Bank Arts Complex.

Although London has many interesting theaters, ranging from John Nash's restrained Theatre Royal, Haymarket of 1831, to Thomas Collcutt's splendid Palace Theatre of 1890, more have been added this century. They include the Savoy of 1929, Sir Denys Lasdun's Royal National Theatre of 1967–1977, and the re-created Shakespeare's Globe, opened in 1997 (the last two offer tours behind the scenes).

In the 1960s, undistinguished development, coupled with plans to destroy Covent Garden Market, St. John's Wood, and other areas, stimulated the conservation movement and the call for a change of style. Buildings by Frederick Gibberd, James Stirling, Richard Rogers, Terry Farrell, and Nicholas Grimshaw have introduced new ideas. In the 1980s, the Docklands revival began, the commercial "Big Bang" led to City rebuilding, and new life was injected into the riverside. More than 30 major London millennium building projects kick-started the 21st century. And the new City Hall, Portcullis House, and 30 St. Mary Axe keep London ever changing.

PLAQUES & STATUES

Thousands of Britain's heroes and villains people London's streets and squares with their statues, or have memorials set in facades of houses, in walls, or even in fountains.

Some are grand: Nelson's statue stands on a tall column and is set in a square named after his great battle, Trafalgar. Others are remarkably modest: The architect of a great sweep of central London, John Nash, has merely a bust in the colonnade of All Souls Church, Langham Place, which he designed. A few have several memorials: The achievements of Prince Albert were recognized in the splendid Albert Memorial in Kensington Gardens, in Charles Bacon's equestrian statue at Holborn Circus, on the facade of the Victoria & Albert Museum, and elsewhere too. But it is the Duke of Wellington—neither king nor prince but one of Britain's greatest generals—who has three equestrian statues: in St. Paul's

Begun in 1514, Hampton Court combines Tudor architecture with Wren's 1690 Classical royal apartments.

Cathedral, in front of the Royal Exchange, and in front of Apsley House.

GREAT MUSEUMS

London has more than 300 permanent museums and galleries, large and small, general and specialist. Some are custom-built; others are collectors' homes; all exist thanks to remarkable people.

The British Museum, the capital's first great national public collection, is one example. Sir Hans Sloane died in 1753, leaving his extensive library and collections of fossils, coins, minerals, and more to the nation—subject to a £20,000 ($32,000) payment to his daughters. The museum opened in Montague House on January 15, 1759, and moved into Robert Smirke's new building in 1838.

The National Gallery, founded in 1824, exists thanks to the gift of 38 paintings by financier John Julius Angerstein. Other national collections include the National Portrait Gallery, the National Maritime Museum, the Science Museum, and the Victoria & Albert Museum, which holds the national collection of decorative and fine arts. The Tate Gallery is now divided into two sections, British art in Tate Britain on Millbank, and international modern art in Tate Modern in the refitted Bankside Power Station.

More personal collections include the Dulwich Picture Gallery, opened in 1814 as the country's first public art gallery; the Iveagh Bequest in Kenwood House; and the Suffolk Collection in Ranger's House. In the house-museums the stamp of the collector's personality is even stronger, lingering on in his or her residence, whether it is the grand Ham House, Osterley Park, Apsley House, or the Wallace Collection, or the more intimate

Sir John Soane's Museum, Dr. Johnson's House, and Leighton House. Palaces fulfill this role, too, especially Kensington and Hampton Court.

Finally, there are the specialist collections: the Percival David Foundation of Chinese Art; the Design Museum; the Museum of London and Museum in Docklands, which tell the capital's own story; and Julius Wernher's treasures in lovely Ranger's House.

ARTISTS IN LONDON

Artists from the world-famous to the quietly anonymous have recorded almost every important event, building, and person of London's history since the 16th century: What the Globe Theatre and Old St. Paul's Cathedral looked like, the extravagance of the Lord Mayor's rich pageant, the formal opening of St. Katharine Dock.

Hans Holbein painted portraits of grandees, while Wenceslaus Hollar, from Prague, worked for the Earl of Arundel drawing the best and most detailed views of 17th-century London that exist, working on the roof of the Earl's Strand mansion. Later, patronage reached a peak under Charles I, who employed Sir Anthony Van Dyck for nine prolific years, and also commissioned Sir Peter Paul Rubens to paint the ceiling of Banqueting House. Thomas Rowlandson and William Hogarth caricatured the city's seamier side. In contrast, Canaletto, Claude Monet, Joseph Mallord, William Turner, James Whistler, and André Derain all eulogized the Thames.

A considerable number of paintings by artists working in London are to be found in Hampton Court and Buckingham Palaces, as well as in some museums and galleries.

The Museum of London has 20,000 paintings, prints, drawings, and other exhibits, usually chosen for their image rather than their artist. One is a spectacular canvas of the Great Fire of London in 1666, by an eyewitness Dutch artist. Another is a picture by Abraham Hondius of the Thames frozen over in 1677—as it did periodically until 1828, when Old London Bridge was demolished and the Thames was allowed to flow faster, an action further reinforced by the building of the Embankments (see p. 48). Roderigo Stoop

depicts Charles II's triumphant coronation procession, while Henry Moore records the impact of war on Londoners taking refuge in Underground stations during 1941 and 1942.

Holbein the Younger came to London in 1526, and later entered the service of Henry VIII. At Henry's Bridewell Palace on Fleet Street, he painted his remarkable double portrait, "The Ambassadors," now in the National Gallery (see p. 101). Here, too, are pictures by Van Dyck, Sir Peter Lely, who arrived here in the 1640s, and Thomas Gainsborough, who first came to London in 1740. Next door, the National Portrait Gallery has plenty of personalities painted in their home city, such as John Hayl's portrait of the diarist Samuel Pepys and Tom Phillips's of the theater director Sir Peter Hall. The Imperial War Museum has a rich collection of 20th-century pictures by artists such as Paul Nash, Stanley Spencer, William Roberts, Edward Ardizzone, Richard Eurich, and David Bomberg. Among the smaller museums, Sir John Soane's stacks up the Hogarth series, and Kenwood House has paintings by Sir Joshua Reynolds, who lived in London from the 1740s.

Occasionally, a London artist's home survives as a house-museum. Lord Leighton's splendid indulgence is in Holland Park, Linley Sambourne's overstuffed home is preserved in Kensington, and Hogarth's country cottage hides between a noisy roundabout and elegant Chiswick House.

Tate Britain has plenty of London artists' work on view. Turner, a Londoner by birth, studied at the Royal Academy and always returned to London after his European tours. His London addresses included one on Chelsea's Cheyne Walk overlooking the river. The Tate's Clore Gallery houses his works, while the main Tate buildings may at any time have on display John Constable's "The Opening of Waterloo Bridge," Charles Ginner's "Piccadilly Circus," and works by R. B. Kitaj, Peter Blake, Howard Hodgkin, and younger artists such as Rachel Whiteread, Damien Hirst, and Fiona Rae.

Today London is seething with artists coming from all over the world; one estimate puts 10,000 working in the East End alone. Howard Hodgkin, Lucian Freud, Richard Hamilton, Gilbert & George, and Maggie Hambling are among the older generation of artists living in London. Hambling's sculpture of Oscar Wilde was set in Leicester Square in 1998.

The annual Turner Prize is the most prestigious contemporary art award and a yardstick for the way art is moving. Hodgkin was an early winner; Damien Hirst (famous for his pickled and chopped-up animals) and Rachel

Albert, Prince Consort, sits in Sir George Gilbert Scott's Albert Memorial in Hyde Park, looking down over the South Kensington museum complex.

Whiteread (who represents inside spaces as dense matter) have both won it, and 1998's winner, Chris Ofili, marked a return to representational two-dimensional painting. The many others to look out for include Gillian Wearing, Garry Hulme, and Jenny Saville, who paints the best flesh since Rubens.

To see the new movements in the art world, visit the shows at the Whitechapel Art Gallery (see p. 199), which also holds information on the biannual Whitechapel Open, when hundreds of East End artists open their studios to the public. Near here, the new commercial galleries in Truman's Brewery building in Brick Lane and others in Hoxton Square show the cutting edge of contemporary art. In the West End, shows at the

Photographers Gallery and Anthony d'Offay are always worth seeing—others are listed in the London Galleries Guide (free from most commercial galleries). Farther west, the Serpentine Gallery in Kensington Gardens is a wild card in conservative Kensington.

LITERARY LONDON

Throughout its 2,000-year history, Londoners and visitors have documented the city in diaries, chronicles, poetry, and fiction. Reading some of these is one way of getting under the skin of London, of evoking its atmosphere at different historical periods. Many are now reprinted, either in their entirety or in anthologies.

The earliest known description is by the Roman historian Tacitus. Loyally he wrote that during Boudicca's revenge "the enemy massacred, hanged, burned and crucified with an energy that suggested…retribution would soon be visited upon them." From a later age, detailed descriptions of the city include the remarkable one of Elizabethan London by retired tailor and self-taught historian John Stow, *A Survey of London,* published in 1598.

Meanwhile, the first English-language poem about London, *To the City of London* (circa 1501), once attributed to Scottish poet William Dunbar, begins with "London, thou art of towns A per se" and ends with the accolade "London, thou art the flower of cities all." The elaborate entertainments offered by Elizabethan theaters prompted Lupold von Wedel, a German visitor, to write about the "dog fights" and "rockets and fireworks."

Some remarkable diaries survive from the 17th and 18th centuries. The little known John Manningham described Elizabeth I's calm death in his diary: "At about three clock her Majesty departed this life, mildly like a lamb, easily like a ripe apple from a tree." Samuel Pepys's diary of 1660–69 is better known. In it, the details of his daily life hopping on boats to move from the City to Whitehall Palace, or playing music and going to church, vividly conjure up the Stuart Restoration, and are as interesting as his spectacular account of the Great Fire of 1666. In the same way, John Evelyn, whose diary spans the years from 1640 to 1706, is as keen to describe William and

Mary's new Kensington Palace as the beaching of a whale at Greenwich or Cromwell's funeral—"the joyfullest funeral that I ever saw." The Scot James Boswell kept his *London Journal* in 1762–63, in which he is depressed by the "tumultuous scene" in Parliament, enjoys a friendship with the popular actor-manager David Garrick, and is, like Pepys, indiscreet on the subject of love.

Diaries were kept by many 19th-century Londoners, from schoolboy John Thomas Pocock to Queen Victoria, and by visitors, from the Frenchmen Gustave Doré and Blanchard Jerrold to American Nathaniel Hawthorne. London life comes alive in the great Victorian novels. Thackeray's *Vanity Fair* paints social London during the Regency period, when Knightsbridge was almost in open country and Belgravia did not exist. In contrast, Charles Dickens's novels sum up deprivation, squalor, and hardship, and gave us the word Dickensian. In *Sketches by Boz,* St. Giles slums are described as "wretched houses with broken windows patched with rags and paper…filth everywhere—a gutter before the houses and a drain behind them."

To get a flavor of the variety of London lives in the 20th century would require a dip into, perhaps, Oscar Wilde's letters, Beatrice Webb's diary, Bertrand Russell's autobiography, and Arnold Bennett's journals. George Orwell's journal, Laurie Lee's autobiography, Raymond Chandler's letters, Sir Winston Churchill's copious writings, John Betjeman's poems, and Martin Amis's novels make an equally diverse set.

But it is William Wordsworth's radiant celebration of the city in his sonnet "Upon Westminster," written in 1802 after he crossed Westminster Bridge in the dawn coach, that still encapsulates the romance of London beginning with: "Earth has not anything to show more fair;…This City now doth, like a garment, wear/The beauty of the morning; silent, bare,/Ships, towers, domes, theaters, and temples lie/…All bright and glittering in the smokeless air."

Few contemporary authors can match the outpouring of quality prose about London written down the centuries. This explains why so much of it is still in print. Martin Amis is an exception, seen in his novels *Money* and *London Fields,* as is Michael Moorcock, whose many books set in London include *Mother London.* Peter Ackroyd writes both biography (on Dickens, for instance, and a recent one on London itself) and novels set in a mixture of contemporary and historic London; his *Hawksmoor* is set in Spitalfields, while *The House of Doctor Dee* concerns an Elizabethan

For nine years Samuel Pepys, a senior naval administrator (1633–1703), recorded everything—his love life, court intrigue, details of naval business—in his diary.

alchemist. But perhaps it is Iain Sinclair who touches the raw nerve of London today, setting many of his books in the City and Docklands. His novels include *Lud Heat* about the founder of London. *Lights Out for Territory* is his collection of walks around the lesser known areas of the capital. As for modern diaries, Alan Clark's insights into Parliament and Sir Roy Strong's into the world of art and society are tremendously good reads.

PERFORMING ARTS

Up to a thousand concerts are given in London every week. There are also operas, plays, musicals, and ballets performed in theaters, rooms, gardens, churches—almost any kind of space.

London has always offered plentiful and

innovative entertainment, bewildering visitors with its sheer quantity of plays and shows available. In 1599, Thomas Platter, a visitor from Basle, remarked that "every day at two o'clock in the afternoon…two and sometimes three comedies are performed at separate places, wherewith folk make merry together, and whichever does best gets the greatest audience."

A watercolor of the original Globe Theatre, Southwark

The Elizabethan stage was, at this period, in its infancy, mixing traditions of secular plays performed in the yards of inns with dancing, singing, and the baiting of bears and bulls. The Puritan City fathers banned theater from the City in 1574. Two years later, James Burbage built London's first permanent playhouse at Shoreditch City. In 1587 the Rose was the first of four theaters to open at Southwark, which soon became London's entertainment center. Here Burbage opened his Globe in 1599. More than 2,000 people would cram into the circular, tiered, wooden theaters to watch plays by Shakespeare, Ben Jonson, and Thomas Dekker, although use of the open-air auditoriums depended upon good weather. Meanwhile, over Christmas 1603, more than 30 plays were staged in the Great Hall of Hampton Court Palace for James I.

With Charles II's restoration, theater returned to the city. Plays were an almost daily event at Whitehall Palace. The King granted two men permission to produce plays for the public: Thomas Killigrew, who opened the Theatre Royal, Drury Lane, in 1663, and William D'Avenant, whose theater at Lincoln's Inn Fields had the first proscenium arch, and facilities to set and strike scenery during a play.

Throughout the 18th century, there were only two legitimate theaters and companies inside the city, Drury Lane and the Opera House in Covent Garden; the many others were illegal. London theater later suffered its second persecution, when Henry Fielding's crude satires at the old Theatre Royal in the Haymarket caused the Lord Chamberlain to introduce powers of censorship in 1737, lifted only in 1968.

Despite strict censorship, theater and entertainment flourished. David Garrick was the actor-manager who revived classical theater, and treated Shakespeare with a new respect. He demanded that actors learn their parts, improved production, and transformed audience behavior, which had often been raucous—people would walk across the stage to chat with friends during performances. Programs changed nightly. The main play began about 6 p.m., followed by an "after piece" of pantomime, farce, or comic opera. In 1728 the first performance of John Gay's *Beggar's Opera* marked the arrival of English opera. Meanwhile, 18th-century London was full of musical activity, both amateur and professional. Concert rooms and theaters were opened to cater to the increased demand for concerts, opera, and masquerades: Mozart appeared at the Hanover Square Rooms, J. S. Bach and Haydn conducted their own compositions, and Handel composed operas, concerts, and chamber works.

From the 1840s onward, London witnessed an explosion in theater, music halls, and entertainment of all kinds. The music halls grew out of informal sing-alongs held in taverns. By the end of the century, huge halls were being built. The lavish, newly renovated Hackney Empire flourishes in north London. The Coliseum,

The West End continues Britain's long-standing theater tradition.

opened in 1904, had a stage large enough to hold a chariot race, with an audience capacity of 2,558, still London's largest. These variety theaters attracted a new audience, the middle-class visitor to London. Gradually, the vulgarity was tempered, so that Sarah Bernhardt played at the Coliseum, Sir Thomas Beecham conducted excerpts from *Tannhäuser* at the

The "Proms," a six-week program of concerts in the Royal Albert Hall, still brings affordable music to all Londoners every summer.

Palladium, and one music hall even put a cricket match on stage.

In theater, the great actor-managers dominated. Herbert Beerbohm Tree built Her Majesty's Theatre and staged *A Midsummer Night's Dream,* with real rabbits hopping about the Athenian woods set, and, in 1895, Oscar Wilde's *An Ideal Husband.* Sir Henry Irving made Ellen Terry his leading lady at the Lyceum, which he managed for 24 years from 1879. Richard D'Oyly Carte staged Gilbert and Sullivan operettas, including *The Mikado,* at his Savoy Theatre with such success that the profits financed the building of his deluxe Savoy Hotel next door.

Landmark events in London theaterland included Richard Wagner conducting his *The Ring* at the Royal Opera House in 1867, and Anna Pavlova making her London ballet debut at the Palace Theatre in 1910. This theater, restored by Andrew Lloyd Webber, is where his *Jesus Christ Superstar,* written with Tim Rice, became London's longest-running musical until it was eclipsed by another of his productions, *Cats.*

Meanwhile, Harley Granville-Barker dazzled Londoners at the Royal Court in Chelsea, where he staged 32 plays from 1904 to 1907, including the first performances of George Bernard Shaw's *Candida.* More recently, Sir Peter Hall was the first director of the National Theatre when it finally opened in 1976, the realization of an idea put forward by Garrick.

Today, some of London's most interesting theater is found in the "Off-West End" and "fringe" venues. The Royal Court, Almeida Hampstead, Old Vic, Young Vic, and Donmar Warehouse theaters stage many of London's most innovative quality productions. Avant-garde fringe theaters, often housed in pubs, warehouses, and small upstairs rooms, are dotted across the capital. Ones at the forefront include the King's Head, Riverside Studios, The Bush, BAC, and Tricycle; others, often more offbeat, include the Etcetera Theatre, Old Red Lion, and The Finborough (for more information see the Entertainment section on p. 263).

Back in the mainstream, the three auditoriums of the state-funded Royal National Theatre and Shakespeare's Globe show traditional and contemporary plays, and some musicals, in repertory. This enables visitors to see a number of productions in any week. The traditional Victorian and Edwardian theaters of the West End stage more conventional productions and long-running musicals. These include Andrew Lloyd Webber's *Phantom of the Opera* and his *Les Misérables,* which plays at his lavishly restored Palace Theatre. Other restorations include the art deco Criterion and Richmond theaters, while the entirely rebuilt Sadler's Wells Theatre reopened in 1998 to focus on ballet and some opera and stage productions. Currently, opera is staged at the lavishly renovated Royal Opera House, the Coliseum, the Savoy Theatre, Sadler's Wells, and Hackney Empire. ■

The great River Thames twists and turns past structures that testify to its role in history—custom houses, quays, palaces, parliamentary buildings, power stations, and the Tower of London.

The Thames

A barge tows containers downstream.

The Thames

THE MAP OF THE THAMES TELLS MUCH ABOUT LONDON. THE RIVER IS still narrow as it runs northward from Hampton Court Palace, becoming subject to the tides of the distant North Sea below Teddington Lock. It passes in great curves through the once rural villages of Twickenham, Richmond, Kew, Chiswick, and Barnes, now swallowed up by the vast amorphous mass of Greater London. The Thames then swings eastward into the city center. The last eight of London's 34 Thames bridges cluster close together, serving the capital's heart, Westminster and the City. Beyond the final one, Tower Bridge, the waters of the widening river slip slowly round the Isle of Dogs peninsula and through the great metal fins of the Thames Barrier, London's safety net against nature's floods.

Along the Thames stand buildings that testify to the river's role in history. For centuries, the river was the main highway for Londoners, and a facade within view of it was prestigious, as it still is. St. Paul's Cathedral, the Tower of London, and Westminster's Houses of Parliament are all close to the Thames.

Kings and queens, accompanied by boatloads of courtiers and musicians, would be rowed up and down the Thames between

their riverside palaces at Greenwich, the Tower of London, Whitehall, Westminster, Richmond, and Hampton Court. Aristocrats often chose rural locations on the river, upstream from the city, for their homes— Ham House, Syon House, and Marble Hill House are the most impressive survivors. And there are several riverside parks:

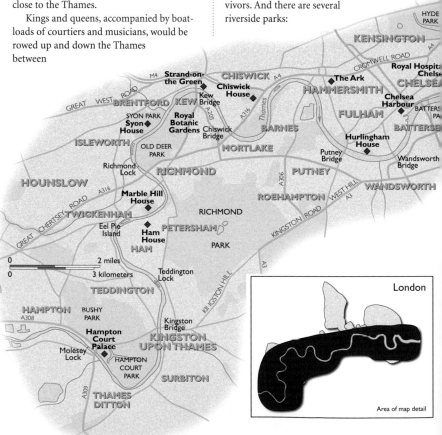

Greenwich downstream, and Battersea, Kew, Richmond, and Hampton Court's Home and Bushy Parks upstream.

Today, energetic riverfront building marks the rediscovery of the Thames. The redevelopment of the Docklands, in particular the Isle

of Dogs, has been infectious. Riverside buildings that have lost their original purpose, such as Bankside Power Station and County Hall, breathe again as they are put to new uses. Dramatic modern buildings are being added, including City Hall at Southwark.

Forgotten harbors, such as St. Katharine and Chelsea, have been redeveloped. River taxis beat rush-hour roadblocks, and the new Millennium Bridge spans the Thames from St. Paul's to Bankside. As for strolling, the newly designated riverside walk has brought Londoners back close to their river again. ■

Teddington Lock, the end of tidal Thames

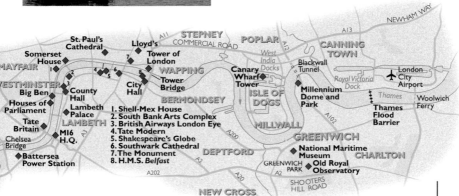

Quinlan Terry's Riverside development at Richmond uses neo-Georgian design to fit in with the original houses in this highly popular London suburb.

The historical port

Once the biggest port in the world, London no longer sees laden ships coming and going up the Thames. And the boats riding it now, for pleasure or transport, are few compared to those of the past, when much of Britain's wealth flowed in and out of the river.

The Roman port flourished on what is now Cornhill, with a wooden bridge, warehouses, and quays. The Anglo-Saxons traded with France and the Rhineland, then ventured farther to the Baltic and Middle East. In Tudor times, merchants built up the port to the point where about 40,000 people lived off the river, from bargemen and boatbuilders to stevedores and porters—and 2,000 boats ferried people up and down the river highway. Trade soared in the 17th and 18th centuries, and London became the world's largest port. In 1802 the enclosed docks opened, relieving the Thames of its shipping jam. By 1900, a million people worked in the port, but when the port moved to Tilbury in 1965, London's river fell silent.

Amid all the bustle of trading, London's river pageantry was always impressive. Henry VIII's ostentatious minister, Cardinal Wolsey, would dress in crimson satin to be rowed in his barge from Westminster to Greenwich to visit the king. The best shows on the Thames were those staged by the Lord Mayor. From 1422 to 1846, each year Livery Company barges escorted the Lord Mayor elect to Westminster, to seek the sovereign's approval.

By the mid-19th century, the river was little more than an open sewer, slowly carrying the industrial and domestic effluent of London out to sea. But after Queen Victoria's lawyers won back the Crown's river rights from the City Fathers in 1857, engineer Joseph Bazalgette designed London's first city-wide sewerage system. He also found a solution to the Thames's poor state of hygiene and the frequent winter freeze-ups that threw London into chaos. Inspired by Wren's suggestion of a river wall, he devised a land-reclamation scheme that narrowed the Thames and made the water flow faster. This embankment had a road on top to relieve the congested city, public gardens, and a tall river wall to combat floods.

Above: "The Thames on Lord Mayor's Day,"
circa 1747, by Giovanni Antonio Canaletto.
Left: Oarsmen in the Doggett's Coat &
Badge race wear traditional livery. Below:
In the 1930s carts stand by to unload sand
and gravel from Thames barges at low tide.

THAMES REVIVAL

When the docks moved and industry was no longer allowed to dispose of its waste straight into the river, London's river-water quality improved dramatically. In 1950 it was biologically dead. Today, more than 100 species of fish now live in the city stretch, including perch, sea stars, mussels, and eco-fragile salmon. With cleaner water, overhauled bridges, and new riverside buildings, Londoners have rediscovered their riverscape.

The revival began in the 1980s. The government's Docklands project was born in 1981. The aim was to reshape the 8.5 square miles of disused docklands with houses and offices. Soon individual developments were under way the length of London's riverbank. Old warehouses were converted to apartments. New office blocks arose, reflected in the waters of the old docks, which have been kept for their recreational potential.

Up at Hammersmith, architect Richard Rogers converted an oil depot into offices and apartments in 1987, creating a new working community. Nearby, Ralph Erskine's fun-shaped The Ark, of 1991, is a brave attempt at an ecologically sound office building.

Chelsea Harbour, where coal barges unloaded their cargo until 1960, was developed in 1986–87 into a luxurious riverside community. On the opposite bank, a simple concrete-and-glass building by Norman Foster houses his own architectural practice.

At Vauxhall, Terry Farrell's new MI6 headquarters, Vauxhall Cross, was completed in 1993, with a public riverside walk in front of its terraced floors.

In central London, Farrell's Embankment Place, built in 1987–1990 as an office block dramatically suspended over Charing Cross railway station, was the first of several major riverside projects. Michael Hopkins's severe Portcullis House at Westminster and Lifschutz Davidson's remodeling of Hungerford Bridge followed upstream; and a string of South Bank transformations and creations appeared, from County Hall to the Oxo Tower.

Downstream from here, there is the dynamic revival of Somerset House, the new Thames span of the Millennium Bridge, and the remodeling of Bankside Power Station into the new Tate Modern. Beyond lie Foster's elliptical City Hall and the converted warehouses of Shad Thames and Docklands. ■

Above: The Millennium Bridge, with St. Paul's and Southwark beyond.
Right: Canary Wharf Tower is the centerpiece of Dockland's redevelopment.
Below: Terry Farrell's Embankment Place, built over Charing Cross Station

London landmarks—and the London Eye—highlight a river cruise.

General riverboat information
www.tfl.gov.uk

Thames Cruises
To the Thames Barrier
(1 hour, 15 minutes)
☎ 7930 3373
www.thamescruises.com
🕐 March–Nov.

City Cruises
To the Tower of London
(20–25 minutes)
☎ 7930 9033

Two Thames boat trips

TAKING A PLEASURE BOAT TRIP ON THE THAMES ON A sunny day is a delightful and relaxing way to appreciate how this great river was the backbone of the capital's development. From Westminster pier, the short, urban journey downstream passes the City of Westminster and the City of London, stopping at the Tower of London and, beyond the Docklands, Greenwich. Some boats continue to the Millennium Dome and Thames Barrier. The rural journey upstream is longer, leaving the city and gliding through increasingly green areas of outer London, past villages and country mansions to stop at Kew, Richmond, and finally Hampton Court Palace. From here, you can take a train back into town.

DOWN THE THAMES: WESTMINSTER TO GREENWICH

Starting from Westminster pier, some boats swing round beneath Westminster Bridge for a view of the Houses of Parliament before moving downstream, with County Hall on the right. Bazalgette's Victoria Embankment, left, has

the Portcullis House, castlelike Whitehall Court, and the National Liberal Club, built in the 1880s. Behind Whitehall Stairs—there were once hundreds of river stairways like this giving access to the river—stood Whitehall Palace.

Under Hungerford Railway Bridge, Farrell's new offices are suspended above older Charing

Cross Station, to the left. The South Bank Arts Complex is right, Charing Cross Pier and Embankment Gardens left, where the Duke of Buckingham's water-gate survives to evoke the Strand's past glories. From here, Victorians took steamboats on vacation day trips down to seaside towns on the Thames estuary. On the skyline you see the Shell-Mex House of 1932, with clock, and Macmurdo's 1903–04 bedroom wing of the Savoy Hotel. Monet painted his views of Waterloo Bridge from one room. At Victoria Embankment the misnamed Cleopatra's Needle—London's oldest monument, dating from 1450 B.C.—is an obelisk of pink granite from Heliopolis in Egypt.

Under Waterloo Bridge, the Royal National Theatre is to the right. Somerset House is to your left, then Inner Temple Gardens and the riverside, cast-iron griffins marking the boundary of the City. After Blackfriars Bridge, you can see Millennium Bridge and, on your left, St. Paul's and the City's vast, egg-shaped 30 St. Mary Axe. Bankside Power Station, now Tate Modern, is on the right, with the new Shakespeare's Globe beyond.

Southwark Bridge and Cannon Street Railway Bridge come next, then the Doric column of the Monument, to the left, commemorating the Great Fire, a modern London Bridge marking Roman London's beginnings, Hays Galleria, H.M.S. *Belfast*, and the curved glass of City Hall.

The medieval Tower of London is on the left and Tower Bridge spans the river beside it. The revived Docklands line the widening river as it sweeps through the Pool of London, until recently filled with ships. To the right are the areas of Shad Thames, Bermondsey, Rotherhithe, and

Deptford. To the left are the districts of Wapping, Shadwell, and Limehouse. The soaring towers of Canary Wharf, on the Isle of Dogs peninsula, face across the Thames to Greenwich. Beyond soars the Millennium Dome, the massive new structure on

Greenwich Peninsula. Farther downstream, the shining fins of the Thames Flood Barrier, a series of stainless steel gates, straddle the river at Woolwich.

UP THE THAMES: WESTMINSTER TO HAMPTON COURT

From Westminster pier, the boats pass under Westminster Bridge. The Houses of Parliament and Victoria Tower Gardens are on the right, with Lambeth Palace and the floating fire station on the left. After Lambeth Bridge, Bazalgette's embankments support Tate Britain on the right.

Beyond Vauxhall Bridge and Farrell's MI6 headquarters, waste energy from Battersea Power Station, left, used to heat Dolphin Square's apartments, right. After Chelsea Bridge the banks look more rural: Battersea Park, with its Peace Pagoda, on the left, and, on

Westminster Passenger Service
Upstream to Kew & Hampton Court
☎ 7906 2062
🕐 April–Oct.

Camera time—
passing under
Tower Bridge

Catamaran Cruisers
☎ 7987 1185
www.catamaran cruisers.co.uk
🕐 April–Oct.
Hop on, hop off bet. Westminster & Greenwich

Circular Cruise
☎ 7936 2033 or 7839 2111
🕐 April–Oct.
Hop on, hop off between Westminster & the Design Museum

The glorious end to a summer's day on the Thames

the right, the gardens of the Royal Hospital Chelsea, the site of the Chelsea Flower Show. Albert Bridge springs from the core of old Chelsea village, right. After Battersea Bridge, familiar from Whistler's paintings, is Chelsea Harbour. Turner painted sunsets from the tower of riverside St. Mary's church, Battersea.

Round a great bend in the river, Hurlingham House (right), built in 1760, and its gardens are now a private sports club. Bazalgette's Putney Bridge replaced the 1729 wooden one, which was the Thames's second longest span but well out of London when it was built. Bishops Park is on the right, boathouses for avid rowers on the left—the Oxford and Cambridge Boat Race starts here. The offices of British architect Sir Richard Rogers and Ralph Erskine's The Ark are on the right, before you arrive at castellated Hammersmith Bridge.

Chiswick's Malls, on the right,

are lined with handsome houses; pretty Barnes village is to the left. After Duke's Meadows, right, comes Chiswick and its elegant bridge, then Kew railway and road bridges, with Strand-on-the-Green's charming cottages, on the right. The Royal Botanic Gardens (see p. 180) at Kew follow, left, with their riverside palace, and on the opposite side gleaming Syon House (see p. 185). After Richmond Half-Tide Weir and Footbridge come Twickenham and Richmond Bridges. Here stand the remains of Richmond Palace, behind the riverside Asgill House, built in 1758 by City merchant Charles Asgill. Richmond Park and Ham House follow, left, with Marble Hill House on the right.

Teddington Lock and Weir mark the end of the tidal stretch of the Thames. After Kingston Bridge and the great sweep past Home Park, Tijou's grand river gates announce Hampton Court Palace (see p. 187). ∎

Churches by Christopher Wren and skyscraper offices huddle in a maze of narrow lanes that date from the capital's origins as a small port in the Roman empire, a far cry from the frenzied financial capital it is today.

The City

Decorative detail from the Victorian screens at Smithfield market

The City

MUCH OF THE CITY'S 2,000 YEARS OF BUSY HISTORY CAN BE TRACED ON THE map. The two defendable hills that attracted the Romans to this spot are still clear to see: Ludgate, on which St. Paul's Cathedral now stands, and Cornhill. Here, 40 miles up the Thames from the sea, the river could be forded and the gravel riverbed bridged. The north bank was firm, and streams from Highgate and Hampstead provided fresh water—the Walbrook ran through the new settlement, the Fleet formed the western boundary.

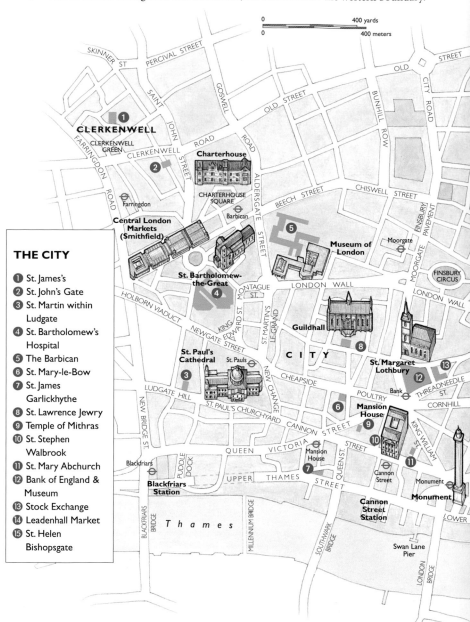

THE CITY

1. St. James's
2. St. John's Gate
3. St. Martin within Ludgate
4. St. Bartholomew's Hospital
5. The Barbican
6. St. Mary-le-Bow
7. St. James Garlickhythe
8. St. Lawrence Jewry
9. Temple of Mithras
10. St. Stephen Walbrook
11. St. Mary Abchurch
12. Bank of England & Museum
13. Stock Exchange
14. Leadenhall Market
15. St. Helen Bishopsgate

The Romans' basilica and forum stood on Cornhill, where Lombard Street now runs; the remains of one of their temples, dedicated in A.D. 240 to Mithras, the god of a mystery cult, can be seen on Queen Victoria Street. Around A.D. 200, the Romans encased their 330-acre city with a tall, thick, tapering wall of Kentish ragstone, 3 miles long and pierced by 7 gates. Today, chunks of wall, with medieval repairs, survive in the Barbican Centre, the Tower of London, Noble Street, and elsewhere. The gateways survive in place-names only: Aldgate, the poet Geoffrey Chaucer's home (1374-1386); Bishopsgate, whose road led all the way to Hadrian's Wall in the north of England; Moorgate, beyond which lay marshy land; Cripplegate, which led to a medieval suburb and to Islington village; and Aldersgate, which led to the monasteries of Clerkenwell and to Smithfield market.

When medieval London burst out of the walls, it crept westward toward its rival, Westminster. The City boundaries barely changed at all. Even today, the City's nickname, "the Square Mile,"

is a roughly accurate description of the Roman settlement.

Then two dramatic events occurred. Plague was endemic to London, but in April 1665, what was to be the worst outbreak since the Black Death of 1348–1350 began. All who could fled—Charles II went to Oxford—but the Lord Mayor stayed to direct relief work. It was a hot, dry summer, and during the worst week 12,000 died, their naked bodies being carried to pits on plague carts. The Great Plague killed an estimated 110,000 before the cold weather brought it to a halt.

The next year, on September 2, fire broke out about 1 a.m. at Thomas Farrinor's bakery on Pudding Lane. By morning, 300 houses and part of London Bridge were alight. The strong east wind was fatal. It fanned the fire as it greedily gobbled up the pitch-coated, timber buildings. People grabbed their valuables and ran, often to the nearest boat. Over the next two days, the flames ate up Lombard Street, Cheapside, St. Paul's Cathedral, and Inner Temple. On September 5, the wind dropped and the fire was checked, but not before four-fifths of the City—including 13,000 houses, 87 churches, and 44 livery halls—had been burned. Luckily, only a handful of people died.

While the embers were still glowing, Charles II pledged that the city would be rebuilt. Sir Christopher Wren's dream of a city of wide avenues radiating from a new St. Paul's was impractical, partly because the guilds would not give up their pockets of land. Instead, fireproof, brick houses were built following the medieval street plan. ■

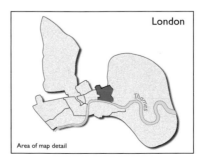

London

Area of map detail

Wren's City churches

THE DOUBLE DISASTER OF THE GREAT PLAGUE OF 1665 AND the Great Fire of 1666 changed the City forever. The wealthy left, initiating the development of the elite residential area of St. James's. The rebuilt City was safer, with wider streets and better constructed houses. The markets, furniture shops, and other suppliers moved west, toward their customers. Sir Christopher Wren's new cathedral and churches gave a cohesive architectural character to the City that can still be felt today despite ponderous Victorian and soaring 20th-century buildings.

The interior of St. Bride, local church to the journalists and printers on nearby Fleet Street

Wren's 51 City churches, built from 1670 onward, made a huge impact. Today, 23 churches still remain—19 were destroyed in World War II bombing, and nine have been lost at other times.

Their designs vary considerably. There are the domed and centralized **St. Mary-at-Hill** *(Lower Thames St., tel 7626 4184)* and **St. Stephen Walbrook** *(Walbrook, tel 7283 4444)*, the grandly baroque **St. Bride** *(Fleet St., tel 7353 1301)*, and **St. Lawrence Jewry** *(Guidhall, tel 7600 9478)*, whose facade is based on Wren's great model for St. Paul's Cathedral. **St. Magnus the Martyr** *(Lower Thames St., tel 7626 4481)* is a good one to visit for its classic design and sumptuous interior, described in T. S. Eliot's *The Waste Land* (1922) as "inexplicable splendour of Ionian white and gold." He refers to the colonnades supporting the tunnel vaulting of the nave, which leads to the finely carved original reredos. Among the baroque statues, shrines, and gilded sword rests, do not miss two other original features: the font and the organ case. The steeple, added in 1705, is one of Wren's best; his other notable ones surviving today are on St. Bride (added 1701–03) and St. Mary-le-Bow.

Some of Wren's interiors have their own—or another, older or ruined church's—fittings.

St. Margaret Lothbury

(Lothbury, tel 7606 8330) fulfills both criteria. Outside, Wren has perched his obelisk tower on a domed base. Inside, the rectangular nave's magnificent furnishings include Wren's design for the finely carved tester and screen, whose barleystick columns and soaring eagle were originally built for All Hallows-the-Great (demolished 1876). The reredos, communion rails, and font, attributed to Grinling Gibbons, come from St. Olave, Old Jewry (demolished 1888).

Almost every Wren church has something special about it. For the interior of his very pretty **St. Mary Abchurch** *(Abchurch Lane, tel 7626 0306)*, Wren gathered a team of his most talented friends, and their work remains almost unaltered. Beneath William Snow's paintings on the shallow dome, some of the City's finest 17th-century wood carving survives, all retaining its original oxblood stain. There are William Emmett's door cases, font cover, and rails, Christopher Kempster's font, William Gray's pulpit, and—the church's glory—Grinling Gibbons's reredos, the City's only authenticated piece by him.

St. Margaret Pattens

(Eastcheap, tel 7623 6630), so-called because wooden clogs or pattens were made nearby in the 13th century, also has a special interior. Here are some of London's few remaining canopied pews, and the one carved with "CW 1686" is thought to have been Wren's own. There is also an hourglass beside the pulpit for timing sermons, a punishment bench for the parish miscreants, and, in the side chapel, hooks for gentlemen to hang their wigs on hot days. Wren's slender lead steeple rises above another fine interior, that of **St. Martin within Ludgate** *(Ludgate Hill, tel 7248 6054)*. The altarpiece, pulpit, font,

and organ case are magnificent examples of late 17th-century carving and protected from the dirt of Ludgate Hill by a screen inside the entrance.

Finally, a visit to **St. Mary Aldermary** *(Queen Victoria St., tel 7248 5139, appointment necessary)* is an eccentric contrast. The pinnacled tower, added in 1702–04, gives a clue. Paid for by Henry Rogers, who presumably influenced the design, this is Wren's only Gothic-style church. The elaborate plaster fan vaulting, the only work of its kind made in the City in the 17th century, was probably Wren's free interpretation of the pre-Fire church. Beneath it, original woodwork includes the pulpit, font, and a wooden sword rest. ■

The steeple of St. Mary-le-Bow: To be born within the sound of its bells was the definition of a cockney Londoner

St. Paul's Cathedral

THIS IS THE CATHEDRAL CHURCH OF LONDON DIOCESE—
a church for Londoners, while Westminster Abbey serves the nation.
St. Paul's was founded by King Aethelbert of Kent for the missionary
monk, Mellitus. This, the fifth church on the site, is England's only
baroque cathedral, the only one with a dome, and the only one built
between the Reformation and the 19th century. It was also the first
to be constructed entirely by a single architect, Sir Christopher Wren.

St. Paul's Cathedral
- 🅰 Map p. 56
- ✉ Ludgate Hill, EC4
- ☎ 7236 4128
- www.stpauls.co.uk
- 🕒 Closed Sun. except for services, & for special events
- 💲 Cathedral & crypt: $$. Galleries: $$ extra
- 🚇 Tube: St. Paul's, Mansion House, or Blackfriars
  Rail: City Thameslink

The foundation stone was laid on
June 21, 1675. Boatloads of Portland stone from Dorset were delivered to the nearest wharves, the
cost partly met by a tax on coal
coming into the port. The bulk
of the cathedral was built by 1679.
Wren's son put the last stone on
the lantern supporting the triple-
layered dome in 1708, and the
cathedral was completed in
January 1711. The entire building
is undergoing a £40 million ($68
million) restoration and cleaning
of stonework, statues, and mosaics
for its 300th anniversary.

EXTERIOR
Before going in, stand well back on
Ludgate Hill and look at St. Paul's
in its entirety. The building is
arranged in four volumes: the
dome and crossing, the nave and
choir, the transepts, and the west
end. The dome rests on a wide
drum—which provides an open
terrace—and is made of an inner
brick dome, an intermediate brick
cone that supports the lantern, and
an outer wooden casing covered in
lead. The grand facade has a pediment relief of the Conversion of St.
Paul. Pilasters and pediments give
the building baroque movement.

Opposite:
View down the
nave and choir to
the window of the
American
Memorial Chapel

INTERIOR
Standing just inside the building,
you get a good first view looking
straight down the length of the
nave and choir to the modern tow-
ering altar. This stunning setting

has contributed to memorials such
as the funerals of Nelson in 1806
and Churchill in 1965; to celebrations such as Queen Victoria's
Diamond Jubilee in 1897, the
Queen's Silver Jubilee in 1977, and
the marriage of Prince Charles and
Lady Diana Spencer in 1981.

Dome & crossing
The crossing is irresistible. Sit
beneath it and rest as you look up
at the dome. It is supported on
eight huge arches. Corinthian
columns rise up to the dome, where
the grisaille frescoes of the life of
St. Paul by Sir John Thornhill,
painted 1716–19, are the only
original decorations. The mosaics
in the spandrels—the prophets by
Alfred Stevens and the evangelists
by G. F. Watts—were added in the
19th century, after a visit by Queen
Victoria, who criticized the building as dreary and uncolorful.

Wren produced several designs
for St. Paul's. These are on display
in the **crypt,** reached from the
south transept. There is a model of
grand Old St. Paul's, which Wren
had been due to restore before the
1666 fire. After the fire, Wren was
appointed Surveyor General in
1669 and was already designing
new City churches when he produced his first model for St. Paul's
in 1670. This was judged to be too
modest; his Great Model of 1673–
74 showed his ideal design of a
Greek cross. When this was rejected
by the clergy as unsuitable for the

bishop's processions, Wren made a third design, with a small dome and long nave. Once the clergy had approved it and he had received the King's Warrant to go ahead in 1675, he enlarged the dome, removed the spire, raised the nave walls, and chopped off three bays—thus returning as closely as he dared to his Great Model design. All the foundations were laid out at the start so that no changes could be forced upon him at a later stage.

There is much more in the crypt, including an audiovisual program, the Treasury, and Wren's own tomb, inscribed *lector, si monumentum requiris, circumspice* (reader, if you seek his monument, look around you), words repeated on the floor beneath the dome. Admiral Lord Nelson and the Duke of Wellington lie here, and near Wren lie the artists Joshua Reynolds, J. M. W. Turner, and John Singer Sargent.

The monuments in the nave are a roll call of British heroes of the 19th and 20th centuries. Francis Bird's font of 1727 stands in the north transept and Jean Tijou's screens close off the Sanctuary; the **American Memorial Chapel** is behind the altar; and Wren's original high altar is kept in the **Lady Chapel.** Near it is the monument to the poet John Donne (1571–1631), who was Dean of St. Paul's and the greatest preacher of his day. Both choir stalls and organ case were carved by a team headed by the young Grinling Gibbons. In the south aisle is Holman Hunt's painting "The Light of the World," the artist's copy of his original version (in Keble College, Oxford).

GALLERIES

The stairs to the galleries and dome are the big climb, an effort rewarded with some magnificent views over London. The 560 stairs begin with gentle steps leading to the

Whispering Gallery. There is a diagram of the dome construction on the stairway wall. Unless you arrive early, there will not be enough peace and quiet for the whispers to carry round the gallery. Steeper steps, with views of the cone supporting the lantern, lead to the wide outside **Stone Gallery,** resting on the dome's drum. From here, you can see how the second story of the screen around the building is blind, built for effect, with nothing behind it. Finally, a spiral staircase leads up to the **Golden Gallery,** narrow and not for the fainthearted, but giving stupendous views of the City, the twisting Thames, and Parliament's many spires at Westminster. ∎

West portico

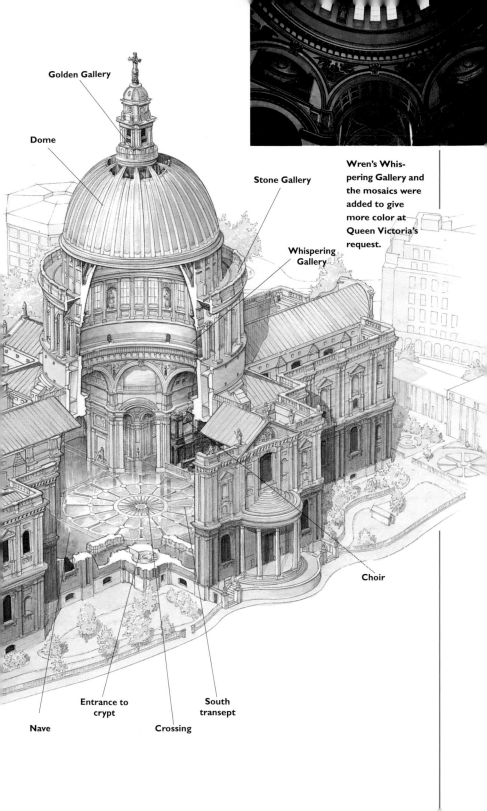

Golden Gallery

Dome

Stone Gallery

Whispering Gallery

Wren's Whispering Gallery and the mosaics were added to give more color at Queen Victoria's request.

Choir

Nave

Entrance to crypt

Crossing

South transept

A City walk

This walk gives a good idea of the dense, medieval compactness of the City and its range of fine buildings of all periods. Go on a weekday for life, on weekends for quiet.

From Monument Tube station, walk down Monument Street to the **Monument ❶**, which commemorates the Great Fire of London of 1666 and can be climbed.

Turn right onto Fish St. Hill. At the bottom is Wren's glorious church, **St. Magnus the Martyr** (see p. 58) on Lower Thames Street; in the porch, see a fragment of the Romans' road leading to their bridge. Farther east, walk up St. Mary at Hill, veering right onto St. Dunstan's Lane, to the remains of **St. Dunstan-in-the-East**—a Wren tower of 1697, and a garden.

Beyond St. Margaret Pattens (see p. 59), turn left at Fenchurch Street, then right onto Lime Street to find the covered arches of Leadenhall Market, the City's food market, opened in 1881. Continue on Lime Street past Richard Rogers's colorful **Lloyd's building ❷** of 1978–1986, with its elevators and stairs hung on the outside walls. Cross Leadenhall into St. Mary Axe to inspect the vast egg-shaped building at No. 30 before turning left to find peace in medieval **St. Helen's Bishopsgate,** with fine monuments. Cross Bishopsgate to find Richard Seifert's 600-foot-tall **International Financial Centre (NatWest Tower),** the world's tallest cantilevered building when completed in 1981.

Turn left down Old Broad Street, cut through Finch Lane, and proceed across Cornhill and into the narrow court opposite to find **St. Michael Cornhill,** where Wren and Hawksmoor added to the medieval tower. Now go right, onto Lombard Street, whose banking signs evoke medieval origins. Hawksmoor's **St. Mary Woolnoth ❸** of 1716–1727 faces onto Mansion House Square, the core of financial London: the **Mansion House** of 1739–1753, the Lord Mayor's official residence, and the Bank of England. Walk around the **Bank of England museum** on Bartholomew Lane, close to **St. Margaret Lothbury** (see p. 59).

Lothbury runs into Gresham Street, where **St. Lawrence Jewry** (see p. 58) stands in front of the **Guildhall ❹**. The medieval crypt is open to the public; the Clockmakers' Company's clocks are exhibited on the ground floor. The Guildhall on Aldermanbury is the seat of the City's government by the Lord Mayor and Aldermen. You can visit the magnificent Hall, and also the **Guildhall Art Gallery,** whose new building displays the City's impressive art collection and incorporates a section of Roman London's amphitheater discovered during building *(Guildhall Yard, tel 7332 3700, www.guildhall-art-*

gallery.org.uk). Farther along Gresham Street, the Goldsmiths' Company has its hall on Foster Lane (exhibitions open to the public). Haberdashers' Hall is on Staining Lane, and there is a chunk of Roman wall on Noble Street. A bridge across London Wall road leads to the **Museum of London** **5** (see p. 68).

Now walk down St. Martin's-le-Grand to **St. Paul's Cathedral** **6** (see p. 60). South of the cathedral, steps lead down to Millennium Bridge. But to continue the walk, go east of the cathedral, along Watling Street, to Bow Lane, with **St. Mary-le-Bow** at the top. If born within the sound of its bells, you are a true Cockney. Up Queen Victoria Street is the Roman **Temple of Mithras** **7**. St.

Stephen Walbrook stands behind Mansion House, off Bucklersbury, while **St. Mary Abchurch** **8** (see p. 59) is set in a square down St. Swithin's Lane. Cannon Street leads to Monument station. ■

🅼	Inside front cover F4
▶	Monument Tube station
↔	3.75 miles
🕐	3 hours if just walking, a day with visits
▶	Monument Tube station

NOT TO BE MISSED
- Guildhall
- Museum of London
- St. Paul's Cathedral

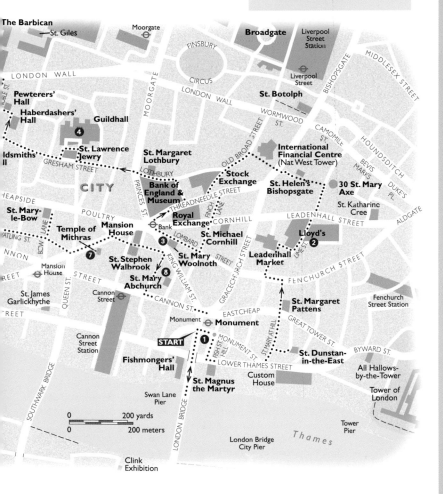

Smithfield & Clerkenwell

Smithfield & Clerkenwell

 Map p. 56

THESE TWO EARLY OVERSPILLS FROM THE CROWDED medieval City survived as a north London backwater while fashionable London moved west. Today, Clerkenwell has more medieval buildings than any other district; and London's only wholesale food market, Smithfield Meat Market, has been glamorously restored.

A Smithfield bummaree

A visit to Smithfield is best made very early indeed—5 to 8 a.m. Follow it up with a hearty breakfast in one of the surrounding pubs.

Smithfield Meat Market, EC1

Map p. 56

Closed Sun.

Tube: Barbican, Farringdon
Rail: City Thameslink

The 12th-century horse market on "Smooth field" (Smithfield) grew into a full-scale livestock market—the scene of terrific noise, drunkenness, brawls, braying, mooing, and blood from slaughtered animals. It was moved to Islington in 1855 when the sale and slaughter of live animals was banned; only the magnicificent **Smithfield Meat Market,** built in 1851–1866, survives. Bummarees (porters) still move the huge hunks of meat that arrive from all over Europe, but hygiene regulations now keep them inside the market.

The original open space was the scene of some major events:

Edward III's tournament for the French king in 1357; Richard II and Mayor Walworth's confrontation with Wat Tyler in 1381 to quell the Peasant's Revolt; and Bartholomew Fair, England's international cloth fair, held annually from 1133 to 1855. Around the edges, seek out the fine medieval St. Bartholomew-the-Great (see p. 67), Cloth Fair's 17th-century houses and tiny alleys, and beautiful St. Etheldreda Church, tucked into Ely Place and built in 1300 for the Bishops of Ely.

Charterhouse Square is northeast of the market, with cobbles, gates, 18th-century houses, and, at the back, the substantial remains of **Charterhouse Monastery's** cloisters and washhouse, used by the Carthusian monks *(Tel 7251 5002 for guided tours).* In St. John's Square, off St. John Street, stands Prior Docwra's grand **St. John's Gate** of 1504. With the church's crypt and chancel, it was part of the Priory of St. John of Jerusalem *(Tel 7324 4070, www.sja.org.uk).*

Clerkenwell was a refuge for monks and for craftsmen fleeing the restrictions imposed by the City's guilds. The village center was the Green, a focus for the many jewelers, watchmakers, milliners, and metalworkers who are now returning to this area. Little of St. Mary's Nunnery survives, but James Carr's **St. James's Church** *(Clerkenwell Close, tel 7251 1190, www.jc-church.org),* built in 1788–1791 to replace the nunnery, has good benefaction boards and a fine organ. ■

St. Bartholomew-the-Great

MEDIEVAL PIETY AND PILGRIMAGES HAD A PROFOUND effect on London. Henry I's court jester Rahere, having been cured of malaria caught during his pilgrimage to Rome, became an Augustinian monk and, in 1123, founded St. Bartholomew's Hospital and Priory. Both were funded by tolls from the annual Bartholomew Fair. What remains of this foundation today is London's oldest church, its only 12th-century monastic church, and its best piece of Romanesque building.

St. Bartholomew-the-Great

- Map p. 56
- West Smithfield, EC1
- 7606 5171
  www.greatstbarts.com
- Closed Sat. p.m. & Mon.
- Tube: Barbican

THE PRIORY

The evocative priory church of St. Bartholomew-the-Great, built in 1123, was restored in 1880–1890 by Sir Aston Webb. It is reached through a 13th-century stone arch, originally the entrance to the nave. The half-timbered Tudor gatehouse is post-Dissolution (1559). The path to the church's door runs past what was once the ten-bay nave, and the cloisters were on the right.

Inside, Rahere's choir, ambulatory, and Lady Chapel survive, showing the magnificence of medieval London's wealthy religious houses. The honey-colored walls, squat columns, unmolded arches, and simple decoration create an atmosphere for contemplation far from the city's bustle.

Rahere was buried here in 1143; his tomb (of a later date) is beside the altar. William Bolton, one of the last priors, gave the Tudor Window in 1515. Soon after, Sir Richard Rich acquired the dissolved priory, destroyed most of it, and lived in the Lady Chapel, which is found through Webb's wrought-iron screen. It later became a printer's office—the writer Benjamin Franklin worked here in 1725.

THE HOSPITAL

St. Bartholomew's *(West Smithfield, tel 7601 8152 for guided tours, www.brlcf.org.uk)* was London's first hospital, built on land given by King Henry I. After the Dissolution, the hospital became secular. It acquired buildings by James Gibbs in 1730–1759, and two murals by Hogarth. Inigo Jones, the architect, was born in nearby Cloth Fair in 1573, and baptized in the hospital church. ∎

A Tudor gatehouse leads to the medieval church.

Museum of London

Museum of London

⬛ Map p. 56

✉ London Wall, EC2

☎ 7600 3699.
   Information:
   7600 0807
   www.museumof
   london.org.uk

🕐 Closed Mon.

💲 Charge for some
   special exhibitions

🚇 Tube: Barbican,
   St. Paul's, Moor-
   gate, or Bank

**An 1875 day
dress by court
dressmaker
Madame Elise
of Regent Street**

LONDON'S LOCAL MUSEUM HOLDS AN ASTOUNDING collection. Its agenda is to tell the story of the commercial and political capital of Britain from prehistoric times to the present. Treasures on display range from a wealthy Roman's floor mosaic, a medieval merchant's counting table, a model of the Tudor and Stuart sovereigns' lost Whitehall Palace, and dresses made of Spitalfields silk. London's glories, atrocities, and failures are all represented here. Above all, the impression is one of Londoners, themselves, speaking to us across the centuries. Special events during which objects can be handled, archaeological site visits, and walks led by museum staff bring a new vividness to London's story.

THE LAYOUT

The museum, currently undergoing renovation and expansion, is housed in part of the Barbican, an arts and conference center, in a building designed in 1975 by Powell and Moya. Opened in 1976, the core collection is an amalgamation of the Guildhall Museum, founded in 1826 for City-related objects, and the London Museum at Kensington Palace, which since 1912 has focused on London's cultural history, especially costume. London's frantic rebuilding during the 1980s and '90s, and developers' willingness to halt work while archaeologists excavated, extended the collection far beyond manageable limits. Only part is on display; more can be seen in the Museum in Docklands (see p. 201).

Rooms are arranged chronologically, with maps, models, and music putting the objects into context. It is always worth visiting the temporary exhibitions and displays of new acquisitions.

THE VISIT

A rewarding first visit might well take a visual overview of the whole of London's history, dipping into one or two thematic rooms.

On the Upper Level, the **Roman rooms** startle with their sophistication. The detailed models of the port and the forum become even more impressive when you imagine the nearby re-created rooms in buildings across the Roman city. There are mosaic floors, a wall painting from Southwark, kitchens equipped with herbs and spices, an elegant dining room, and some fine sculptures from the Temple of Mithras.

Coins and imported pottery in the **Saxon galleries,** together with weapons left by Viking raiders, prove London by no means ground to a halt when the Romans left. The **medieval rooms** bring alive another London—pilgrims' badges, Black Death crosses, and a merchant's chest, plus models of the Tower of London and old London Bridge. The grandeur of **Tudor**

The glittering
Cheapside Hoard
of jewelry in the
Early Stuart
gallery

London is apparent in the model of the Royal Exchange and tantalizing snippets from Henry VIII's Nonsuch Palace.

Stuart London undergoes the instability of Civil War, while one monarch is executed and another restored to the throne. There are memorial medallions to Charles I, a hoard of jewelry from Cheapside, and models of the lost Whitehall Palace. There is gruesome information on superstitions, food, and water supplies; an enthralling sight-and-sound diorama lets you witness the Great Fire of 1666.

Downstairs, the wealth of Stuart London is displayed in a room from Poyle Park in Surrey, complete with fine virginals, while the Georgian era is recalled in 18th-century newspapers, trade cards, ceramics, and a pawnbroker's shop.

The sheer size of **Victorian London** could overwhelm most of the 2,000 years of London's history. The 19th-century galleries are a deluge of transport, building, public utilities, entertainment, and trains. A re-created street of well-stocked shops brings it all to life. London continued to grow in the 20th century. In this section there is an elaborate art deco elevator from Selfridge's store, the story of the London film industry, and a Ford Model T car. Do not miss the Lord Mayor's gilded coach, still used for his November procession. ■

Head of Mithras,
circa A.D. 180–220,
shown as a young
man in a Phrygian
cap, found in the
1954 excavation
of the Temple
of Mithras

Islington

Camden Passage

✉ Camden Passage, off Upper Street, N1

☎ 7359 0190

🕐 Shops: closed Mon. Stalls: open Wed. & Sat.

🚇 Tube: Angel

UP THE HILL FROM THE CITY, ISLINGTON HAS LONG BEEN associated with fun and frolicking. Some aristocrats set up home here after the Dissolution of the Monasteries in the 16th century, but it was as an 18th-century spa that Islington's character was established. Although the houses of the Georgian merchants soon lost the surrounding fields to a patchwork of Victorian squares, Islington is still synonymous with entertainment—theaters, markets, restaurants, pubs—and has a strong community spirit of its own.

Two contrasting markets capture the spirit of Islington: traditional **Chapel Market,** where locals buy their food and other goods, and sophisticated, international **Camden Passage** (see box below), saved from developers in the 1960s. Duncan Street and Charlton Place lead from Camden Passage to the grand Georgian houses of Duncan Terrace. The successful Tudor merchant Hugh Middleton has his statue on Islington Green, opposite the Royal Agricultural Hall of 1861–62, now London's Business Design Centre.

Upper Street, reputed to have more restaurants than any other European street, has the landmark **St. Mary's Church** of 1751–54, with a fine steeple. Three of Islington's theaters are around it: the King's Head pub-theater; the Little Angel Theatre for children, near handsome Cross Street; and the avant-garde Almeida Theatre on Almeida Street.

Canonbury, to the northeast, is a delight to walk through: rows of late Georgian terraces, now desirable houses. Canonbury Square, with the grand Canonbury House of 1780, leads to Compton Terrace and Alwyne Villas. Barnsbury, to the west, has a string of Victorian squares, the next wave of building for City business people. ■

Antiques, indoors and outdoors, in Camden Passage

Camden Passage

One of the densest concentrations of antique dealers in Britain crams into this narrow Islington lane, paved with York flagstones. Serious specialist shops line the passage, devoted to clocks, old clothes, prints, and other subjects. Arcades have been squeezed in wherever possible, and you can find a good selection of art nouveau objects, Staffordshire figures, Bakelite, and enamelware. For best fun, go early on Wednesday or Saturday, when stalls fill every inch, goods are piled on the ground, and every last fish fork has its price. ■

The grandeur of Westminster Abbey, the Houses of Parliament, Westminster Cathedral, and Buckingham Palace is offset by the abbey's serene St. Faith's Chapel and the restful pleasures of Victoria Tower Gardens, Green Park, and St. James's Park.

Westminster

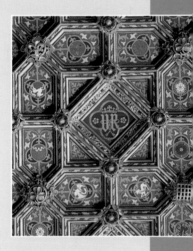

Detail of a ceiling of the Houses of Parliament with VR for Victoria Regina

Westminster

WESTMINSTER, THE NATION'S POLITICAL AND ROYAL HUB, HAS A TOTALLY different atmosphere from that of the commercial City. Lying 2 miles upstream from it, London's second city was born a thousand years later, on a very different type of riverbank and for different reasons. Look at any map and the contrast with the City is immediately clear. Quite unlike the densely packed "Square Mile," this is an area of palaces and large open spaces, of public buildings and public spectacle rather than secret deals; of national politics rather than international finance; of unfenced royal estates instead of a protected, walled port.

ORIGINS OF WESTMINSTER

Westminster was born beside the Thames, on boggy land watered by the River Tyburn. This unlikely spot is believed to be where Sebert, king of the East Saxons, founded the Church of St. Peter, possibly in A.D. 604. This was the same year that his uncle, Aethelbert, founded St. Paul's on the City's Ludgate Hill.

Whatever its cloudy origins, Westminster quickly received royal blessings. Saxon kings gave land and relics; St. Dunstan, Bishop of London, contributed a dozen monks in 960; but it was Edward the Confessor who put it firmly on the map. His dream, inspired by royal foundations on the Continent, was to build a new palace, an extensive monastery, and an abbey church fit for royal burial. William the Conqueror and all subsequent sovereigns have reinforced Westminster's royal, religious, and political role.

WESTMINSTER TODAY

The riverside Palace of Westminster, better known as the Houses of Parliament, has long dominated the day-to-day life of the area. London's second masonry bridge, Westminster Bridge, beside Parliament, was opened in 1750 and rebuilt in 1852–1862. Today, it is the departure point for pleasure boats up and down the river (see p. 52).

Parliament's offices have spilled into neighboring buildings, most recently into Michael Hopkins's fortresslike gray-black Portcullis House. Members of Parliament (MPs) have worshiped at the parish church of Westminster, St. Margaret's, in preference to the much grander Abbey ever since the Puritan Speaker

of the House of Commons worshiped there on Palm Sunday 1614.

Parliament's bureaucratic offices on Whitehall—a street lined with grand, sometimes pompous buildings—would have obliterated all memory of the glorious Whitehall Palace (of which there's a model in the Museum of London p. 68), had Inigo Jones's Banqueting House and John Vardy's Horse Guards not survived.

The abbey is Westminster's second focus and it is the abbey's magnificent building, and the part it has played in Britain's history, that attracts visitors today. Henry III began rebuilding the abbey in 1245 to create a shrine to Edward the Confessor, a royal necropolis, and a royal coronation church. The Archbishop of Canterbury has his London palace right across the river from Westminster.

The geographic proximity of Church and State kept the sovereigns in Westminster. As London grew increasingly polluted, the monarchs left Whitehall Palace for Kensington Palace and Hampton Court, but they always kept Court at St. James's Palace. When George III bought Buckingham House in 1761, he brought the London life of the sovereign back into Westminster. Buckingham Palace has remained the monarch's London home to this day, though St. James's Palace is the official Court residence. ■

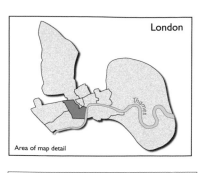

London

Area of map detail

WESTMINSTER

1 U.S. Embassy 2 Royal Mews
3 Queen's Gallery 4 Queen Victoria Memorial 5 Spencer House
6 Lancaster House 7 Clarence House
8 Queen's Chapel 9 Marlborough House 10 Queen Anne's Gate
11 Cabinet War Rooms 12 Central Methodist Hall 13 St. Margaret's
14 Cenotaph 15 Westminster Hall

Westminster Abbey

IT IS ALWAYS WORTH PAUSING IN FRONT OF A GREAT building before entering, and this is particularly true of Westminster Abbey. Today, it takes a leap of the imagination to envisage the impact on medieval London of this soaring church—it is the tallest Gothic church in the country—and of its extensive abbey buildings and grounds.

The West Towers, added to Westminster Abbey in the 18th century

This is not the original abbey church. No evidence has been found of the first church built on this spot, dedicated to St. Peter. Edward the Confessor's, begun in 1050, is gone too. So is the Norman church of 1110–1150, which was gradually demolished to make way for Henry III's church. Today's abbey is largely the result of Henry's devout and hugely expensive building program, begun in 1245. It was he who built the Gothic chancel, transepts, and crossing, and the first five bays of the nave, using soft stone from Reigate in Surrey. Henry was close to the French Court and his architect, Henry of Reynes, may very well have been French. Several basic elements are clearly French-inspired: the polygonal apse with its radiating chapels, the first of its kind to be built in Britain; its amazing height; and its lavish decoration.

Imagine just the chancel, pinned on to the Norman nave. That is how it was for a century. Then, in 1375, Richard II had the Norman nave pulled down so Henry Yevele could begin the new one. The nave was completed in the 1390s, and the great west window was added in the prevailing Perpendicular style. The west towers were not added until the 18th century, designed by Nicholas Hawksmoor.

Henry VII used the leanest possible Perpendicular style when he added his chapel to the east end in 1503–1512. It is well worth viewing from the outside. The great outer piers carrying the buttresses that support the weight of the roof—and so enable the windows to be huge—are folded and paneled.

THE INTERIOR

The first impression is one of extreme richness, in decoration and in monuments. But it was not always so. Imagine the interior empty of all monuments, with a delicate chancel screen—whose function was to divide the monks from the worshippers. Today's rich but heavy Gothic Revival screen, made in 1839, is by Edward Blore; he also designed the elaborate choir stalls, in place by 1848. Multicolored light streams through the stained-glass windows onto the whitewashed walls, and only the carved decoration in red, blue, green, and gold is seen. That is how the abbey was when pilgrims flocked to see the Confessor's shrine, and the cloisters were filled with Benedictine monks.

When Henry VIII dissolved the monasteries, he took the rich Abbey of Westminster for himself in 1534, closed it in 1540, and later sold off two-thirds of its extensive lands. There was a brief reprieve under Mary I, then Elizabeth I sealed the abbey's fate and it became the Collegiate Church of St. Peter at Westminster.

> **A**nd so the building, nobly begun at the King's command, was successfully made ready; and there was no weighing of the costs; past or future, so long as it proved worthy of, and acceptable to, God and St. Peter."
> —Anon. (11th century) ∎

YOUR VISIT

So rich are the abbey's monuments that you should either join a tour or make a list of priorities, allowing time out to rest. Try to arrive early to attend a service in St. Faith's Chapel, or come in the afternoon to join Evensong.

Wandering the nave is like being in an overstocked museum of Renaissance to Victorian sculptures and reliefs. The monument to Sir Isaac Newton, designed by William Kent in 1731, is straight ahead, at the left side of the screen. Michael Rysbrack sculpted the figure of Newton, and those of Ben Jonson and John Milton, both in Poets' Corner. The portrait of Richard II, dated to 1390, is just inside the entrance. Next to it the Tomb of the Unknown Warrior, an unidentified soldier's body from World War I, is the abbey's most recent burial.

Beyond Blore's screen and choir stalls, the deep-cut decoration of Henry III's nave is clear to see. On the way there, at the crossing see James Thornhill's great rose window in the north transept, beautiful

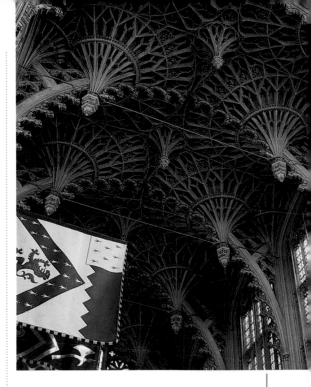

Fan vaulting in Henry VII's chapel

Westminster Abbey

ⓜ Map p. 73

✉ Broad Sanctuary, SW1

☎ 7654 4900
www.westminster-abbey.org

🕐 Closed Sun. except for services.

💲 Nave & Royal Chapels: $$
Chapter House, Pyx Chamber, Undercroft Museum: $
Cloisters: Free

winged angels and ceiling bosses in the south transept, and Sir George Gilbert Scott's high altar of 1868, incorporating Salviati's mosaic of the Last Supper. It is here that the monarch is crowned; for Elizabeth II's coronation in 1952, 250 people took part in nine processions that lasted over four hours in a service based on King Edgar's coronation at Bath in 973.

Henry VII's Chapel is arrestingly beautiful. London's finest late Perpendicular building, it compares with the contemporary chapels at King's College, Cambridge, and the Chapel of St. George at Windsor. The huge windows, together with the cobweb-fine fan vaulting, create a delicate, decorative lightness. The statuary, as elsewhere, was at one time brightly painted and gilded; the choir stalls have richly carved misericords; the banners belong to knights of the ancient Order of the Bath, revived by George I in 1725.

The **Royal Tombs** display some of the abbey's most impressive monuments. An especially poignant one is for Henry VII, who lies next to his beloved queen. The ancient shrine to Edward the Confessor is at the heart of the building. It is surrounded by his royal devotees: Henry III, Edward I, Edward III, and Richard II, with Henry V at the entrance. The Coronation Chair is found beside his grave.

Poet's Corner, by no means restricted to memorials to poets, is in the South transept. Here, with patience, you can find not only Geoffrey Chaucer and Edmund Spenser, but also novelists Jane Austen and George Eliot, composer George Frederick Handel, and actor David Garrick. The walls are decorated with 13th-century wall paintings. Behind lies the quiet, magical St. Faith's Chapel, with a 14th-century wall painting.

Where the South transept joins the Nave, a door leads to the **Abbey Cloisters,** which still give a good idea of the atmosphere that prevailed in London's medieval monasteries. Surrounding the cloisters are several abbey buildings. The Chapter House of 1250–53 is where the abbot would

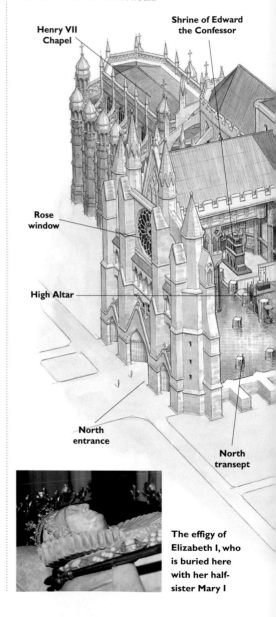

Henry VII Chapel

Shrine of Edward the Confessor

Rose window

High Altar

North entrance

North transept

The effigy of Elizabeth I, who is buried here with her half-sister Mary I give daily instructions to his monks, and it was here that Parliament met in the later 13th and 14th centuries. The **Pyx Chamber** of 1065–1090 and the **Undercroft Museum,** once the monks' dormitories, now house brightly colored wax effigies made for funeral processions: Charles II's is the oldest. More abbey buildings lie outside: In Broad Sanctuary, an arch leads into Dean's Yard, where Westminster School is found. Look for the College Hall of the 1360s, once part of the Abbot's house. ∎

The shrine to Edward the Confessor, who died in 1066

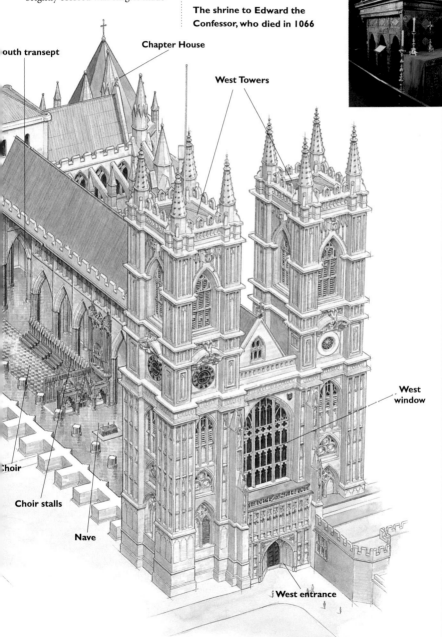

South transept

Chapter House

West Towers

West window

Choir

Choir stalls

Nave

West entrance

Palace of Westminster

COMMONLY KNOWN AS THE HOUSES OF PARLIAMENT, THIS Victorian Gothic riverside palace, with its landmark Big Ben clock tower, is London's newest palace, built on the foundations of its oldest. On October 16, 1834, a fire destroyed the rambling old palace, which had been the principal London royal residence from William the Conqueror to Henry VIII. Even after Henry moved to Whitehall Palace in 1530, Westminster remained the seat of government—as it still does today.

Little survived the 1834 fire: William II's Westminster Hall, the cloisters and crypt of St. Stephen's Chapel, and the 14th-century Jewel Tower, possibly built as a giant safe for Edward III's jewels, furs, and gold. A visit to the Jewel Tower, the only old part that is easily accessible, makes a good start.

There were 97 entries in the competition for the new building— all designs had to be in the fashionable Gothic or Elizabethan Revival styles. Architects Charles Barry and Augustus Welby Pugin won. Their great building had 1,200 rooms, 2 miles of corridor, 11 courtyards, 100 staircases, and a river facade 320 yards long. Almost complete by 1847, this was the symbol of the

Cabinet War Rooms

This maze of underground rooms served as the headquarters for the government's War Cabinet from August 1939 until September 1945. It was from these small, claustrophobic rooms that war operations were directed. They are still furnished, and it is easy to imagine the secret information arriving, the meetings and planning sessions, the transatlantic telephone calls—and Sir Winston Churchill catching a few hours' sleep in his small bedroom. ∎

**Visiting the Palace
of Westminster** To
attend a debate or
Question Time, apply
to your embassy (or
MP). Otherwise, join
the line at the St.
Stephen's Entrance
(best after 5 p.m.).
To go on a highly
recommended guid-
ed tour *(July–Oct.),*
prepurchase a ticket
*(tel 0870 906 3773,
www.firstcalltickets.
com).* A ticket office
opposite the Lords'
Entrance opens in
mid-June.

**The Speaker in
procession into
the House of
Commons**

Mother of Parliaments as the
British Empire enjoyed its apogee.

Although parts of the interior
can be visited (see sidebar p. 78), a
look at the exterior can be rewarding. There are two ways of enjoying
the river facade: from nearby Westminster Bridge; or from across the
river beside Lambeth Palace.

The view from the river is fairy
tale. Pugin, an ardent Gothicist,
coated the classicist Barry's order
with a riot of decoration. Statues of
sovereigns from William the Conqueror to Victoria cover the facade,
while gilded pinnacles catch any
sunlight. Such sumptuousness was
matched inside and is today undergoing long-term refurbishment.

On the left of the palace is
Victoria Tower, over which a flag
flies when Parliament is sitting.
Completed in 1860, it houses a
copy of every Act of Parliament
since 1497. This end of the building,
devoted to the House of Lords, is
decorated in red. The Lords' function is to review, question, revise,
and amend proposed legislation.
Their Peers' Lobby leads to the

Central Lobby. To the right is the
Members' Lobby, where non-
Members (Strangers) can come to
meet their Member of Parliament
(MP) or watch debates from the
Strangers' Gallery. Farther right,
St. Stephen's Hall is the House of
Commons, in somber green. It is
built on the site of the chapel where
Parliament met for 300 years. The
19th-century building kept to the
chapel layout, as did the rebuilding
that took place after World War II
bombing: The Speaker's chair is in
the center, where the altar had been,
the party in government on his/her
right, the Opposition on the left.

The clock tower, known by the
name of its bell, **Big Ben,** symbol-
izes British government for many. If
Parliament is sitting at night, a light
shines on top. The tower was completed in 1858, and the clock, with a
bell cast in Whitechapel (see p. 199),
started on May 31, 1859. Its dials
are 23 feet in diameter, its hour
hand 9 feet long, and the minute
hand 14 feet long. The chimes are
said to be based on Handel's aria, "I
know that my redeemer liveth." ■

A Westminster walk

This half-day walk is strong on street statuary. It's a good one to do on a day of unsure weather, as there is always a remarkable building for shelter if the clouds burst. Start at Westminster Tube station; end at Green Park station. For a shorter walk, finish at St. James's Park station, behind Queen Anne's Gate.

From **Westminster Bridge ❶**, enjoy the river facade of the Palace of Westminster and, downstream, County Hall, home to the London Aquarium. On the north end of the bridge, Thomas Thornycroft's bronze, unveiled in 1902, shows **Queen Boudicca** and her daughters hurtling toward London in their chariot.

Walk past **Big Ben's** clock tower ❷ (see p. 79), then left around the Palace of Westminster, passing first an 1899 statue of Parliamentarian leader Oliver Cromwell (1599–1658), then the Crusader Richard I (R.1189–1199). **St. Margaret's Church, Westminster,** and the **Jewel Tower ❸** stand across the road. In **Victoria Tower Gardens** find three memorials: to the emancipation of slaves in 1833; to the suffragette Emmeline Pankhurst (1857–1928); and Rodin's sculpture, "The Burghers of Calais."

Cross Lambeth Bridge for **Lambeth Palace ❹**, the intriguing little **Museum of Garden History,** and, in front, the finest viewpoint for the Palace of Westminster. The superb **Imperial War Museum** (see p. 213) is a five-minute walk down Lambeth Road.

Back on the north bank, elegant 18th-century Westminster is found down Dean Bradley Street, in Smith Square, where **St. John's Church ❺**, now a concert hall, often has lunchtime concerts. Walk past the fine houses of Lord North Street and down Cowley and Dean Barton Streets to Great College Street, where an arch on the right leads into Dean's Yard. At the far end, another arch opens into Broad Sanctuary, beside the west door of **Westminster Abbey** (see p. 74). Opposite, the domed Central Methodist Hall of 1905–1911 and the Middlesex Guildhall of the same date stand on either side of Powell Moya and Partners' **Queen Elizabeth II Conference Centre ❻**, opened in 1986.

Parliament Square, down Broad Sanctuary to the right, is a political sculpture court. Abraham Lincoln and the great orator George Canning (1770–1827) stand in front of Guildhall; statesmen Sir Robert Peel (1788–1850), Lord Beaconsfield (born Benjamin Disraeli, 1804–1881), Lord Derby (1799–1869), and Lord Palmerston (1784–1865) overlook the central square, ending with Field Marshal Jan Smuts (1870–1950) and the old, bearlike Sir Winston Churchill. Sir George Gilbert Scott's Foreign Office (Old Treasury), built in 1868–1873, fills the north side of the square and represents the triumph of classical over Gothic in the Victorian battle of tastes.

Past Big Ben again, find two annexes for MPs: new Portcullis House and, on Victoria Embankment road, Richard Norman Shaw's striped 1880s building. Farther along, a section of old Whitehall Palace's terrace can be seen in the gardens, behind the statue of General Gordon (1833–1885). Turn up Horse Guards Avenue to Whitehall; the

Richard the Lionhearted guards the Houses of Parliament.

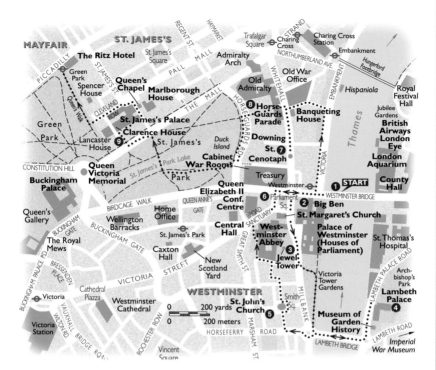

Banqueting House (see p. 82) stands on the corner. Whitehall has three monuments in the road: Sir Edwin Lutyens's **Cenotaph** and equestrian statues to Field Marshals Earl Haig (1861–1928) and the 2nd Duke of Cambridge (1819–1904).

Across Whitehall and left, **Downing Street** ❼ lies behind its great gates on the right. Prime Minister Tony Blair's official residence is No. 11, better suited to his young family than the traditional No. 10. Back up Whitehall, William Kent and John Vardy's **Horse Guards** was built 1745–1755. The guard is changed twice daily. Go through to **Horse Guards Parade** ❽ to see the building's park facade that forms the backdrop to royal pageantry such as Trooping the Colour.

St. James's Park lies ahead, surrounded by an assortment of buildings. To the left, near the statue of Clive of India (1725–1774), are the **Cabinet War Rooms** (see p. 78). The bridge over the lake gives fine views toward Whitehall and leads to the Mall. From here look left, up past the Queen Victoria Memorial to Buckingham Palace. **Clarence House** ❾,

- Inside front cover D3
- ► Westminster Tube station
- 3.4 miles
- 3 hours
- ► Green Park Tube station

NOT TO BE MISSED
- Parliament Square
- Banqueting House
- Downing Street
- St. James's Park

formerly the Queen Mother's home, is now refurbished as the Prince of Wales's London home (www.princeofwales.gov.uk). Its reception rooms are open to the public in summer (tel 7930 4832, 7799 2331, www.royalresidences.com & www.royal.gov.uk). Marlborough Road runs between them to **St. James's Palace**, whose Queen's Chapel is to the right. Walk around the palace, turning into Cleveland Row, which leads to Green Park, where Queen's Walk goes up past The Ritz hotel's park facade to Green Park Tube station. ■

Inigo Jones gave Westminster a room fit for royal entertaining.

Banqueting House

Banqueting House

🅰 Map p. 73

✉ Whitehall, SW1

☎ 7930 4179

www.hrp.org.uk

🕒 Closed Sun. & for government functions

💲 $$. Recorded tour for rent

🚇 Tube: Westminster, Charing Cross, or Embankment

MORE A GRAND ROOM WITH A BASEMENT THAN A HOUSE, this huge, double-cube space, lit by floor-to-ceiling windows on the Whitehall side, has its entire ceiling painted by Peter Paul Rubens, and is perhaps London's most beautiful room.

James I built it between 1619 and 1622, employing architect Inigo Jones, who was already working on Queen's House at Greenwich (see p. 205). Later Jones would design Queen's Chapel for St. James's Palace, and Covent Garden's St. Paul's as well as the Piazza (see p. 113). The king wanted to rebuild the whole of Henry VIII's rambling, brick Whitehall Palace, but this was the only part to be completed. The Banqueting House survived the fire of 1698, when the rest of the palace was destroyed. London's first building to be partly encased in Portland stone, it set a new design tone.

The crypt was for the king's informal parties. The grand room upstairs was for masques, banquets, Court ceremonies, and diplomatic functions. On entering the room,

the visitor would see the decoration of two orders, Ionic below and Corinthian above, mirroring the exterior of the building. Ranks of courtiers standing on both sides led the visitor to the enthroned king, ahead. Looking up, he or she would see Rubens's panels, painted in 1634 for Charles I for £3,000 (about $4,500). For these paintings, which honored Charles's father, James I, as the symbol of the union of England and Scotland and celebrated the benefits of wise rule, Charles bestowed a knighthood on Rubens.

Later events were to put Rubens's allegory into question. Charles I was beheaded on a scaffold mounted outside the windows on January 30, 1649; but in 1660, it was here that Charles II celebrated his restoration to the throne. ∎

Westminster Cathedral

BEGIN IN THE CATHEDRAL'S PIAZZA, OFF VICTORIA STREET. Here, the red and white bulk of London's last cathedral rises uninterrupted. The Roman Catholic hierarchy was not reestablished in England and Wales until 1850, 300 years after the Reformation. In 1894, Archbishop Vaughan chose John Bentley to design a cathedral on two conditions: that it had a wide nave for big congregations, and that it looked nothing like nearby (Protestant) Westminster Abbey.

Bentley had been working in the Gothic style. This would not do, being too similar to the abbey. So he toured Italy, Greece, and Constantinople (Istanbul), and returned to create a church that mixed Byzantine and Romanesque ideas using red brick and white Portland stone.

Climb the **Campanile** for views toward Big Ben, Nelson's Column, and Buckingham Palace. The cross on top of the Campanile contains a relic of the True Cross.

Inside the cathedral, incense perfumes the air, mosaics in chapel domes reflect the lights of votive candles, and a great gold cross hangs above the required huge nave. Marble lines the walls, while the domes and apse are held together by bridges supported on columns inspired by Ravenna's seventh-century churches. Eric Gill's "Stations of the Cross," made in 1914–18, are on the nave piers. To see Bentley's scheme complete, peep into the Lady Chapel. ∎

Westminster Cathedral
- Map p. 73
- Victoria Street, SW1
- 7798 9055.
  Tours: 7798 9069
  www.westminster cathedral.org.uk
- Campanile: closed Thurs.–Sun. Dec.–March
- Cathedral: donation Campanile: $
- Tube: Victoria

Mass at Westminster Cathedral

St. James's Palace

St. James's Palace

- Map p. 73
- Cleveland Row, Marlborough Gate, SW1
- Palace not open to the public. Chapel Royal & Ambassadors Court: Sun. services Oct.–Easter. Queen's Chapel: Sun. services Easter–July
- Tube: Green Park

The Tudor gatehouse of St. James's Palace

A VISIT TO ST. JAMES'S PALACE SHOULD BEGIN IN FRIARY Court, watching the Queen's color trooped, as the old guard forms up during the Changing of the Guard ceremony. The original palace, which had four courts, was built in the 1530s by Henry VIII as part of a lavish building program. Despite fires and rebuilding, much of the exterior survives.

The name of one of the courts, Friary Court, betrays the origins of the palace. A medieval Augustinian friary, it later became a women's leper hospital dedicated to St. James the Less. Henry VIII bought the hospital and its grounds, built the palace, and enclosed 300 acres of land (now St. James's Park).

After the Whitehall Palace fire of 1698, St. James's became the sovereign's principal London residence. Two nearby palatial mansions were built after that date: Sir Christopher Wren's Marlborough House in 1709–1711, and Benjamin Wyatt's Lancaster House in 1827. After George III's move to Buckingham Palace in 1762, St. James's remained the official royal residence. Today, a new sovereign is proclaimed here, and makes his or her first speech here. Foreign ambassadors are appointed to the Court of St. James's, and ride from here in the glass coach to make their first courtesy call on the Queen.

Opposite Friary Court stands **Queen's Chapel.** Built in 1623 for Charles I's Catholic wife, Henrietta Maria, it was England's first Italian-inspired classical church. Inigo Jones designed it and, as at Banqueting House, made the interior a simple double cube.

Henry's four-story **Gatehouse,** with its clock, octagonal towers, and linenfold-paneled doors, gives an idea of what fairy-tale palaces Tudor Whitehall and Greenwich must have been. It is sometimes possible to peek into Ambassadors Court and, on some Sundays, to visit the **Chapel Royal,** whose painted roof may have been done by Holbein. The rest was lavishly redecorated in the 1830s.

It was at St. James's Palace that the Court custom of having a poet-laureate as an official part of the royal household began. John Dryden was the first; subsequent poet laureates have included William Wordsworth, Alfred Lord Tennyson, Sir John Betjeman, Ted Hughes, and, currently, Andrew Motion. ∎

Buckingham Palace

THE DUKE OF BUCKINGHAM'S RELATIVELY MODEST mansion built in 1705 is now lost behind successive additions of regal rooms, splendid art, and an imposing facade. Outside the railings, people gather on momentous occasions to cheer the Queen and the Royal Family, who come out onto the balcony between the great central columns. The sovereign's London home is a focal point of the capital.

THE VIEW

The best view of Buckingham Palace is from the Mall, near Sir Aston Webb's "Queen Victoria Memorial" created in 1901–1913. Thomas Brock's marble statue of the Queen looks up the Mall, surrounded by allegorical figures of such Victorian virtues as Charity, Truth, Progress, and Manufacture; a gold-leaf Victory figure soars above. The circular Memorial Gardens that surround it, symbolizing the Empire, have gates given by Canada, West and South Africa, and Australia.

Straight ahead, across the parade ground where the Changing of the Guard ceremony takes place, the Palace's Portland stone facade seen today was constructed by Sir Aston Webb in just three months in 1913. Before that, Buckingham Palace and its surroundings had been far less imposing. John Sheffield, Duke of Buckingham,

Buckingham Palace with its gardens on the left, the Queen Victoria Memorial on the right, and Green Park in the background

The Royal Standard flying above the palace indicates that the Queen is in residence.

Buckingham Palace

Map p. 73

The Mall, SW1

7930 4832 or 7799 2331.

Tickets for the State Rooms: 7321 2233 & at ticket office opposite the palace. Royal Mews: 7839 1377. Queen's Gallery: 7321 2233 www.royalresidences.com, www.royal.gov.uk

built a country house here in 1705. After George III bought it in 1761 for his wife, Queen Charlotte of Mecklenburgh-Strelitz, Sir William Chambers remodeled it, retaining its private character; ceremonial functions continued to take place at St. James's Palace.

THE BUILDING

It was George IV who began aggrandizing the house in 1826. He instructed John Nash to transform it into an appropriately grand palace where he could hold his courts and official ceremonies. The elderly Nash, hampered by inadequate funds and the need to incorporate the old building, added a string of new rooms along the garden side, with State Rooms up on the first floor. Nash's Bath stone garden facade is particularly delightful in its light, French neoclassic style, but his Mall facade was obscured by Edward Blore's east wing, added in 1847–1850 to provide more space for Queen Victoria—nurseries, bedrooms, kitchens, and a huge ballroom 123 feet long.

THE INTERIOR

While the Queen keeps a mere dozen rooms overlooking Green Park for herself, visitors can enjoy the grand scale and lavish furnishings of the **State Rooms.** George IV's taste for opulence is displayed in sculptured panels, elaborate ceilings, and bright colors such as raspberry pink and lapis blue. The Blue, White, and Green Drawing Rooms, the Music Room, and the

Throne Room are some of the grandest. George's palace was completed only after his death, and William IV never lived there. So it was the young Victoria who, in 1837, moved into a fresh, new palace.

The palace is a treasure house of art; the Royal Collection is one of the world's finest. When George V and Queen Mary came to the throne, they employed Sir Aston Webb to improve the exterior while they arranged the contents. Queen Mary's organized approach to this task resulted in sets of furniture being reassembled from all over the Royal residences and restored.

In all, the palace has 600 rooms, including 19 State Rooms, 52 royal and guest bedrooms, 188 staff bedrooms, and 78 bathrooms. More than 400 people work here, and each year more than 40,000 are entertained here. Used for state ceremonies, official entertaining, and royal garden parties, it is one of the world's few remaining working royal palaces.

THE TOUR

Today, it is possible to visit some of the State Rooms, a move initiated to raise funds after Windsor Castle's 1992 fire (see p. 222). Visitors enter Buckingham Palace through the **Ambassadors Court,** where Nash's facade is visible. Go up the grand Carrara marble double staircase to see the Green Drawing Room and the Throne Room. Next is the Picture Gallery, where Van Dyck's "Charles I" of 1633 is among 50 major

All openings subject to change. State Rooms: Aug.–Oct. The Royal Mews (entrance on Buckingham Palace Rd.): March–Aug. Tues.–Thurs., Aug.–Oct. Mon.–Thurs., & Oct.–March Wed.

State Rooms: $$$
Royal Mews: $$
Queen's Gallery: $$

Tube: Green Park, Victoria, or St. James's Park

Since 1993 the palace's State Rooms have been open to the public in summer. The visit includes the opulent White Drawing Room.

paintings from the Royal Collection hung in the top-lit room. The Silk Tapestry Room leads into the East Gallery, and so to the rooms overlooking the 45 acres of glorious gardens. The State Dining Room comes first, then the Blue Drawing Room, the Music Room with its great bow window, and the White Drawing Room. You leave down the Ministers' Stair and across a corner of the gardens.

OTHER PALACE AREAS

You can see more of the Royal art collection at the newly rebuilt and enlarged Queen's Gallery, designed by John Simpson. Here, changing exhibitions display a selection of the Queen's own art, one of the

world's finest private collections. At the nearby Royal Mews on Buckingham Palace Road, Nash's stables and coach house still contain the painted State Coach of 1761, the horses that pull it today, the harness, and other royal ceremony apparel. ■

"It was like a triumphal entry … The windows, the roofs of the houses, were one mass of beaming faces, and the cheers never ceased … I was deeply touched and gratified …

No one ever, I believe, has met with such an ovation as was given to me, passing through those six miles of streets."—Queen Victoria in her journal, June 21, 1897, about her Diamond Jubilee parade.

Royal parks

London's nine royal parks are a great source of pleasure. These lands were once private, personal possessions of the sovereign, used for hunting and other pastimes. Gradually, under pressure, they were opened to the public. Charles II began with St. James's Park.

The parks have various origins. Henry VIII took Hyde Park in exchange for land in Berkshire. Primrose Hill was also an exchange deal, this time with Eton College. Richmond Park was a series of farms bought by Charles I. William and Mary added Kensington Gardens to Nottingham House.

Today, an informal atmosphere is preserved, though park law and regulations are enforced by a parks security force. Gardeners maintain a labor-intensive but impressive style—40,000 tulips are planted annually in front of Buckingham Palace, 250,000 more at Hampton Court. There are also naturalists looking after the animals, trees, and lakes. Volunteers record the large numbers of birds.

You can walk through nearly 2 miles of parkland—from Westminster to Notting Hill—through St. James's, Green, and Hyde Parks to Kensington Gardens. ■

Right: Peace and quiet in the rose-scented Queen Mary's Rose Garden in Regent's Park

Royal London

London is full of contradictions. Although a democratically elected government sits at Westminster, with the sovereign merely a figurehead, the royal presence is strongly felt. At a time when the very existence of a royal family is under question, the capital is littered with royal reminders.

It was Edward the Confessor, king of England 1042–1066, who first made Westminster his capital. Queen Elizabeth II traces her blood-descent back to Egbert of Wessex, king of the English from 829. London's palaces, pageantry, statues, and symbols result from this history.

Homes & gardens

The choice of royal homes to visit in London begins with Buckingham Palace (see pp. 85–89), followed by Clarence House (see p. 81), both lived in today. Then there are Whitehall Palace's surviving Banqueting House (see p. 82), Westminster's Jewel Tower (see p. 80), Kensington Palace (see pp. 146–47), and the fortress-palace, the Tower of London (see pp.

By Appointment

More than 800 shops in Britain have a royal coat of arms fixed above the door. This indicates that the business holds a royal warrant to supply "By Appointment" to the Queen, Queen Mother, Duke of Edinburgh, or the Prince of Wales. Dating back to the Middle Ages, the tradition remains strong today. The highest concentration of these official royal suppliers, who use their position to promote the quality of their goods, is in St. James's and Mayfair ■

The Queen rides in an open carriage, driven by a postillion, to the Trooping of the Colour. Right: The Royal Coat of Arms

194–97). Farther afield, magnificent Hampton Court Palace (see pp. 187–90) lies upriver, beyond Kew Palace and Marble Hill House. Greenwich (see pp. 202–206) is downstream, while the riches of Windsor Castle (see pp. 222–23) are a 40-minute train ride away. On Sundays, the Chapels Royal at St. James's, Hampton Court, the Tower, and the Queen's Chapel are occasionally open to worshipers. St. James's Palace, Westminster Hall, Clarence House, and Marlborough House can be enjoyed just from the outside, but only tantalizing fragments remain of Richmond, Rotherhithe, and other lost palaces.

The Royal Parks were once royal hunting grounds. Garden lovers should not miss Queen Mary's Rose Garden in Regent's Park, the Tudor and Dutch gardens at Hampton Court, or the Royal Botanical Gardens at Kew.

Pageantry

Despite some scaling down of royal pageantry, there is still plenty to see. The Changing of the Guard takes place at Buckingham and St. James's Palaces, and at the Tower, either daily or every other day. The Ceremony of the Keys has been performed nightly for more than 700 years at the Tower. Annual events include Trooping the Colour, Beating the Retreat, and the State Opening of Parliament in November. The Queen still follows the Court Year, and entertains visiting heads of state in April, July, and November. ■

Regency shop fronts are part of the elegance of Burlington Arcade.

St. James's, Mayfair, & Piccadilly

THE HEART OF ARISTOCRATIC LONDON HAS ENJOYED A reputation for exclusiveness since its development by the aristocrats themselves, when they moved westward from the City and leased land to speculative builders.

Spencer House

🅰 Map p. 73

✉ 27 St. James's Place, SW1

☎ 7499 8620

www.spencerhouse .co.uk

🕐 Open Sun. only. Closed Jan. & Aug.

$ $$

🚇 Tube: Green Park

ST. JAMES'S

Today, St. James's Square, laid out by Henry Jermyn in the 1660s, is home to the discerning bibliophiles' refuge, the **London Library** at No. 14. **Christie's,** the international art auctioneers, is on nearby King Street, surrounded by art dealers who break from their shops to lunch at their clubs (see sidebar p. 93) or shop on Jermyn Street. Guests of the Ritz, Stafford, and Duke's hotels echo the lifestyle once enjoyed in such mansions as **Spencer House,** painstakingly restored by Lord Rothschild.

Asprey & Co.

This lavishly refurbished shop, with its long, curving, old windows, epitomizes Mayfair shopping (169 New Bond St., tel 7493 6767, www.asprey.com). Charles Asprey, of French Protestant Huguenot descent, opened a shop here in 1848, and until recently his family has supplied the royal family with jewelry, silver, and objets d'art. Designers and craftsmen working in the shop create some of the unquestionably luxurious and beautiful objects on sale. But for most people, the solid silver swizzle sticks and gold-plated peppermills will remain in a windowshopper's dreamland. ■

Gentlemen's clubs

The 18th-century coffeehouses and gambling clubs of Mayfair and St. James's developed into somber gentlemen's clubs. Large clubhouses along Pall Mall and St. James's Street became homes-away-from-home for members who tended to share the same interests. On Pall Mall, the Athenaeum is known for academics and bishops, while the Reform attracts liberal thinkers (it was the first to give full membership to women). On St. James's Street, the Carlton is for Tories, Brooks's is more liberal, and White's is for the very grand. ■

MAYFAIR

Essentially a development of six great estates, Mayfair's residential grandeur is enhanced by deluxe hotels: The Dorchester, Claridges, and The Connaught. The Mayfair home of composer George Frideric Handel from 1723 to 1759 is now **Handel House Museum** (*25 Brook St., W1, Tel 7495 1685, www.handelhouse.org*). Sotheby's, Mayfair's art focus, is on the most stylish shopping strip, New and Old Bond Streets, where Asprey's, Versace, and the Fine Art Society create dazzling shop windows to lure spenders.

PICCADILLY

Dividing Mayfair and St. James's, Piccadilly runs from Piccadilly Circus to Hyde Park Corner. Here, the Duke of Wellington's **Apsley House** is a rare survivor of Mayfair's mansions, with Adam fireplaces and pictures by Goya and Rubens. Quality pleasures line the street's core: The Ritz hotel and Hatchard's bookshop on one side; the **Royal Academy of Arts** and Burlington Arcade on the other.

The academy was founded in 1768, with George III as its patron and Sir Joshua Reynolds its first president. Gainsborough was a founding member; Constable and Turner were students. The tradition of newly elected Academicians presenting one work to the academy began early, and the exhibition of these is the origin of the annual Summer Exhibitions.

At the show in 1855, Queen Victoria bought Frederick, Lord Leighton's painting, "Cimabue's Madonna," thus securing the young artist's reputation. Even today, international exhibitions make way for the great Summer Exhibition, when Royal Academicians exhibit their work alongside amateur and professional artists who enter in competition.

Burlington Arcade runs alongside the academy. Samuel Ware's covered shopping arcade, completed in 1819, was a Continental idea welcomed by fashionable, often rain-drenched London. Piccadilly, Royal Opera, Prince's, and Royal Arcades are all in this area, each containing boutiques. ■

The grand entrance hall of the Reform Club

Apsley House
- Map p. 72
- Wellington Museum, Apsley House, 149 Piccadilly, SW1
- 7499 5676
- www.apsleyhouse .org.uk
- Closed Mon.
- $$
- Tube: Hyde Park Corner

Royal Academy of Arts
- Map p. 73
- Burlington House, Piccadilly, W1
- 7300 8000
- www.royalacademy .org.uk
- Open daily during exhibitions
- Cost varies with the exhibition
- Tube: Green Park, Piccadilly Circus

Wallace Collection

Wallace Collection
- Map p. 72
- Hertford House, Manchester Square, W1M 6BN
- 7935 0687
  www.the-wallace-collection.org.uk
- Closed Sun. a.m.
- Tube: Bond Street, Marble Arch

ONE OF THE CAPITAL'S FINEST PRIVATE ART COLLECTIONS is found at Hertford House, a palatial 18th-century mansion just north of Mayfair in Manchester Square.

The house was built for the Duke of Manchester in 1777. But it was four generations of the art-loving Hertford family who created the collection. The 1st Marquess was patron to the 18th-century Scots painter Allan Ramsay and bought works by Canaletto. The 2nd Marquess bought the house in 1797 and hung Gainsboroughs upon its walls. The 3rd, who enjoyed a high society life with the Prince Regent, added Sèvres porcelain and Dutch canvases. And the 4th, an eccentric living in Paris in post-revolution chaos, bought Fragonards, Watteaus, and Bouchers, plus furniture, and installed the Parisian staircase. As a postscript, the 4th Marquess's illegitimate son and inheritor, Richard Wallace, renovated the house and added his Italian majolica and Renaissance armor, bronzes, and gold. His widow gave both house and collection to the nation.

Hertford House is a joy to visit; Rick Mather's glazed roof spans the inner courtyard and Café Bagatelle. The lower ground floor houses four new galleries, a lecture theater, studio, and visitors' library.

A composite 15th-century suit of German armor for man and horse made of low-carbon steel in the spiky Gothic style

When you first enter, it is difficult to resist going straight up the opulent double staircase, whose balustrade of wrought iron and bronze was made for Louise XV's Palais Mazarin in Paris. Do not miss the Boucher paintings on the walls. Up on the next floor, treats include a roomful of Venetian paintings by Canaletto and his pupil, Guardi, and another room of Dutch pictures by Ruisdael, Hobbema, and Wijnants. The finest collection of French paintings outside France includes Fragonard's "The Swing." Frans Hals's "The Laughing Cavalier" is among the familiar paintings in the 100-foot Long Gallery. Back downstairs, enjoy the English paintings, Boulle furniture, and clocks. Also shown here are Limoges enamels, Venetian glass, porcelain, and finally the armor. ■

W estminster, Covent Garden, Bloomsbury, Marylebone, and Mayfair encircle this concentration of theaters, restaurants, national galleries, first-run cinemas, and state-of-the-art amusements.

Trafalgar Square & Soho

Soho at night: London's clubland

Trafalgar Square & Soho

THIS SMALL AREA OF UNCOMPROMISINGLY URBAN LONDON, CUT OFF FROM the river and parks, has few great public buildings. It is, nevertheless, a microcosm of the capital's passive and active reaction to Londoners' demands for change over the centuries.

A close-up view of Nelson's stony face from his statue on the 185-foot column in the middle of Trafalgar Square

In Tudor times, farms, fields, and woods—the possessions of various monasteries—lay north of royal Westminster. To improve his hunting around Whitehall Palace, whose stables until the 19th century covered much of today's Trafalgar Square, Henry VIII appropriated the land that later became Soho. The focus for London's commercial entertainment was established.

Shaftesbury Avenue, completed in 1886, divides Soho into two distinct halves. The narrow streets to the north have in the 20th century been home to newly arrived Greeks, mainland Italians, and Sicilians, creating a slightly exotic and friendly Continental atmosphere. Today, most of the seedy clubs have been turned into chic bars and restaurants, and there are plans to pedestrianize some of the narrow streets. To the south, a handful of streets makes up Tong Yan Kai (Chinese Street), as one of London's newest immigrant populations calls it. The Chinese, fleeing poverty in Hong Kong, arrived here from the 1950s forward and quickly created an atmospheric Chinatown.

Moving farther south, 19th-century Leicester Square had transformed from residential square to entertainment center by the 1950s, with Turkish baths and a full-scale circus. And when the picture palaces arrived from America, several great halls offered their clients the cheap but gloriously escapist Hollywood dreams. Nightclubs soon abounded, where Noel Coward, Gloria Swanson, and Marlene Dietrich entertained and encouraged the inter-war fashionable set to dance fast and forget the looming clouds of social change and the onset of another war. Today, cinemas still dominate the square, and Madame Tussaud's (Rock Circus) and the great Trocadero entertainment center are nearby.

Oxford Circus

Trafalgar Square, to the southeast, makes an uneasy transfer from entertainment center to more somber London districts. James Gibbs's St. Martin-in-the-Fields, 1721, was the blueprint for colonial churches, especially in America. It stands on the corner of the 19th-century square, conceived as a vast crossroads for routes to Buckingham Palace, the Houses of Parliament, Whitehall, and the City. The square's walls are Smirke's porticoed Canada

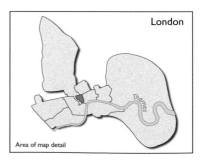

London

Thames

Area of map detail

House, Baker's fine South Africa House, and William Wilkins's National Gallery, which was built in 1832–38; the Sainsbury Wing was added in 1988–1991. In the center of the square, Horatio, Viscount Nelson, the hero of the Battle of Trafalgar in 1805, looks down on an unchanging London scene of visitors, statues, fountains, and hundreds of pigeons. ∎

The Empire Theatre in Leicester Square, one of the great Victorian theaters, is now a cinema.

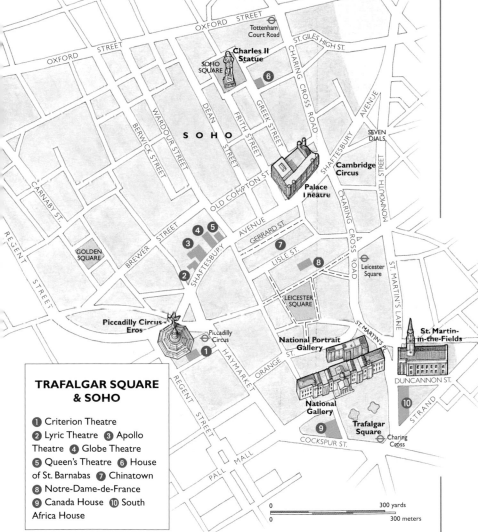

TRAFALGAR SQUARE & SOHO

① Criterion Theatre
② Lyric Theatre ③ Apollo Theatre ④ Globe Theatre
⑤ Queen's Theatre ⑥ House of St. Barnabas ⑦ Chinatown
⑧ Notre-Dame-de-France
⑨ Canada House ⑩ South Africa House

The impressive portico of the National Gallery overlooks Trafalgar Square and fountains by Sir Edwin Lutyens.

National Gallery

THIS IS ONE OF THE WORLD'S MOST IMPRESSIVE NATIONAL galleries. Indeed, the National Gallery's collection of about 2,000 paintings is a succession of masterpieces that tell the story of European painting from the 13th to the 19th centuries. Because the collection is relatively small and the rooms compact, the visitor can stroll through all the galleries, pick out some highlights, and choose areas to return to another day for an in-depth look.

National Gallery

- 🅰 Map p. 97
- ✉ Trafalgar Square, WC2
- ☎ 7839 3321. Information: 7747 2885
- 💲 Charge for some special exhibitions. Crowded on weekends
- 🚇 Tube: Charing Cross, Embankment, Leicester Square

It was George IV who, observing the enlightened progress of public art galleries in Paris, Amsterdam, Vienna, Madrid, and Berlin, suggested to a government reluctant to fund the arts that there should be a National Gallery of England. Fortunately, prompted by the promised gift of a fine collection, it stumped up £57,000 ($91,200) in 1824 to pay for the 38 pictures left by John Julius Angerstein, a Russian-born financier living in London. At first, his pictures were exhibited in his Pall Mall house; then in 1838 they were moved into William Wilkins's classic building overlooking Nash's newly laid-out Trafalgar Square. The Sainsbury Wing, opened in 1991, has expanded gallery space with 16 rooms, home for the magnificent early Renaissance paintings of Italy and northern Europe.

OVERVIEW

Every painting in the impressive collection—unless on loan or in restoration—is on display. If a room is closed, its contents will usually be displayed elsewhere;

simply ask. The 66 galleries are divided into four sections: paintings of 1260–1510 in the Sainsbury Wing; paintings of 1510–1600 in the West Wing; paintings of 1600–1700 in the refurbished North Wing; and later paintings in the East Wing. Twentieth-century art is displayed at Bankside's Tate Modern (see p. 216), while most of the British paintings are at Tate Britain (see p. 174) in Pimlico.

SAINSBURY WING (ROOMS 51–66)

The place to start is the Sainsbury Wing. The gallery's earliest Renaissance paintings are hung here, a mixture of northern and southern European works. One of the earliest is Giotto's "The Pentecost" (1306–1312), in Room 51. With his murals in Florence and Padua, this work marks the beginning of a new artistic era, one in which painting became realistic, three-dimensional, and dramatic. Rooms 52–56 illustrate this further, notably with "The Wilton Diptych" (1395–99), possibly commissioned by Richard II of England for his private devotions; Paolo Uccello's "Battle of San Remo" (circa 1450), showing a Florentine victory over the Siencse; and Rogier van der Weyden's almost surreal naturalistic "The Magdalen Reading" (1399). As for portraits, there are the groundbreaking heads by Robert Campin, and Jan van Eyck's "The Arnolfini Marriage" (both from the 1430s).

Rooms 57–60 contain more complex technical challenges, such as Carlo Crivelli's "The Annunciation, with Saint Emidius" (1486), with its deep perspective and political overtones, and "An Allegorical Figure" (circa 1460) by Cosimo Tura, an Italian who had absorbed the northern precision technique.

Botticelli's "Venus and Mars" (1480–1490) is one of the Florentine artist's few secular works, still decorative, but achieving a wonderfully translucent gown for Venus. The two by Raphael, "Saint Catherine of Alexandria" (1507–1508) and "The Ansidei Madonna" (1505), were painted when the artist was in his early twenties, yet already they display the influence of ancient Greco-Roman art, as well as the search for ideal beauty that marks the High Renaissance.

At this point, go into the darkened chamber in Room 51, containing Leonardo da Vinci's large, fragile drawing of "The Virgin and Child with Saint Anne and Saint John the Baptist" (circa 1499–1500). Return to the main room for "The Virgin of the Rocks" (circa 1508).

Rooms 61–66, at the end of this section, contain a number of familiar Renaissance paintings. From the Veneto, there is Andrea

The Victorian glory of the refurbished North Wing, where 17th-century European paintings hang

"A Scene on Ice near a Town" by the Dutch painter Hendrick Avercamp (1585–1634)

Mantegna's "The Agony in the Garden" (circa 1460) and his brother-in-law Giovanni Bellini's picture of the same subject, painted five years later. Portraits grow in number and refinement—for instance, Alisso Baldovinetti's "Portrait of the Lady in Yellow" (1465) and Giovanni Bellini's "The Doge Leonardo Loredan" (circa 1501). Finally, don't miss the two

sedate Piero della Francesca panels, "The Baptism of Christ" from the 1450s and "Nativity" (1470–75).

WEST WING (ROOMS 2–12)

The High Renaissance artists represented here include Raphael, Michelangelo, Bronzino, and Correggio. All were influenced by Leonardo da Vinci. Inspired by

---

Dulwich Picture Gallery

✉ College Road, SE21
☎ 8693 5254
www.dulwichpicture
gallery.org.uk
🕐 Closed Mon.
💲 $$. Free on Fri.
🚆 Regular trains from Victoria and London Bridge Stations to North Dulwich or West Dulwich

Dulwich Picture Gallery

Opened in 1814, Sir John Soane's custom-designed neoclassic gallery was England's first public art gallery. It owes its astounding collection to the failure of the British government to accept the offer of 400 pictures collected by the art dealer Noel Desenfans. The collection was intended for the projected National Gallery of Poland in Warsaw, but when the Polish king was forced to abdicate in 1795, Desenfans offered it to Britain. Unbelievably, the government refused the offer. Desenfans

then gave the paintings to Sir Francis Bourgeois, who later bequeathed them to Dulwich College, already the owners of a good art collection. Wandering the dozen top-lit rooms today, you can enjoy in peace what might have been exhibited in Trafalgar Square: Van Dyck's "Emmanuel Philibert of Savoy," Poussin's "Triumph of David," Rembrandt's "Girl at a Window," Cornelius Bol's view of London, sketches by Rubens, and several Gainsboroughs. There are also temporary exhibitions. ■

Bellini, Venetian artists such as Titian explored color and worked increasingly in oil paints on canvas, cloth used for sails. Subject matter broadened to include bigger portraits, mythological and allegorical compositions, still lifes, and landscapes. The age of collectors began and the artist's skills were valued as much as his subject matter.

Two Italian artists in Room 2 demonstrate these changes: Correggio in "The School of Love" and Parmigianino in his "Madonna and Child with Saints John the Baptist and Jerome" (both circa 1520). The Holbeins in Room 3 include "The Ambassadors" (1533), an early portrait of two full-length figures. Room 8 contains paintings by three of the leading artists of 1500–1550: Michelangelo's "The Entombment," Sebastiano del Piombo's "The Raising of Lazarus," and Bronzino's "An Allegory with Venus and Cupid." Venetian color dominates in Room 9, where Titian's works include "Bacchus and Ariadne" (1522–23) and "The Vendramin Family" (1543–47); there is more Venetian portraiture in Paolo Veronese's "The Family of Darius before Alexander" (1565–1570) in Room 11.

NORTH WING (ROOMS 14–32)

The richness of 17th-century painting fills the next 19 rooms. Landscape had become a favorite subject of collectors and patrons, and northern artists such as Cuyp, Ruisdael, and Rubens produced some of the most sublime canvases. Under the influence of northern artists, Italians reduced the size of pictures, while Italy's classical art and southern light inspired such northerners as Poussin, Claude, and Rubens. Van Dyck, Velazquez, and Rembrandt took the portrait tradition a step further, while the

"Ballet Dancers" by Edgar Degas (1834–1917)

most innovative painting schools were the Spanish and Dutch, typified by Velazquez and Rembrandt.

Claude Lorraine's landscapes in Rooms 15 and 19, such as "Seaport with the Embarkation of the Queen of Sheba" (1648), were hugely influential in 18th-century English painting and landscape gardening. The Turner pictures in Room 15 are proof of this. Among the domestic Dutch scenes in Rooms 16–18, Vermeer's "A Young Woman Standing at a Virginal" (1670) is especially intimate. Dutch landscape comes later, with Aelbert Cuyp's pastoral "River Landscape with Horseman and Peasants" (circa 1650) in Room 21, after the French painter Nicholas Poussin's golden-lit "The Adoration of the Golden Calf" (1634) in Room 20. French paintings in Room 22 include Philippe de Champaigne's magnificent 1637 portrait of Cardinal Richelieu. The Dutch pictures in Rooms 23–27 culminate with a roomful of Rembrandts. Here is "Self Portrait at the Age of 34" (1640) and "Belshazzar's Feast"

"Ruth in Boaz's Field" (1820) by the Leipzig painter Schnorr von Carolsfeld, an artist much admired by the Pre-Raphaelites (Room 42)

(1636–38). Equally stunning are Rooms 28–30, a collection of Rubens canvases that range from the allegorical "Peace and War" to his powerful "Samson and Delilah" of 1609. Royal portraits reach new grandeur in Velazquez's "Philip IV of Spain" (1631–32) and Van Dyck's "Equestrian Portrait of Charles I" (1637–38).

EAST WING (ROOMS 33–46)

The subject matter of 18th- and 19th-century painting is both colorful and accessible—beach scenes, flowerpots, the writing of a letter. It retains many traditional genres, such as portrait, landscape, still life, domestic scenes, and narrative.

In Room 33, French painter Jean Siméon Chardin sustained domestic intimacy in his "The House of Cards" (1736–77). British paintings fill Rooms 34–36. Portraits are

especially strong, and include Sir Joshua Reynolds's "Lady Cockburn and Her Three Eldest Sons" (1773), Thomas Gainsborough's "The Morning Walk" (1785), and Thomas Lawrence's aging, delicate Queen Charlotte, painted four years later. Turner's "Fighting Temeraire" (1838–39) takes landscape painting into new territory. Spanish portraits in Room 38 include Francisco de Goya's "The Duke of Wellington" (1812–14), and French paintings in Room 41 feature Ingres's sumptuous "Madame Moitesser" (1856). Lyrical Impressionist paintings fill Rooms 43 and 44, including Claude Monet's "The Beach at Trouville" (1870), Pierre-Auguste Renoir's "Boating on the Seine" (1879–1880), and Georges-Pierre Seurat's "Bathers at Asnières" (1884). The collection ends in Rooms 45 and 46 with such works as Vincent van Gogh's "Sunflowers" (1888). ∎

National Portrait Gallery

THIS IS WHERE YOU CAN PUT FACES TO FAMILIAR NAMES, from a Tudor king to the inventor of the steam engine or a favorite novelist. Here you can see the faces of the personalities who have influenced all facets of British history. From top to bottom, this is a chronological parade of the brilliant, talented, or high-achieving, of the beautiful and ugly, of the good and devious. Each is fascinating, and the clear labeling helps explain the significance of those people who may not be so familiar. Seen all in one visit, even casually, the collection makes an excellent, visual skip through the island's history.

National Portrait Gallery

- 🅰 Map p. 97
- ✉ St. Martin's Place, WC2
- ☎ 7306 0055. Information: 7312 2463 www.npg.org.uk
- 🆂 Charge for some special exhibitions
- 🚇 Tube: Charing Cross, Leicester Square

Founded in 1856 in the Victorian spirit of idealism, heroism, and didactic hopes of education by example, the collection's aim was to assemble and display portraits of the British great and good as an inspiration to others. The portraits moved around London until they came to rest here in 1896, in Ewan Christian's building behind the National Gallery.

At first, a person had to be dead to be eligible for inclusion here, allowing time to assess his or her worthiness. Today, that rule has been broken, and living inspirations include Baroness Thatcher, soccer player Bobby Charlton, and barrister–writer John Mortimer; visitors renting the CD guide can hear some of these contemporary sitters and artists talking frankly about their portraits. More than 10,000 portraits are in the collection, although not all are on show. Even allowing for the fact that some people have more than one image, that is a considerable number of significant people, and a wide enough selection for visitors to find their ideal hero.

THE VISIT

Because the portraits are arranged chronologically, with the earliest at the top of the building, the best way to visit the gallery is to take the elevator to the second floor and walk down. Here in Rooms 1–20, personalities run through the 16th to 19th centuries. On the first floor in Rooms 21–32, you'll find portraits of people who lived in the 19th and 20th centuries, while members of the royal family are in Room 33. The ground floor is a daring selection of recent and contemporary contributors to

Tucked away behind the National Gallery, the National Portrait Gallery has an impressive doorway.

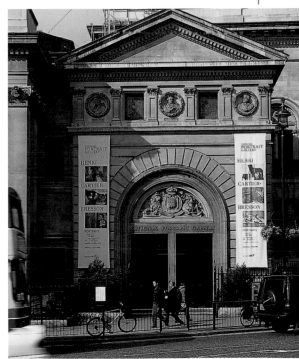

An anonymous portrait of Elizabeth I, painted around 1575, when she was in her early forties

British society, both painted and photographed. Special exhibitions in the Wolfson Gallery, also on the ground floor, include the annual BP Portrait Award (sponsored by British Petroleum, in summer) and, in the Photography Gallery, the annual wintertime John Kobal Photographic Portrait Award.

The gallery's recent new extension includes an atmospheric new Tudor room, and the rooftop Portrait Restaurant has spectacular panoramic views across London.

For added enjoyment, it is worth renting the specially created CD soundguide, which has intriguing interviews with painters and their subjects—who were not always contented sitters.

SECOND FLOOR

Here are a few stars to look out for. The Tudor Galleries open with Holbein's great portrait of Sir Thomas More and his family in their Chelsea home.

Seek out William Scrots's anamorphic portrait, "Edward VI" (1546), meaning that it has been painted to be viewed from a sharp angle to correct the perspective. Elizabeth I portraits include one by Marcus Gheeraerts the Younger to mark her visit to Ditchley Park, near Oxford—her feet are planted on Oxfordshire. The portrait of Shakespeare is the only known contemporary portrait of the playwright, and was the gallery's first acquisition. Do not miss the group of exquisite miniatures by Nicholas Hilliard of the Elizabethan heroes Sir Francis Drake, Sir Walter Raleigh, Robert Dudley, Earl of Leicester, and their good queen. "Star players" in the English Civil War (Oliver Cromwell) and Restoration (Charles II) hang along with the diarist Samuel Pepys, painted in a rented Indian outfit and holding a music score he com-

posed. Britain's dynamic 18th century produced a host of exceptional figures. You can find Jonathan Swift, Sir Christopher Wren, Sir Joshua Reynolds, George Stubbs, and Dr. Johnson, not forgetting explorer Capt. James Cook and Admiral Lord Nelson. The Romantic poets John Keats, Samuel Taylor Coleridge, and a contemplative William Wordsworth are here, too, as well as Sir Richard Arkwright and other heroes of the industrial revolution. Lawrence's portrait of George IV nicely captures that king's decadent elegance.

FIRST FLOOR

Victorian and Edwardian personalities start with early Victorians such as the Brontë sisters, who were painted by their brother, Branwell. Heroes of the empire include linguist and explorer Sir Richard Burton, painted by Leighton. Prince Albert, Queen Victoria's consort, epitomizes 19th-century cultural-scientific advances, whereas William Morris, Thomas Carlyle, and Benjamin Disraeli are proponents of later Victorian culture. For the Edwardian arts, you can discover what Rudyard Kipling, G. B. Shaw, and Edward Elgar looked like.

Architect Piers Gough has refurbished one room. The vista down the whole great room is retained by hanging the early 20th-century portraits on glass panels. Near here, a splendid picture by John Lavery of George V, Queen Mary, and their family at Buckingham Palace in 1913 is usually on display.

GROUND FLOOR

These rooms are some of the most exciting, for they contain images of people who are alive today, still playing their part in our lives. It

is here that the CD guide is so useful: You can hear just how miserable John Mortimer was during his sitting and just how difficult the artist found him to paint. There is plenty of action in this part of the building, where paintings and photographs are changed regularly. New acquisitions are displayed here before joining the collection. One recent group had Meredith Frampton's George VI, theater director Sir Richard Eyre depicted by Peter Snow, and Polly Borland's photograph of politician Peter Mandelson. ∎

"That an humble Address be presented to Her Majesty, praying that Her Majesty will be graciously pleased to take into her Royal consideration the expediency of forming a Gallery of the Portraits of the most Eminent Persons in British History."—Proposal by 5th Earl of Stanhope for a National Portrait Gallery, 1856

Piers Gough's early 20th-century gallery with portraits hung on glass panels

Piccadilly Circus

Piccadilly Circus is the hub of Soho's amusements. It was laid out by Nash in 1819 as part of the Prince Regent's dream to link Carlton House and Regent's Park (see p. 132). This busy intersection of streets, with Eros in its center, was transformed when Shaftesbury Avenue was built in the 1880s. When the Eros statue was added in 1893, its nudity outraged Victorian sensibilities, but it quickly became a symbol for London.

Alfred Gilbert's aluminum figure in fact portrays not Eros the god of love, but the Angel of Christian Charity. It commemo-

Watching the world go by on a summer night in busy Piccadilly Circus

rates Antony Ashley Cooper, 7th Earl of Shaftesbury, 1801–1885, a philanthropist and statesman who fought hard to improve conditions for factory and colliery workers, chimney sweeps, and the insane.

Such was the significance of Piccadilly Circus that London's first illuminated advertisements blazed here in the 1890s, promoting Bovril and Schweppes. More theaters arrived, including one right beside Eros, the basement Criterion. This theater, and its street level restaurant, are decorated with Thomas Verity's beautiful mosaics and tiles, well worth a look. ■

Shaftesbury Avenue

The backbone of London's commercial theaterland, Shaftesbury Avenue was driven through the Soho slums, necessitating the rehousing of 3,000 people. Opened to traffic in 1886, it quickly attracted theatrical impresarios who built theaters suitable for staging fashionable musical farces. Today, a modern impresario, Andrew Lloyd Webber, has bought and restored to glory the **Palace Theatre,** originally designed by Collcutt and Holloway in 1888–1891. A cluster of theaters down the street begins with **Queen's Theatre** of 1907, subsequently rebuilt, and the **Globe,** built in 1906. The French Renaissance **Apollo** rose five years earlier, while the **Lyric,** one of the first theaters on the street, was built in 1888 with profits from a hit musical playing in Leicester Square.

Entertainment of a different sort lies at the bottom of the street. The **Trocadero,** built as a dance hall in 1895, is now an entertainment complex that includes Sega World, Funworld, and four themed restaurants. In this area, young travelers of the world meet, chat, and relax in the pedestrianized Leicester Square and Piccadilly Circus. ∎

Trocadero
- Map p. 97
- Piccadilly Circus, W1
- 0891-881100
- www.troc.co.uk
- Tube: Piccadilly Circus

Soho

Until Westminster Council began its crackdown in June 1986, Soho was one of London's raunchiest areas. It appeared to the outsider never to sleep, nor to be as dangerous as one could have expected. The maze of narrow streets, passages, and courts were the haunts of prostitutes; seedy bars lurked on the corners; basements housed peep shows, striptease clubs, clip joints, and pornographic bookshops. Collectively, it was known as the Vice, and the council decided to do away with it. As each lease expired, its renewal was refused and the property sold off, usually to become a restaurant, office, or flat. Within a year, the prostitutes had moved off, and the number of sex establishments had been halved. Today, the bright lights of Raymond's Revuebar, a lame survivor, advertise entertainment safe enough for schoolboys. Madame JoJo's, nearby, perhaps offers something slightly more fun and risqué. However, the numerous new residents, restaurants, sleek bars, and fashion shops have reawakened some of Soho's round-the-clock liveliness. It is a good area to wander.

NORTH OF SHAFTESBURY AVENUE

At the west end of the grid of streets north of Shaftesbury Avenue, the stallholders of Berwick Street's lively fruit and vegetable market stand in front of pretty 18th-century houses. On Old Compton Street, once the heart of French London, more recent Italian immigrants run Camisa Stores and

Soho's streets glow with neon signs proclaiming sundry entertainments.

**The dragon dance
snakes through
Soho streets to
celebrate Chinese
New Year.**

the Sicilian bakery, Patisserie
Valerie. Italians left their mark on
Dean Street, too, at P. G. Leoni's
Quo Vadis restaurant, which
opened in 1926. Ronnie Scott's, on
Frith Street, continues to host top
jazz stars despite the death of its
mentor. On Greek Street, the plain
facade of the House of St.
Barnabas, built in 1746, belies a
magnificent interior. Beside it,
Charles II's statue in Soho Square
testifies to Soho's noble beginnings.

CHINESE SOHO

Almost all the tall, narrow houses
of London's Chinatown have a shop
or restaurant at street level. There
are Chinese medical shops, news-
agents selling the British-published
Sing Tao, and video rental shops
with piles of kung fu tapes. But

mostly, there are restaurants. In
addition to stir-fried or steamed
Cantonese food, specialties include
dim sum snacks and wind-dried
meats.

In this area, where the Chinese
have succeeded in keeping alive
their mother tongue, the atmosphere is enhanced by Chinese-style
telephone boxes, benches, and red-
and-gold gateways between
Shaftesbury Avenue and Gerrard
Street. It makes a great setting for
the Chinese New Year celebrations.

The French once dominated
this area, hence its nickname Petty
France. Tucked down Leicester
Place is Notre-Dame-de-France—
once a theater but converted in
1865 by art nouveau pioneer
Auguste Boileau. In 1960, Jean
Cocteau added some frescoes. ∎

**Chinatown has
its own street
market where
stallholders deal
in Chinese
vegetables and
specialty foods.**

Between the City and Westminster, this area has always been a giant service depot: Its courts of law, theaters, shops, markets, and entertainments have fulfilled the same functions for centuries. Only the printing presses have fled.

Covent Garden to Ludgate Hill

Market barrow in Covent Garden

Covent Garden to Ludgate Hill

HUGGING THE CURVE OF THE THAMES, THIS PART OF LONDON FILLS THE space between the capital's two cities: Westminster and the City. Ancient buildings such as Temple Church and Lincoln's Inn Gateway, Covent Garden's restored market, the Adelphi Theatre, and the new Royal Opera House show how it has moved continuously to keep pace with its customers.

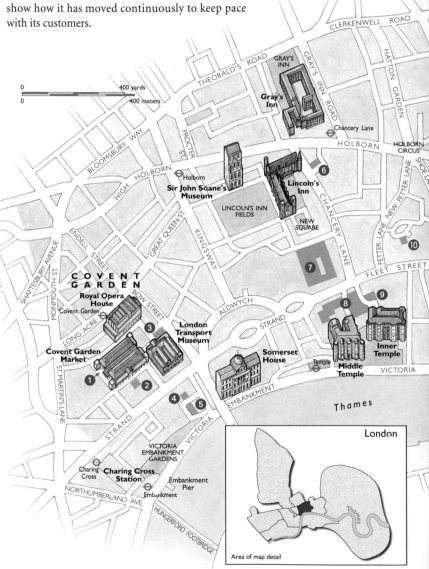

When Westminster became the seat of royal and political power, a riverside path linked it to the merchants' City of London. The sweep of the Strand, so called because it ran close to the north bank of the Thames, and Fleet Street, named after the river it crossed, became a favorite address for medieval bishops. Later, after the Dissolution of the Monasteries, the two parts took on slightly different characters.

Along either side of Fleet Street, toward St. Paul's Cathedral, some bishops' houses evolved into barristers' inns of court, while early printers and booksellers established themselves around the churches of St. Bride and St. Dunstan. Newspaper presses thundered on Fleet Street from 1702 until the 1980s. The printers have gone, but the law remains. Lawyers defend their clients in the great courts, while their pupils hurry through the streets with armfuls of files.

Along the Strand, Tudor and Stuart rulers presented the bishops' former houses and waterside gardens to favored courtiers. George Villiers, a favorite of both James I and Charles I, enlarged the palace of the bishops of Norwich to include a watergate, which survives today in Embankment Gardens, testifying to both the grandeur of these residences and the pre-

Trace the history of the London double-decker bus in the London Transport Museum, Covent Garden.

Embankment width of the river Thames.

The Savoy Theatre reflects the changing roles of the Strand down the centuries. The first building on the site, the sumptuous 14th-century Savoy House, fashionably faced the river. In Covent Garden's 17th-century heyday, the Strand was a smart promenade, but by the late 19th century it had degenerated into a seedy mixture of prostitutes, coffeehouses, and cheap theaters. When Richard d'Oyly Carte built his Savoy Theatre in 1881, he put the entrance on the newly built, clean, and smart Embankment rather than on the Strand. Later, in 1929, the entrance was turned to face a much-improved Strand; the Aldwych crescent had replaced a swath of slums in 1905.

Today, the heart of the area is again Covent Garden. Originally the garden of a convent attached to Westminster Abbey, it was given to the Earl of Bedford after the Dissolution of the Monasteries. Covent Garden Piazza, laid out in 1631, became the blueprint residential London square. Half a dozen others followed nearby, including Lincoln's Inn Fields, to house the gentry who were moving out of the City after the Great Fire. When society moved farther west, the aristocratic tone of the Piazza changed to a commercial one with the arrival of the main London fruit and vegetable market, coffeehouses, and gambling dens. When the market moved to south London, the area was cleaned up and became a lively mixture of shops, restaurants, and museums encircled by a dozen theaters. ■

FARRINGDON ROAD
HOLBORN VIADUCT
FARRINGDON ST.
City (Thameslink)
OLD BAILEY
Central Criminal Court (Old Bailey)
LUDGATE CIRCUS
LUDGATE HILL
11
NEW BRIDGE ST.
EMBANKMENT
BLACKFRIARS BRIDGE

Sir John Soane's Museum

Sir John Sloane's Museum

- 🗺 Map p. 110
- ✉ 13 Lincoln's Inn Fields, WC2
- ☎ 7405 2107
  www.soane.org
- 🕐 Closed Sun.–Mon.
- 💲 Donation. Tours $
- 🚇 Tube: Holborn

Note: Appointment required for groups of six or more.

ONE OF LONDON'S MORE ECCENTRIC AND ATMOSPHERIC house-museums, this was where architect Sir John Soane lived from 1813 until his death in 1837. It is still redolent of his personality. Soane designed No. 12 Lincoln's Inn Fields for himself in 1792; later he bought No. 13 and rebuilt it as a timeless, intensely personal home for his collection. Now the museum owns No. 14, where Soane's collection of architectural models and the Adam brothers' architectural drawings will be displayed.

The best way to arrive is to walk around Lincoln's Inn Fields, a large square laid out in the 1630s, go through the gardens to the north side, and ring the bell at No. 13.

On the ground floor, flanking the library fireplace, are John Flaxman's reliefs "The Silver Age" and "The Golden Age," two fine pieces of Soane's rich collection of English sculpture. Through the corridor, lined with antique marbles, lies the Picture Room. In this tiny room Hogarth's paintings for his "The Rake's Progress" and "The

Election" series are stored against the walls in layers that unfold to reveal a view of Soane's model for the Bank of England.

Down in the basement, one of Inigo Jones's original capitals for his Banqueting House was rescued by Soane when it was refaced. Beyond, the Sepulchral Chamber containing the sarcophagus of Seti I, made in 1300 B.C. and found in the Valley of the Kings, reflects Europe's new excitement about Egypt. When the piece arrived in 1824, Soane threw a party. ■

Appropriately for an architect, Sir John Soane's Museum is as remarkable for its use of space as its exhibits.

Covent Garden

THE RESTORED MARKET BUILDINGS, CHIC SHOPS, AND entertainers in the piazza typify this much-changed area, bordered by the Strand, Kingsway, High Holborn, and Charing Cross Road.

The 1st Earl of Bedford acquired this land in 1552, after Westminster Abbey was dissolved. But it was the 4th Earl who laid out London's first residential square of high society houses. When the aristocrats moved west, the 5th Earl won a license for a fruit and vegetable market in 1671. Traders, prostitutes, and members of the literary coterie, including Richard Sheridan and James Boswell, met here. Stalls selling everything from lavender to birdcages sprawled over the square.

Order of a sort began in 1831, with the building of the Central Market. Floral Hall (1860), the Flower Market (1870–72), and the Jubilee Market (1904) followed. This was the Covent Garden of George Bernard Shaw's *Pygmalion*: of "low life" in the piazza but high life in the Royal Opera House, first built in 1732; of actors working in local theaters and being buried in St. Paul's Covent Garden.

When the market moved in 1974, protests ensured that the buildings were restored, not demolished, and the area has been revitalized. Central Market, now the **Market,** is full of shops, restaurants, and stallholders. Street entertainers and comedians perform in the traffic-free piazza. **Jubilee Hall** has antique and crafts stalls. The **London Transport Museum** occupies part of the old Flower Market; the rest is filled by the **Theatre Museum,** the Victoria & Albert Museum's outpost for its collection of posters, props, and costumes. The completely refurbished Royal Opera House opened in December 1999. ■

Covent Garden's restored Market has moved on from its origins.

London Transport Museum

▲ Map p. 110

✉ 39 Wellington St., WC2

☎ 7379 6344. Information: 7836 8557
www.ltmuseum.co.uk

$ $$

Ⓜ Tube: Covent Garden

Theatre Museum

▲ Map p. 110

✉ Russell Street, WC2

☎ 7943 4735
www.theatre museum.org

🕐 Closed Mon.

$ $$

Ⓜ Tube: Covent Garden

Note: Some archive material is at the National Archive of Art and Design, 23 Blythe Road, W14, tel 7603 1514, open by appt.

Middle Temple Hall (1573) is still in daily use by members as a dining hall.

Inns of Court & Old Bailey

LONDON HAS FOUR INNS OF COURT. EACH ONE IS AN independent society governed by Benchers who call their students, known as pupils, to the Bar—hence the word barristers. Such orders were gradually established after Edward I's Ordinance of 1292 put all men of law under the judges' control, thus ending the clergy's position as lawyers and reducing their power.

The Inns have records going back to the 15th and 16th centuries. Each was originally a great mansion, where students and barristers lived. In Tudor times, when litigation was as popular as the arts, lawyers trained at the Inns of Court sat at courts throughout London but enjoyed a high life back at their halls and chambers. Members of Middle Temple entertained Elizabeth I to a performance of *Twelfth Night* in their magnificent hall with a hammerbeam roof.

Gray's Inn (*High Holborn, tel 7458 7800, www.graysinn.org.uk*), whose students were established in Reginald de Grey's mansion by 1370, has a Tudor screen in its hall. In summer, the garden walks are open to visitors at lunchtime. Early

lawyers of **Lincoln's Inn** (*Chancery Lane, tel 7405 1393, www.lincolnsinn.org.uk*), which took over a mansion on the Earl of Lincoln's property, lived in the surviving Old Hall, built in 1490–92; later lawyers included Oliver Cromwell and William Penn (founder of Pennsylvania).

Inner and **Middle Temples** (*Fleet Street, tel 7797 8250 or 7427 4800, www.innertemple.org.uk and www.middletemple.org.uk*) derive their names from the Knights Templar, a French-founded brotherhood whose members protected pilgrims bound for Jerusalem. At the Dissolution of the Monasteries, their lands became Crown property, which the Benchers leased in perpetuity in 1608. Today, their labyrinth

---

Royal Courts of Justice (Law Courts)

- 🅰 Map p. 110
- ✉ Strand, WC2
- ☎ 7947 6000
- www.open.gov.uk
- 🕐 Closed Sat.–Sun. & Aug.–Sept.
- 🚇 Tube: Temple, Chancery Lane
- Note: No cameras, cell phones, jeans, or children under 14 allowed in the courts.

Central Criminal Court (Old Bailey)

- 🅰 Map p. 111
- ✉ Newgate Street, EC4
- ☎ 7248 3277
- www.cjsonline.org
- 🕐 Closed Sat.–Sun.
- 🚇 Tube: St. Paul's
- Note: List of day's program by main door. No children under 14. No large bags, radios, cameras, pagers, or cell phones allowed in Viewing Galleries.

of courts and buildings includes Middle Temple's **Hall** *(Middle Temple Lane, call for hours)*, the Inner Temple gateway of 1610–11, and Wren's King's Bench Walk of 1677–78. The **Temple Church** *(Inner Temple Lane, tel 7353 3470, www.templechurch.com)*, originally a round Norman building with a nave added later, has marble effigies of 13th-century Templars. When the Embankment's land reclamation (see p. 48) provided the barristers with Inner Temple Gardens, they hosted the Royal Horticultural Society's annual flower show, now held at Chelsea (see p. 169).

In the 19th century, a new interest in legal education forced barristers to use their inns more for work than for pleasure. The courts were centralized in the **Royal Courts of Justice.** Today, the Inns are sandwiched between these courts and the Central Criminal Court, known as the **Old Bailey** after the street running beside it. Built in 1900–1907, its dome is topped by a bronze statue of Justice. ■

The Old Bailey, designed by architect E.W. Mountford

Fleet Street printing

The Law Courts mark the beginning of Fleet Street, which until recently has been synonymous with the printing industry. After the death of William Caxton, who published the first book printed in England in 1477, his commercially acute pupil Wynkyn de Worde moved the presses from Westminster to Fleet Street. De Worde set up England's first press with movable type near St. Bride's Church, close to his clergy customers. Between 1500 and 1535, he published about 800 books and also ran one of the many bookshops in St. Paul's Churchyard. Printers, bookbinders, booksellers, and writers soon filled the lanes off Fleet Street. Dr. Samuel Johnson lived in one (see p. 116) and patronized the coffeehouses and pubs around it.

On March 11, 1702, Fleet Street added to its ecclesiastical, literary, scientific, and political output by publishing its first newspaper, *The Daily Courant*. But the newspaper industry did not really take off until Alfred Harmsworth, pioneer of popular journalism, bought the *Daily Mail* in 1896 and pushed its circulation up to a million. He later founded the *Daily Mirror* with his brother.

Fleet Street remained the hub of the national newspapers until the 1980s. Then international press baron Rupert Murdoch pushed through the technological revolution that resulted in all newspapers leaving Fleet Street for offices linked to their presses by computer. ■

A walk through legal London & Covent Garden

This walk is best done on a weekday, when activity in legal London adds atmosphere; but Covent Garden, although busy on a weekday, is at its most bubbly on Saturday, with entertainers and markets. The walk begins at Temple and ends at Covent Garden Tube stations. The first part is a loop, which could be a walk in itself, or which could be omitted.

IN & AROUND THE STRAND

From the Temple Tube station, walk up to the Strand and turn left past Somerset House containing the Courtauld Gallery (see p. 118). Turn left again onto **Waterloo Bridge** ❶, where there are good views east to the City towers and south toward Westminster.

Return to the Strand and turn left. The **Savoy Hotel** and **Theatre** ❷ lie down their own lane to the left. Richard D'Oyly Carte built the theater in 1881, where Gilbert and Sullivan's operas, including the successful *Mikado,* financed the adjoining deluxe hotel as well as Claridges. Both buildings later benefited from work by the art deco architect Basil Ionides.

Along the Strand, opposite Stanley Gibbons (stamp dealers) and the Vaudeville and Adelphi Theaters, turn left by the Coal Hole pub, with its rich Edwardian interior, and go down Carting Lane to Embankment Gardens. Inside the gardens, turn right at the statue of Robert Raikes. At the end of the paths is **York Watergate** on the right, a survivor from grand riverside York Mansion of 1626.

Backtrack through the garden to the statue of composer Sir Arthur Sullivan (1842–1900) at the far end. Leave the gardens there, cut up Savoy Street, then turn right to venture past Aldwych. **St. Mary-le-Strand** ❸ stands mid-road, James Gibb's first London church (1714–17). This was the first of 50 churches Queen Anne planned (she achieved 12) for the capital's growing population, which was being tempted into nonconformism or lapsing into atheism. St. Clement Danes, another island church, lies beyond. The Strand ends with the magnificent **Royal Courts of Justice** ❹ (see p. 115) on the left, and Thomas Twining's tea store and the 1882–83 Lloyd's Bank banking hall, lined with Doulton tiled panels made at Lambeth, on the right.

THE LAW COURTS & COVENT GARDEN

At the start of Fleet Street, a mid-road memorial topped by a griffin rampant marks the ever tense boundary between the Cities of London and Westminster, between the monarchy and its source of finance. Opposite Chancery Lane, an archway leads into **Inner** and **Middle Temples** ❺ (see p. 114). Going straight ahead, then right, find Fountain Court and Middle Temple's Hall (another court); going straight, then left, find **Temple Church** (1160–1185 and 1220–1240) with splendid effigies of Knights Templars; the Inner Temple Gardens; and Wren's King's Bench Walk, 1677–78. An opening here leads to Bouverie Street and back to Fleet Street.

Across the road, both Bolt and Hind Courts lead into Gough Square, a patch of 17th-century alleys and houses. Dr. Samuel Johnson lived here from 1749 to 1759, during which period he compiled his dictionary, helped by six amanuenses working on the top floor. Now a museum, **Dr. Johnson's House** ❻ *(17 Gough Square, tel 7353 3745, closed Sun.)* is both simple and atmospheric inside.

At the back of the square, go to Fetter Lane, then along Norwich and Furnival Streets to High Holborn. Staple Inn's half-timbered houses are to the left. The way into **Gray's Inn** ❼ (see p. 114) is opposite, its narrow entrance next to the Cittie of Yorke Pub; squares lead to the grassy Walks (gardens). Down Chancery Lane, dozens of silver shops make up the London Silver Vaults (*Tel 7242 3844, closed Sun.*). Farther down, the Gatehouse (1518) leads into **Lincoln's Inn** ❽ (see p. 114). Here New Square leads into Lincoln's Inn Fields and so to **Sir John Soane's Museum** (see p. 112).

From here, Remnant Street and Great

Queen Street lead across Kingsway to Bow Street, home of the **Royal Opera House.** Russell Street, on the right, goes past the **Theatre Museum** (see p. 113) into **Covent Garden Piazza** **9** (see p. 111). The **London Transport Museum** (see p. 113), with fine displays including complete trams and buses, is on the left; the **Central Market** (see p. 113) is straight ahead.

On the far side of the Piazza, go along Henrietta Street and turn right on Bedford Street. Inigo Jones's classical **St. Paul's Church** (1631–33) has memorials to such actors as Edith Evans, Charlie Chaplin, and Vivien Leigh. Garrick Street, where the Garrick Club honors actor David Garrick, leads to Long Acre and Covent Garden Tube

station. Long Acre and parallel Shelton Street and Shorts Gardens are good for shopping. ■

- Inside front cover E4
- Temple Tube station
- 3.9 miles (total)
- 3 hours
- Covent Garden Tube station

NOT TO BE MISSED
- Inner and Middle Temples
- Temple Church
- Dr. Johnson's House
- Gray's Inn
- Lincoln's Inn
- Covent Garden Piazza

A WALK THROUGH LEGAL LONDON & COVENT GARDEN

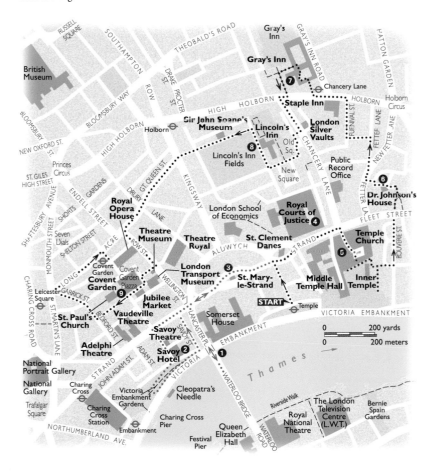

Somerset House

THREE EXTRAORDINARY ART COLLECTIONS AND A LARGE public piazza that is a fountain in summer and an ice rink in winter have reawakened Sir William Chambers's sumptous palace built in 1776–1786 for government bureaucrats.

Somerset House

- Map p. 110
- Strand, WC2
- 7845 4600
  www.somerset-house.org.uk
- $$ for each museum
- Tube: Temple, Embarkment, Covent Garden

Ice rink

- 7845 4670. Tickets: 0870 0423
- $$$ for ice-skating
- Open Nov.–Jan.

One corner of huge Somerset House is the setting for the Courtauld's Gallery.

Central London's most successful new arts complex is in a refurbished and forgotten building. The 16th-century palace of Edward Seymour, Protector of Somerset, was later home to various Tudor and Stuart royals. Demolished on the orders of George III to make way for London's most impressive 18th-century public building, here the Navy Board, Inland Revenue, a handful of learned societies, and the Register General of Births, Deaths, and Marriages enjoyed luxurious offices until 1989. Today, the courtyard draws locals and visitors to enjoy ice skating in winter and cafés in summer. The River Terrace has more café and restaurant tables.

Inside, the **Courtauld Institute Galleries** (7848 2526, www.courtauld.ac.uk) opened first. Samual Courtauld, industrialist and art patron, founded the Courtauld Institute in 1931 in his Adam mansion in Portman Square, aiming to help art history students experience great paintings in fine settings. His French Impressionist and Postimpressionist canvases were later joined by the Princes Gate Collection's Rubens, Tiepolo, and Van Dyck paintings; by the Lee Collections's Botticellis, Goyas, and Gainsboroughs; and by more than 7,000 old master prints and drawings. Here you can enjoy a roomful of Rubens, Manet's "Bar at the Folies Bergère," magnificent silver, and Derain's paintings of London.

Across the courtyard, past John Bacon's bronze statue of George III, the riverside buildings house the **Gilbert Collection** (7240 4080, www.gilbert-collection.org.uk), Sir Arthur Gilbert's lifelong assembly of decorative arts, from silver and snuff boxes to Italian mosaics; and the **Hermitage Rooms** (7845 4630, ticketmaster: 7413 3398, www.hermitagerooms.co.uk), where rotating exhibitions from the Hermitage Museum in St. Petersberg are displayed. ∎

Eighteenth-century squares form the back-bone of Bloomsbury. Their gardens provide relaxation for academics and visitors to the British Museum. There is also a handful of fascinating individual small collections for special interests.

Bloomsbury

The massive columns of the British Museum's entrance welcome visitors to its collections of treasures.

Bloomsbury

BLOOMSBURY'S AIR IS FILLED WITH CALM CONTEMPLATION AND WONDER, a mood set by the presence of the University of London and the British Museum plus their satellite institutions. It is hard to believe that Soho's bars, Covent Garden's entertainment, and the bustle of north London's busy railway stations are but a five-minute walk away.

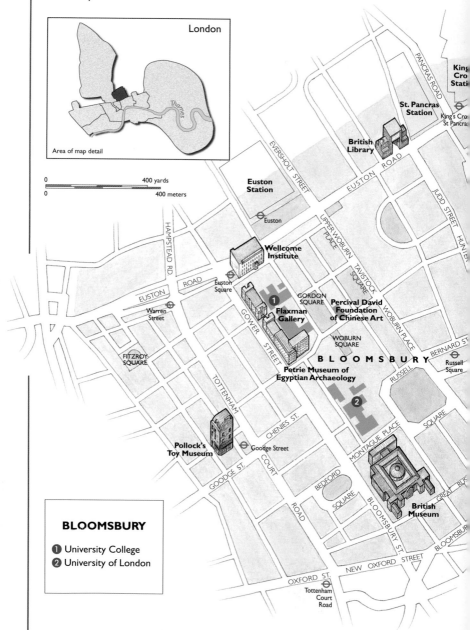

London

Area of map detail

0   400 yards
0   400 meters

BLOOMSBURY

❶ University College
❷ University of London

Like much of central London, Bloomsbury's story has agricultural, monastic, and aristocratic chapters. The Domesday Book, William the Conqueror's 11th-century inventory of his English possessions, records a wood for 100 pigs and vineyards here. Later, Edward III gave the land to the Charterhouse monks. After the dissolution, Henry VIII gave it to his Lord Chancellor, the Earl of Southampton. The 4th Earl of Southampton laid out the square that is now Bloomsbury

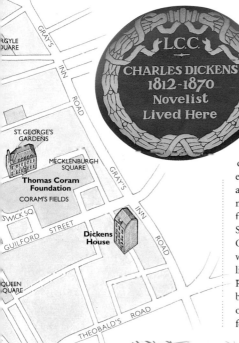

The Charles Dickens Blue Plaque on Doughty Street is just one of many such plaques in Bloomsbury.

Square in 1660. A clever marriage linked the Southampton family with the Bedfords. The 4th Duke of Bedford's widow built Bedford Square in the 1770s, while her son was a minor. After he became the 5th Duke, he recognized the area's potential and, around 1800, began building Bloomsbury.

Land was parceled off to developers, principally James Burton, an ambitious Scot. He was succeeded by his architect son, Decimus Burton, and Thomas Cubitt (see p. 171). The sequence of elegant squares then progressed rapidly: Bloomsbury Square was redeveloped, Russell Square was begun in 1800, Tavistock in 1806, Gordon in 1820, and Woburn in 1825.

Meanwhile, in 1823 work began on replacing Montague House, the British Museum since 1759, with a specially built museum. Soon after, in 1836, England's first nondenominational university, the University of London, was founded in Bloomsbury. East of the patchwork is Mecklenburgh Square, laid out in the 1790s by the Governors of the Thomas Coram Foundation for Children, a hospice for abandoned children founded by Captain Coram in 1732 and endowed by Hogarth, Gainsborough, Handel, and others. It overlooked the hospital's land, now Coram's Fields, and set a different tone from the nearby streets—delightful Queen Square, Great James Street, and Lamb's Conduit Street. Handsome Doughty Street was completed in 1812; later Charles Dickens lived here. West, across Tottenham Court Road, Fitzroy Square was laid out by the Adam brothers in the 1790s. Almost an extension of Bloomsbury, it later became a magnet for artists. ■

Britain's temple of history—the British Museum

British Museum

British Museum

📍 Map p. 120

✉ Great Russell Street, WC2; rear entrance on Montague Place

☎ 7636 1555. Information: 7323 8783 www.thebritish museum.ac.uk

🚇 Tube: Tottenham Court Road, Holborn, or Russell Square

💲 For some exhibitions

BRITAIN'S LARGEST MUSEUM IS NOT TO BE TAKEN ON lightly. Put simply, its nine departments look after the national collection of archaeology and ethnography. It covers 13.5 acres, employs 1,200 people, has more than six million visitors a year, and looks after more than four million objects ranging from prehistoric bones to chunks of Athens' Parthenon, from whole Assyrian palace rooms to exquisite gold jewels. This is a living museum: It changes daily as different pieces are put on display, special exhibitions are held, and new discoveries force adjustments to opinions on other objects. It also grows almost daily: Most British archaeological discoveries come here; bequests are frequent; and the museum buys new pieces.

THE MUSEUM

This astounding treasure-house began as the simple idea of one man, Sir Hans Sloane. A physician who lived at nearby Bedford Place, he collected minerals, coins, books, and other objects with rare obsessiveness. On his death in 1753, he suggested the government buy all 80,000 bits and pieces, which they did. The same year, the British Museum Act was passed, creating London's first public museum. Money was raised by public lottery, Montague House bought, and the museum doors opened in January 1759. Entry was by written application, but the curators were not interested in the public. Groups were escorted through the galleries in just half an hour, and not permitted to linger or gaze at the objects.

The foundation collection also included the library and finds of

Above left: Greek sculpture from the Nereid monument at Xanthos (Room 7)

Above right: Huge bulls with human heads at the entrance to the Assyrian Gallery (Room 16)

antiquarian Sir Robert Cotton and the manuscripts of politician Robert Harley. It expanded alarmingly fast. Even before the museum opened, in 1757 George II donated most of the Royal Library's 12,000 volumes. The Hamilton antique vases, Townley classical sculptures, Elgin marbles, George III's extensive library, Capt. James Cook's collections from his voyages, and the Bank of England's coins all came to Montague House.

The house overflowed. So Robert Smirke's great classical temple to learning was built around the house in 1823–1838. Then the house was demolished to make way for the entrance colonnade and portico, which closed the courtyard, known as the Great Court. The domed Reading Room was built in 1854–57, and all remaining space was filled with galleries and book stacks. Even then, the museum overflowed. In 1881 the Natural History department went to South Kensington (see p. 162); and in 1973 the Printed Books and

Manuscripts department went to the British Library, confusingly situated in a part of the museum.

By the latter part of the 20th century, a radical solution was needed. First, the British Library was given its own building at St. Pancras, just north of Bloomsbury. This released 40 percent of the museum's space, which, crucially, included the Great Court. A program of expansion and renewal was completed in 2003, the museum's 250th birthday. The centerpiece is the Great Court in the middle of the museum. Cleared of all but the Reading Room and roofed in glass, it is another light-filled public Bloomsbury square, this time a covered one. This is the information area for the museum's 100 galleries, a central bureau for its educational events, and a space where visitors can rest, shop, refresh themselves, and cross from one part of the museum to another.

Galleries have been reorganized in response to the Grand Court's reemergence. In particular, the

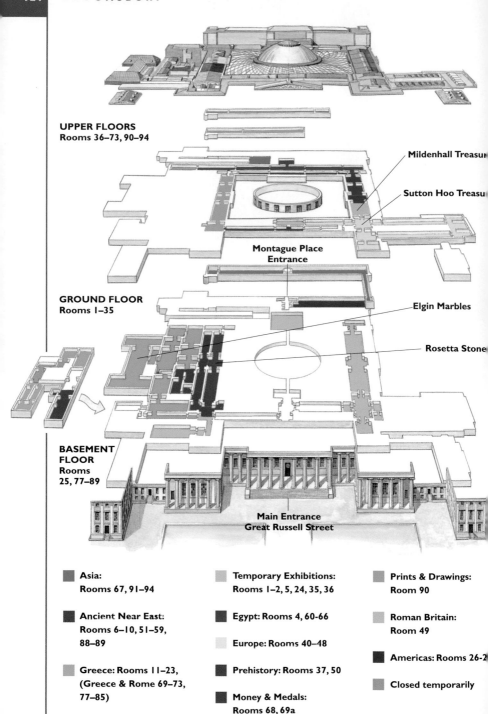

UPPER FLOORS
Rooms 36–73, 90–94

Mildenhall Treasur⃨

Sutton Hoo Treasu⃨

Montague Place
Entrance

GROUND FLOOR
Rooms 1–35

Elgin Marbles

Rosetta Stone⃨

**BASEMENT
FLOOR**
Rooms
25, 77–89

Main Entrance
Great Russell Street

■ Asia: Rooms 67, 91–94	■ Temporary Exhibitions: Rooms 1–2, 5, 24, 35, 36	■ Prints & Drawings: Room 90
■ Ancient Near East: Rooms 6–10, 51–59, 88–89	■ Egypt: Rooms 4, 60-66	■ Roman Britain: Room 49
	■ Europe: Rooms 40–48	
■ Greece: Rooms 11–23, (Greece & Rome 69–73, 77–85)	■ Prehistory: Rooms 37, 50	■ Americas: Rooms 26–2⃨
	■ Money & Medals: Rooms 68, 69a	■ Closed temporarily

Ethnography Department returns to the museum after decades in a Mayfair annex, the Museum of Mankind.

THE VISIT

Clearly, this is not a "do-in-a-day" museum. Many visitors have a very clear idea of what they want to see and will pick up a map and seek out their objects. For others, the museum is overwhelming. In the Great Court, there is information and lists of the day's events. To help transform this into a manageable, stimulating experience, here is a trail that focuses on just a few objects.

From the Great Court, turn left and go to the west side to find Room 25. This great, long gallery contains the cream of the finest collection of **Egyptian antiquities** outside Egypt—some 70,000 objects (a few are displayed upstairs in Rooms 60–66). Sculpture fills this gallery, and among the heads of Rameses II, Amenophis II, and other ancient rulers is the small but significant Rosetta Stone, carved in 196 B.C., when Egypt's pharaohs were all dead and the land was ruled by the Greek Ptolemy kings. On it, the same information is written in first Greek, then Egyptian, in both hieroglyphic and demotic scripts. By comparing scripts, modern scholars were able to decipher ancient Egyptian and thus read the inscriptions. The upstairs galleries contain funerary models for the afterlife, painted mummies, books of the dead, and Coptic portraits.

Next to the Egyptian sculptures is the **Western Asiatic** department in Rooms 16–21. This covers the civilizations that rose and fell in the huge area between Egypt and Pakistan. The Assyrian friezes are especially beautiful. Excavated last century, they have come from palaces built in the ninth century in the successive capitals of Nimrud,

Khorsabad, and Nineveh. Room 19, the Nimrud Gallery, has some colossal, protective winged lions and narrative scenes of the king hunting, the army swimming across a river, and an attack on a town. Room 17, the Assyrian Saloon, tells the story of a royal lion hunt and features the animals being released, the people of Nineveh watching from a hill, and a strip cartoon of the kill.

The remaining rooms in this part of the museum, Nos. 1–15, are devoted to **Greek** and **Roman antiquities.** One of the world's finest collections, covering every aspect of life, it ranges from the early simplicity of Cycladic figures to the sophistication of Greek vase paintings. The sculpture is exceptional and includes pieces from two of the world's best-known buildings. Room 8 contains sculptures from the **Parthenon's Temple**

Children gaze at the desert-dried body of an Egyptian man, called "Ginger" for his tuft of red hair, buried more than 5,000 years ago.

Gold shoulder clasp from the Anglo-Saxon ship-burial at Sutton Hoo (Room 41)

of Athena, built in the fifth century B.C. as part of a plan to beautify Athens. Using money intended for the navy, the sculptor Phidias oversaw the decorative work on the most harmonious and magnificent building from the golden age of ancient Greece. It remained perfect until gunpowder stored there exploded in 1687. In the early 19th century, Lord Elgin brought many of the surviving sculptures to London: The great frieze of the procession to celebrate Athena's birthday, plus sculptures from the pediments and metopes. The other outstanding piece is in Room 7: the **Nereid Monument,** the front of a tomb built like a miniature Greek temple.

Now go up the stairs to the upper levels. In Room 68, the **HSBC Money Gallery** (supported by the Hong Kong Shanghai Banking Corporation) displays 2,000 years of British coinage in commerce, history, and portraiture.

Rooms 37 and 49–50 display the **Prehistoric** and **Romano–British Antiquities** spanning early history to the Christian period. There is a gold torque from Norfolk, a bronze mirror, and gaming pieces. At the top of the stairs, a mosaic floor found in Dorset in 1963 contains the

earliest known representation of Christ in a mosaic floor in the Roman empire.

Some precious and delicate objects from the **Medieval and Later Antiquities** department fill the corner Rooms 41–47. Several special treasures are worth seeking out here. In Room 41, early pieces include the **Sutton Hoo Treasure,** an Anglo-Saxon royal burial ship that survived intact in Suffolk and was excavated in 1939. Room 41 also includes Byzantine and Early Christian objects, Celtic bowls, Merovingian coins, and high-quality locally made jewelry, all illustrating the international diversity and sophistication of Anglo-Saxon high society. Room 42, one of the **Medieval Rooms,** has European items from the 9th to 15th centuries, spanning the Carolingian to the Gothic periods. Included here are the **Lewis Chessmen,** possibly carved in Scandinavia in the 12th century and found on the Hebridean island of Lewis in 1831.

Cut down the east side of the museum through Rooms 49–52 to the North Wing. There are four levels, connected by stairs and elevators. On the top floor, exhibitions from the **Prints and Drawings** collection are held. Down one level, the **Oriental** collections, some of the world's finest, fill the remaining North Wing rooms. Nos. 92–94 are devoted to **Japanese art.** On the floor below them, Room 33 is the Joseph E. Hotung Gallery, which begins at the west end with early **Indian Buddhist sculptures** and moves through the cultures of **Southeast Asia.** Beneath this, the ground floor contains the John Addis Gallery of **Islamic arts.** ◼

The museum trail

THE BRITISH MUSEUM IS THE INSPIRATION FOR A HOST of other fascinating museums scattered throughout Bloomsbury and around Covent Garden. Telephone the smaller ones to confirm opening times before visiting.

Start at the **British Library.** Professor Sir Colin Wilson's red brick empathizes with Scott's Victorian St. Pancras station next door. Edouard Paolozzi's sculpture of Newton in the courtyard introduces the headquarters of the world's most important library collection, composed of more than 150 million items—George III's 65,000 volumes are housed in a magnificent six-story glass-walled tower. Galleries include the **John Ritblat Gallery,** displaying rare treasures such as the Magna Carta, a charter setting out some basic liberties that King John was forced by his barons to sign at Runnymede in 1215. The **Pearson Gallery of Living Words** looks at such themes as the Story of Writing; and the hands-on displays of the **Workshop of Words, Sounds, and Images** enable visitors to design a book and understand sound recording.

From here, there are two routes to the British Museum. The first will take you via the **Thomas Coram Foundation for Children** (see p. 121), where the courtroom of the original hospital, decorated by Hogarth and his friends in the 1740s, has been saved, plus many good pictures. Doughty Street is a five-minute walk to the east. Charles Dickens lived at No. 48 (see p. 130).

The alternative route visits the dependably fascinating science exhibitions at the **Wellcome Institute** (*183–193 Euston Road, tel 7611 8231, www.wellcome .ac.uk, closed Sun.*). Next stop is the **Percival David Foundation of Chinese Art,** where exquisite Chinese porcelain fills a simple, terraced house. More tricky to find, and visit, are two little museums at the University of London's University College: the **Flaxman Gallery** (*Slade School of Fine Art, Gower Street, tel 7679 2540, www.ucl.ac .uk/slade, by appt.*) displays a hundred models by neo-classic sculptor John Flaxman. The informal **Petrie Museum of Egyptian Archaeology** (*University College, Malet Place entrance, tel 7504 2884, www .petrie.ucl.ac.uk, closed Sun. & Mon.*) intrigues both the curious and the knowing. Finally, **Pollock's Toy Museum** (*1 Scala St., tel 7636 3452, www.pollocks web.co.uk, closed Sun.*) fills two houses to capacity with a multitude of childhood treasures, including dolls, teddy bears, puppets, and an 18th-century Noah's Ark.

Both routes now join, pass the British Museum, and cross to Drury Lane to find the **Theatre Museum** (see p. 113), a rich collection of theatrical props, costumes, posters, playbills, and more. Around the corner, the **London Transport Museum** (see p. 113) tells the story of travel within the capital. Visitors can clamber around the buses, trace the evolution of trams, try out Underground train controls, and see the quality posters that persuaded 1930s Londoners to take a train out of the city to the country. The trail ends at the **Somerset House** (see p. 118) across the Strand. ∎

British Library
- Map p. 120
- 96 Euston Road, NW1
- 7412 7332
- www.bl.uk
- Open daily. Tours Mon. & Wed.–Sun. Advance reservation recommended
- Tube: King's Cross

Thomas Coram Foundation for Children
- Map p. 121
- 40 Brunswick Square, WC1
- 7841 3600
- www.coram.org.uk
- Open Mon.–Fri. by appointment
- Donation. Fee for guide
- Tube: Russell Square

Percival David Foundation of Chinese Art
- Map p. 120
- 53 Gordon Square, WC1
- 7387 3909
- www.pdfmuseum .org.uk
- Closed Sat.–Sun.
- Donation
- Tube: Euston Square, Russell Square

London squares

Bloomsbury's squares of flat-fronted, brick houses overlooking gardens of lawns, trees, and the odd statue have a rhythm that sets the tone for much of London. The London square is a very specific piece of urban design, which suited the English social system, love of gardens, and, once the Enlightenment took hold, its sense of order. Introduced in the 17th century, the square reached its peak of popularity in the 19th century. More than 150 of them are spread across central London.

Inigo Jones, Charles I's favorite architect, laid out Covent Garden Piazza in 1631 for the Earl of Bedford. While the Earl was inspired by Paris's Place des Vosges, Jones was remembering Palladio's work in Italy. The result was a handsome residential square whose houses, built behind a uniform facade, overlooked an airy central space. It was quite different from anything the tight-knit City offered, and it was popular. By 1700, a dozen squares had been built for London's wealthy, including Lincoln's Inn Fields, Soho, Leicester, Bloomsbury, St. James's, and several in the Inns of Court.

The squares often proved to be nuclei for 18th-century development, the period when squares were given their most satisfactory sizes and proportions. This is the case in Mayfair, where the concept developed as St. James's Square leaped across Piccadilly to appear as Hanover, Berkeley, and Grosvenor Squares. More isolated gems were built, too, such as the Charterhouse (on the edge of the City) and Smith (in Westminster).

But it is Bedford Square, one of the early Bloomsbury squares, that reached near-perfection, and survives complete. A daring piece of speculative development in the 1770s, Bedford was London's first square to be planned and built as a single architectural unit. Each side follows a simple design, a great palace facade with a pediment in the middle, overlooking a central oval garden.

The classical grandeur of Eaton Square in Belgravia

Originally, the square was gated and guarded, to preserve residents' privacy. Only the residents had keys to the gardens—a practice still in use in many London squares. Tradesmen used the back entrances in the mews lanes behind the buildings, where the stables were. Coal was delivered to the front of the house, however, and poured down coal holes in the pavement, so that it reached the basement kitchens without dirtying the main house. You can still see the metal lids for these coal holes in some sidewalks.

During London's rampaging 19th-century expansion, developers constantly utilized the square. Islington's 18th-century terraces were joined first by Canonbury Square in around 1800, then, gradually, the unpretentious squares of Barnsbury. But something on a new

scale of grandeur was simultaneously being built to create Belgravia. Belgrave Square, the centerpiece for Thomas Cubitt's development (see p. 171), begun in 1825, is huge and unashamedly pompous. Mansions mark each corner, each terrace is four stories high, and columns and pilasters are rampant. Working with George Basevi, Cubitt broke the facades up, giving individuality to the houses by varying the entrances, elevations, and decoration.

The break with the austere Georgian square was complete. But individuality kept the square popular. Eaton Square resembles a triumphal way; Chester Square, long and narrow, is surprisingly intimate; Ladbroke Square's Italianate houses overlook what is possibly London's largest private communal garden. Late 20th-century developments at Chelsea Harbour and Broadgate have kept the idea of the square alive. ■

Berkeley Square in Mayfair was laid out in the late 1760s.

Dickens House

CHARLES DICKENS HAD MANY LONDON HOMES, BUT ONLY this one survives. He, his wife, Catherine, and their young son Charles moved onto Doughty Street in 1837 and lived here for three key years. Dickens wrote the first of his great novels in this house.

The drawing room at 48 Doughty Street, the only surviving London home of Charles Dickens

The house was well located: in a good residential area, yet close to the City and Thameside streets where he did his research. His daughters Mary and Kate were born here. More significantly, during this time Dickens could emerge from the pseudonym of Boz and take the literary stage in his own right. Not surprisingly, the house holds the world's most comprehensive Dickens library and is a place of pilgrimage for Dickens enthusiasts, many of whom join walks around Dickens's London.

Saved from demolition in 1922 by the Dickens Fellowship, which now runs it, the house has been skillfully arranged to retain its atmosphere of literary output and early Victorian interior decoration. Seeing the writer's desk and chair, marked-up copies of his readings, and Victorian relief scraps, it is easy to imagine him polishing off the *Pickwick Papers*, writing *Oliver Twist* and *Nicholas Nickleby,* or beginning *Barnaby Rudge*—feats all achieved here. ∎

Dickens House

- Map p. 121
- 48 Doughty Street, WC1
- 7405 2127
  www.dickens museum.com
- Closed Sun.
- $$
- Tube: Russell Square, Chancery Lane

The Bloomsbury Group

At the beginning of the 20th century, a handful of artists and writers formed a clique devoted to the philosophy of G. E. Moore, which decreed that the most important things in life were "the pleasures of human intercourse and the enjoyment of beautiful objects. It is they that form the rational ultimate end of social progress." Most of the group had Cambridge connections, but they all gathered in Bloomsbury's Gordon Square, where in 1904 the Stephen family—Virginia (later Woolf), her sister Vanessa (later Bell), Toby, and Adrian—moved into No. 46. The economist John Maynard Keynes was part of the group, as were E. M. Forster, Lytton Strachey, Leonard Woolf (Virginia's husband), and Vanessa's husband, Clive Bell. So, too, was Roger Fry, the artist and critic who left his art collection to the Courtauld Institute. Paintings by him and another Bloomsbury artist, Duncan Grant, are in the Courtauld Gallery (see p. 118). ∎

R esidents of this part of
north London enjoy two
of the city's most glorious
parks. Regent's Park has formal
gardens, a zoo, and stucco terraces, while Hampstead Heath
offers wilder hills, Kenwood
House, and Hampstead and
Highgate villages.

Regency London

**Statues on top of
Cumberland Terrace,
the grandest of
John Nash's designs**

Regency London

WHEN THE PRINCE REGENT BECAME GEORGE IV HE INTRODUCED A NEW order into London in the development of Regent Street and Regent's Park. Not since the great building projects of the Tudors had a royal exercised such influence on the shaping of London. The Prince Regent was the energy and inspiration behind the dream. John Nash, his planner and architect, realized this dream with theatrical panache. A further dose of good luck produced the essential ingredients of land and finance. Regency London got off to a good start. The slopes of Belsize Park and St. John's Wood were soon covered with spacious houses. Development eventually reached to the hilltop spa villages of Hampstead and Highgate, whose residents ensured the next London "lung," Hampstead Heath, remained forever open.

It is clear from the map how innovative this piece of bold, Crown-controlled growth was in a city that until then had developed piecemeal, individual land-owners building modest streets and squares. How did it happen?

When Prince George came of age in 1783, he moved out of St. James's Palace into the modest Carlton House, sited where the bottom of Regent Street is today. The Prince quickly and lavishly transformed it into a stylish entertainment palace. For the next 30 years, the handsome, jobless Prince squandered a fortune on having fun, while his capable father ruled. It was during this period that he employed John Nash, an architect of stucco-fronted houses who had worked with the landscape gardener Humphry Repton on country house projects.

The Prince, influenced by the growing English Picturesque movement, which saw architecture as part of the environment, conceived a scheme that would make sweeping changes to the outer reaches of London. In 1811, when he and Nash were already making plans, three key events happened. The lease on 500 acres of Crown parkland, just north of smart Marylebone and Mayfair, expired; George III became so unwell that his son was made Regent; and the tide turned in the Napoleonic Wars, firing London with optimism and jump-starting a building boom.

The idea was to create a garden city for aristocrats, a park dotted with villas, woods, a royal pleasure palace, a lake, and a canal. The plan also included a wide, mile-long street of suitable size for large carriages to link the park to his own home and thus to the Court and Parliament.

Unlike Christopher Wren's great dream for the post-Fire City, the Prince Regent's dream was realized. Regent Street was built at the expense of hundreds of Soho houses, forever dividing Mayfair and Marylebone from all points east. Today, much rebuilt, it remains a stylish shopping street, and happily links to James Adam's farsighted, immensely elegant Portland Place of 1776–1780. Carlton House was demolished when the Prince moved to Buckingham Palace, and the southern end of Regent Street closed with a staircase leading down to the green space of St. James's Park. At the north end, the great circus planned at the crossing with Marylebone Road was only half-realized in Park Crescent, but even this small part is one of London's finest architectural set pieces.

Regent's Park may have fewer villas than planned, and no pleasure palace, but with its meandering lake, northern boundary canal, zoo, immaculate gardens, and gleaming terraces, it is one of London's most breathtaking royal parks—a much loved garden for more people than the Prince could ever have imagined.

At the southwest corner, Dorset Square's development in 1811 forced the famous Marylebone Cricket Club to move to Lord's in St. John's Wood (now the country's best known cricket ground). North of the park, as buildings covered the hills, Hampstead and, to a lesser extent, Highgate were brought into the London frame. ∎

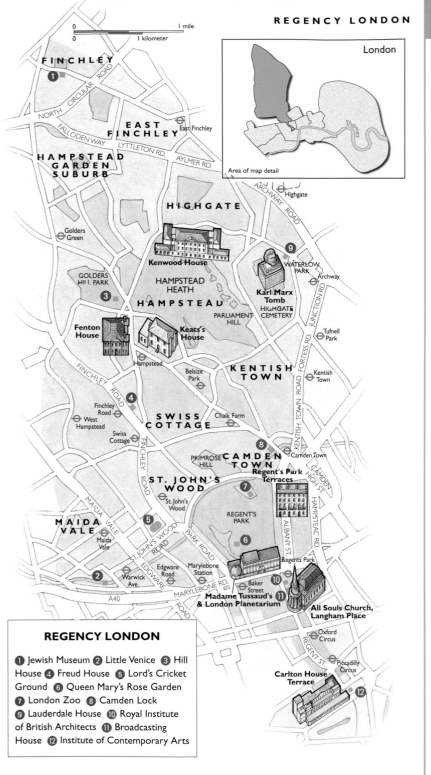

London

Area of map detail

0   1 mile
0   1 kilometer

FINCHLEY ①

NORTH CIRCULAR ROAD

FALLODEN WAY

EAST FINCHLEY   East Finchley

LYTTLETON RD.

HAMPSTEAD GARDEN SUBURB   AYLMER RD.

ARCHWAY ROAD   Highgate

HIGHGATE

Golders Green

Kenwood House

⑨

WATERLOW PARK   Archway

GOLDERS HILL PARK

HAMPSTEAD HEATH

③   Karl Marx Tomb

HAMPSTEAD   HIGHGATE CEMETERY

Fenton House

Keats's House   PARLIAMENT HILL

Tufnell Park

Hampstead   Tufnell Park

Belsize Park

KENTISH TOWN   Kentish Town

FINCHLEY ROAD

④   Chalk Farm

Finchley Road

West Hampstead   SWISS COTTAGE

Swiss Cottage

⑧   Camden Town

PRIMROSE HILL   CAMDEN TOWN

ST. JOHN'S WOOD   Regent's Park Terraces

⑦

St. John's Wood

MAIDA VALE   REGENT'S PARK

⑤   ⑥

Regents Park

Maida Vale   ST. JOHN'S WOOD ROAD

PARK ROAD   ⑩

Edgware Road   Marylebone Station   Baker Street   ⑪

②   Warwick Ave.

EDGWARE ROAD   MARYLEBONE RD.

Madame Tussaud's & London Planetarium   All Souls Church, Langham Place

A40

Oxford Circus

REGENT ST.   Piccadilly Circus

Carlton House Terrace

⑫

REGENCY LONDON

① Jewish Museum ② Little Venice ③ Hill House ④ Freud House ⑤ Lord's Cricket Ground ⑥ Queen Mary's Rose Garden ⑦ London Zoo ⑧ Camden Lock ⑨ Lauderdale House ⑩ Royal Institute of British Architects ⑪ Broadcasting House ⑫ Institute of Contemporary Arts

Regent Street

Regent Street
Map p. 133

Institute of Contemporary Arts
Map p. 133
✉ Nash House, The Mall, SW1
☎ 7930 3647
www.ica.org.uk
🕐 Closed a.m.
💲 $ (Mon.–Fri.), $$ (Sat.–Sun.)
🚇 Tube: Charing Cross

The long curve of Regent Street makes it pleasing to the eye for shoppers.

OXFORD STREET MAY HAVE MORE SHOPS THAN ANY OTHER street in Europe, but Regent Street has the edge for its mix of shops, style, and a drop of culture—all wrapped in architectural grandeur.

At the south end of Regent Street, architect John Nash (see p. 136) tidied up the eastern side, creating Pall Mall East and planning for Trafalgar Square. When the Prince moved to Buckingham Palace, Nash replaced Carlton House with grand Carlton House Terrace (1827–1832). Today, No. 6 is home to the erudite Royal Society, whose presidents have included Wren, Newton, and Sloane. In the middle of the terrace is Benjamin Wyatt's Duke of York's Column. Steps lead to the **Institute of Contemporary Arts,** which shows state-of-the-art exhibitions and films.

Nash compensated for slicing through smart St. James's by creating the Royal Opera Arcade and rebuilding Theatre Royal Haymarket. (The English Tourist Board's center is on this section of Regent Street.)

Northward, **Piccadilly Circus** (see p. 106) marks a change of direction and mood. From here, Nash swings around with full theatrical drama. His colonnade of stores, designed to keep shoppers out of the rain, has been removed, but the high-quality shops remain. Here is Austin Reed, with its art deco basement barber, and Garrard, where sovereigns since Victoria have bought their jewelry. Farther up, Liberty & Co. is known for its quality, exotic goods.

Across Oxford Circus, where Regent Street crosses Oxford Street, the circular portico of **All Souls Church, Langham Place** has a bust of Nash looking down his street. **BBC** (British Broadcasting Corporation) **Broadcasting House** is just beyond, decorated with Eric Gill's sculptures; the BBC gallery and publications shop is inside. After the first broadcast in 1922, the non-commercial BBC was established in 1927 in order to prevent commercial radio from taking hold; by 1939, nine million licenses were held. Farther up Portland Place, the **Royal Institute of British Architects** (*Tel 7580 5533, www. architecture.com*), or RIBA, presents lectures and exhibitions, and awards an annual Gold Medal. ■

Regent's Park

THIS IS WHERE JOHN NASH LEFT THE FRENCH FORMALITY of Regent Street behind and returned to English Picturesque. Almost 500 acres of farmland had been appropriated by Henry VIII from the Abbey of Barking. These were sold by Cromwell, then reclaimed by Charles II and leased out (see pp. 136–37). It was these leases that reverted to the Crown in 1811. Of Nash's 56 planned villas only eight were built, but the terraces at the sides were completed.

Regent's Park has great variety. In the southeast corner, the Victorian complexity and density of planting in Avenue Gardens, laid out in 1864, has been restored to full glory. Beside them the Broad Walk runs the length of the park, bordered by mature horse chestnuts. About 6,000 forest trees grow in the park.

Halfway up the Broad Walk, Inner Circle protects the park's most private and magical area, Queen Mary's Rose Garden. Laid out to celebrate the Jubilee of George V and Queen Mary in 1935, it includes formal and alpine gardens, and a glorious rose garden. More than 30,000 plants and 400 varieties, both old and new, perfume the air with blooms throughout the summer. Rambling and climbing roses encircle beds of flowers, creating peaceful corners.

The **Regent's Park Open-Air Theatre** is in Inner Circle, too, near the modest Rose Garden Restaurant. Regent's Park Lake, a sanctuary for waterbirds, meanders around Inner Circle; the bandstand's music floats over it, and boaters enjoy views of the Holme, a villa designed by Decimus Burton. North across the lawns, the roaring of lions announces **London Zoo,** opened in 1828. A bridge over Regent's Canal leads to Primrose Hill, with views across London. ∎

Savor Regent's Park's royal atmosphere by rowboat.

Regent's Park
- Map p. 133
- 7486 7905
  www.royalparks
  .gov.uk
- Closed at night
- Tube: Regent's Park, Baker Street, Great Portland Street, or Camden Town (especially for zoo)

Open-Air Theatre
- Inner Circle, Regent's Park, NW1
- 7486 2431
- June–Sept.
- $$
- Tube: Regent's Park, Baker Street, or Camden Town

London Zoo
- Map p. 133
- Regent's Park, NW1
- 7722 3333
  www.londonzoo
  .co.uk
- $$$
- Tube: Camden Town

Regency architecture

What architect John Nash did for London became the capital's chief expression of Regency architecture and town planning. Inspired by the Picturesque movement, it was a style of architecture that reacted against the Enlightenment's classical severity. The emphasis turned from quality of building and detail to overall effect; from a preoccupation with interior space to a desire only for impressive facades; from a serious, formal approach to a more capricious, eclectic one that took inspiration from any period or culture, like a painter of stage backdrops.

Born in 1752, Nash produced his best work in his sixties and seventies when, as the Prince Regent's town planner, he brought freedom and imagination to the city's "metropolitan improvements," as the Prince dubbed his project. Nash's gleaming stuccoed streets, terraces, and villas introduced a new theatricality, a new dignity to a city transforming itself from a port with sensible brick houses into the capital of a worldwide empire.

Cornwall Terrace, one of the early Nash terraces on the west of Regent's Park

This Regency style is best displayed in Nash's imposing Regent's Park terraces, which surround the park: York, Cornwall, Clarence, Sussex, and Hanover, built in 1821–23, were followed by Ulster, Cambridge, Chester, and Cumberland, and finally Gloucester in 1827.

York Terrace is strung along the south side of the park in two sections. In the middle, the thoroughly stage-set design of York Gate cleverly frames Marylebone Church, built in 1813 with gilded caryatids supporting the tower's dome. The other early terraces are strung along the west side. York, Cornwall, and Clarence, ambitious conceptions by Nash, were built under his direction by James Burton and his son, Decimus. In Sussex Place, Nash drew on his Brighton Pavilion: The curved end wings, octagonal domes, and polygonal bay windows seem better suited to the seaside. Finally, Hanover Terrace returns to a classical simplicity.

Where the architecture lapses, however, the lighthearted theatrical effect does not. This is even more true of the terraces on the east side, which follow the south side's Ulster Terrace with its simple lines and bay windows at each end. Between the relatively modest Cambridge Terrace and the asymmetrical Gloucester Gate, Chester Terrace's long facade of 940 feet is broken up by giant Corinthian columns; at either end, projecting wings are joined with thin triumphal arches. This is fun, but for architectural frolic Cumberland Terrace tops it. With its seven porticoes, courtyards, and arches, it makes one of the most impressive panoramas in London, a perfect backdrop to aristocratic partying.

Of the eight villas once sprinkled through the park, just three remain. Seen from across the lake, the Holme, designed by Decimus Burton for his father, looks just as it should: part of a suburban idyll of country houses surrounded by spacious grounds. The theatrical conceit still works. ■

Cumberland Terrace in 1831 (above), little changed externally today (below)

Madame Tussaud's & London Planetarium

The distinctive green dome of the Planetarium adjoining Madame Tussaud's

DRAWING SOME OF THE LARGEST CROWDS IN LONDON, these two institutions are especially popular with children, even though each is of relatively minor importance in a city blessed with so many truly amazing museums for history, art, and science. Madame Tussaud's opened in 1835, the Planetarium in 1958.

Madame Tussaud's & London Planetarium

- Map p. 133
- Marylebone Road, NW1
- 0870 400 3000
  www.madame-tussauds.com
- $$$, $$$$ for both
- Tube: Baker Street

Madame Tussaud, whose real name was Marie Grosholtz, fled revolutionary Paris in 1802, toured England with her uncle's waxworks, then settled near here. Fans kept returning because she was always adding people in the news. Her sons moved the collection to this site, and today's owners keep the show up-to-date.

A motley collection of personalities includes 17th-century diarist Samuel Pepys, Lenin, Joan Collins, U.S. Presidents and British prime ministers, and members of the British royal family. The Chamber of Horrors is especially tacky; the Spirit of London ride is not much better.

The Planetarium, on the other hand, is a more interesting experience. The 40-minute-long virtual-reality presentation, "Cosmic Perceptions," is projected onto a vast dome and gives beginners a good overview of the history of astronomy. A permanent display depicts a giant revolving Earth with its satellites, as well as live weather transmissions, space images, and touch-screen computers. ∎

Lord's Cricket Ground

England's most exclusive cricket club, the Marylebone Cricket Club, lies behind high walls. Thomas Lord moved the MCC northwest of Regent's Park when he sold the club's Dorset Square ground for development. The ground hosts club and Middlesex County matches and international Test matches. Visitors may tour the buildings (one designed by Michael Hopkins) and museum (Tel 7432 1033, www.lords.org, closed on major match days). Cricket memorabilia include Donald Bradman's boots, the sparrow killed by Jehangir Khan's ball in 1936, and the tiny urn containing the Ashes. The Ashes, of the stumps burned after Australia's first victory over England in 1882, is a mock trophy awarded to the winner in Test matches between the two countries. ∎

Regent's Canal, Camden Market, & Little Venice

IN THE 18TH CENTURY, ENGLAND WAS CRISSCROSSED BY canals—water highways that transported much of the industrial revolution's new trading wealth. Regent's Canal, built as the park's north border, provided a vital link in the system. It ran from Paddington Basin, where the Grand Union Canal from the Midlands then ended, to the Port of London 8.5 miles away, and quickly became England's busiest stretch of canal. Even after the railways were built, it was used for delivering expanding London's building materials.

Today, Regent's Canal is silent. The towpath is a favorite fishing spot, and pleasure boats ferry passengers between Camden Lock and Little Venice, stopping at London Zoo.

The two destinations are quite different. Camden's modest, small-scale houses are now gentrified. Weekend life with its banter and noise focuses in and around Camden Lock, whose ethnic market began in the 1970s and is now spruced up. Thousands of bargain hunters flock to the markets that have spread up Camden High Street and Chalk Farm Road. Camden Market also opens on Thursdays and Fridays.

Little Venice is, by contrast, a leafy and stylish haven. Painted barges are moored at the canal's end, including one that is a puppet theater (*Tel 020-7249 6876*). It is worth taking a walk here to enjoy the grand houses of the neighborhood of Maida Vale—the elegant ones on Blomfield Road border the canal—and to see a perfectly preserved Victorian pub, the Prince Alfred, on Formosa Street. ■

Regent's Canal pleasure boats

Tube: Camden Town, Warwick Avenue

London Waterbus Company
☎ 7482 2660
🕐 Closed Mon.–Fri. Nov.–March
$ $$

Jason's Trip
☎ 7286 3428
www.jasons.co.uk
🕐 Closed Nov.–March
$ $$

Jenny Wren
☎ 7485 4433
🕐 Closed Oct.–Easter
$ $$

Hampstead

Fenton House

- Map p. 133
- Hampstead Grove
- 7435 3471
- www.nationaltrust.org.uk
- Closed Mon., Tues., Sat. April–Oct., Mon.–Fri. March, & all Nov.–Feb.
- $$
- Tube: Hampstead

DISTANCED FROM THE CENTRAL LONDON DEVELOPERS, Hampstead watched the builders climb up the hill toward its doors but retained its distinct, hilltop village character, which persists even today. Healthy air and panoramic views right across London to the Surrey hills attracted Tudor merchants to Hampstead. By the 18th century, its popularity ran parallel with Islington's, but its position farther from town made it a more select pleasure resort, and it has never lost its fashionable image.

Well Walk recalls Hampstead's origins as a spa.

Burgh House

- New End Square
- 7431 0144
- www.london-northwest.com/burghhouse
- Closed Mon. & Tues.
- Tube: Hampstead

houses and gardens, and made them museums. **Fenton House,** at the top of the hill, is perhaps the grandest. It is a William-and-Mary house of 1693, filled with fine ceramics and musical instruments, and set in a delightful garden. **Burgh House,** located in the village center, is a perfect Queen Anne house of 1703, and was once owned by Hampstead physician Dr. William Gibbons.

Among the writers attracted to Hampstead was the poet John Keats, who lived between 1818 and 1820 in Keats Grove, a modest Regency house (*Wentworth Place, tel 7435 2062, www.keatshouse.org.uk*) now furnished with his belongings. The psychoanalyst Sigmund Freud lived in Maresfield Gardens (*Tel 7435 2002, www.freud.org.uk, closed Mon.–Tues.*), where his analyst's chair is displayed. Finally, the National Trust has bought and opened **2 Willow Road** (*Tel 7435 6166, www.national trust.org.uk*), designed by Erno Goldfinger in 1939.

The wealthy, artistic, and intellectual came to take the health-giving mineral waters at Hampstead's spa, and some stayed—statesman William Pitt and writers Lord Byron, Robert Louis Stevenson, and John Galsworthy all lived here. Despite the restaurants and shops that line High Street today, houses in Hampstead Square, Church Row, Flask Walk, Well Walk, and their surrounding streets still echo with Georgian holiday mood.

Hampstead's contemporary intellectuals have saved several fine

Two other things to do: Walk around **Hampstead Garden Suburb,** an "ideal" garden city of vernacular houses, conceived by Raymond Unwin and Barry Parker in 1907. It was laid out with houses of three sizes, for different income groups. Farther out, the **Jewish Museum** (*80 East End Road, Finchley, tel 8349 1143*) displays particularly good collections of Jewish art and objects. ■

Highgate

LIVING SLIGHTLY IN THE SHADOW OF FASHIONABLE
Hampstead, Highgate's story has always been a similar but quieter
one. A hamlet grew up on land belonging to the bishops of London.
By the end of the 16th century its waters and air were worth the journey from London, as were its open spaces for exercise and fun;
wealthy merchants built their country mansions here. Today,
Highgate is best known for its beautiful cemetery, where many
famous Londoners lie.

Lauderdale House
- Map p. 133
- Highgate High Street, N6
- 8348 8716
- Tube: Highgate, Archway

One of the earliest mansions to be
built here, **Lauderdale House**
(1580) survives in part, with later
additions. The large sloping garden,
confusingly called Waterlow Park,
has great beech, catalpa, and yew
trees shading the heavily scented
summer azalea blossoms.

The nucleus of Highgate, how-
ever, is farther up the hill, where the
eccentric philanthropist William
Blake built houses at Nos. 1–6 of
The Grove in the 17th century.
Nearby, delightful houses fill Pond
Square, and more survive in South
Grove: Old Hall at No. 17 (1690s),
Moreton and Church Houses at
Nos. 10 and 14, and the stuccoed
Literary Institute (1839). Cromwell
House, at 104 Highgate Hill, is a
rare survivor: a large London house
of the 1630s. The High Street has
more 18th-century houses at
Nos. 17–21, 23, and 42, and several
attractive Georgian shopfronts.

Highgate Cemetery, next
to Waterlow Park, is the burial place
of numerous interesting people,
and well worth a visit. Opened in
1839, it was so popular for its
ornate catacombs and fine views
that an extension was opened in
1857, with an under-road tunnel to
take the biers to the graves. In the
eastern part today, obelisks and
other elaborate monuments are
shaded by mature trees.

Memorials in the cemetery
include those to writer George
Eliot, who died in 1880, philosopher
Herbert Spencer (1903), and Karl
Marx, who died in 1883. Tours to
the western side may pass memorials for the Rossetti family, Dickens's
family (he himself is in
Westminster Abbey), Charles
Chubb, who invented Chubb locks,
and Charles Cruft, founder of
Cruft's Dog Show. The most
ostentatious mausoleums, though,
are the Terrace Catacombs,
supposedly the inspiration for
Bram Stoker's *Dracula*. This sacred
ground is closed during funerals;
children are not welcome. ∎

**Parliament Hill is
a favorite spot to
relax because of
its fine views.**

Highgate Cemetery
- Map p. 133
- Swaine's Lane, N6
- 8340 1834
- www.highgate-cemetery.org
- East side: $. West, guided tours: $
- Tube: Archway

Kenwood House & Hampstead Heath

Kenwood House, Iveagh Bequest

- Map p. 133
- Hampstead Lane, NW3
- 8348 1286
- www.english-heritage.org
- Charge for special exhibitions
- Tube: Hampstead, then walk 1 mile

Hill House & Garden

- Map p. 133
- Sandy Lane, by Jack Straw's Castle pub, North End Way, NW3
- None
- Tube: Hampstead

A magical setting for a summer evening concert

FINE ART IN A SPECTACULAR SETTING IS MATCHED BY panoramic views, rolling hills, and woodland, making this house and its surroundings one of the great joys of London.

In 1754 the brilliant lawyer the Earl of Mansfield bought the hilltop, early 17th-century Kenwood House with its fashionable "prospects" as a summer retreat from his city home in Lincoln's Inn Fields. Robert Adam, a fellow Scot, remodeled it in 1764–69. Exhibiting his mastery of both exterior and interior design, Adam added another story to the long, classical garden front and balanced the older orangery with a sumptuous library, one of his best rooms anywhere. The ceiling is decorated with plasterwork by Joseph Rose and paintings by Antonio Zucchi. After Mansfield, the house languished until 1925, when Edward Guinness, Earl of Iveagh, bought it along with 80 acres of park and hung his pictures in Adam's suite of rooms. Guinness left the house and gardens to the nation, along with the paintings, which include Vermeer's "Guitar Player" and Rembrandt's late "Portrait of the Artist."

From the front terrace, the lawns sweep down to an ornamental lake, now the setting for summer concerts; to the left (east), a path leads to the summit for breathtaking views of London. Walkers will itch to step out across Hampstead Heath, a tract of 789 acres fought for in the face of developers and accumulated piecemeal since 1829. Plunge down to **Highgate Ponds,** then climb **Parliament Hill** where Sunday kite flyers make their fragile, colorful paper shapes perform acrobatics in the skies; continue to **Hampstead Ponds** and perhaps take a walk in **Hill House**'s secret garden of heavily scented azaleas. ∎

Kensington Palace and its gardens of childhood magic make the area particularly family friendly. In South Kensington curious people of all ages roam the museums and enjoy concerts, circuses, and shows at the Royal Albert Hall.

Kensington & South Kensington

A sculpture of a pterodactyl decorates the Natural History Museum's roof.

Kensington & South Kensington

IN 1689 THE ASTHMATIC AND BRONCHITIC WILLIAM III LEFT DANK Whitehall Palace with his wife, Mary, for the fresh air of Kensington village, then well outside London. Thus began a royal association with the area that continues, for members of the royal family still live in Kensington Palace. The State Apartments are now open to the public.

William and Mary invited Sir Christopher Wren and Nicholas Hawksmoor to remodel their house as Kensington Palace. They also fenced off some of Hyde Park to create the nucleus of Kensington Gardens, where they indulged their passion for gardening.

The palace still lies at the heart of Kensington. This was a favorite official palace of the 18th-century Hanoverian rulers, until George III moved to Buckingham Palace in 1762. Queen Victoria lived there from her birth in 1819 until she succeeded to the throne in 1837. The proximity of royalty attracted the rich and wellborn: Even today, Kensington contains many of London's most fashionable residential streets.

London's grandest and most ostentatious street, Kensington Palace Gardens, was laid out in 1843 as a gated, tree-lined avenue. Edged with palatial mansions, it was soon nicknamed "millionaires' row." Today it is mostly devoted to foreign missions. Less ostentatious Kensington survives beyond, in the area bordered by two great shopping streets: Kensington Church Street, which curls up the hill to Notting Hill Gate and so to Portobello Road as a continuous parade of antiques shops; and Kensington High Street, which rose to prominence for more practical shopping after the Underground was built in 1868. The large estate of Holland Park was parceled off to become grand Holland Park houses at one end and a leafy idyll for artists such as the 19th-century painter Lord Leighton at the other.

Had you visited Kensington in the year 1851 you would have seen crowds coming to visit the Great Exhibition, held in the specially built Crystal Palace in Hyde Park. Conceived by Prince Albert as a platform for, and celebration of, worldwide industrial enterprise, it ran from May to October and was visited by six million British people, a

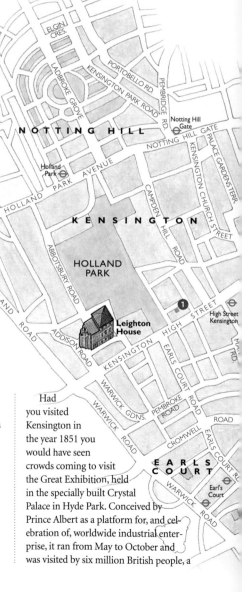

ELGIN CRES.

LADBROKE GROVE

KENSINGTON PARK ROAD

PORTOBELLO RD.

PEMBRIDGE RD.

NOTTING HILL

Notting Hill Gate

NOTTING HILL GATE

KENSINGTON GARDENS TERR.

Holland Park

PARK AVENUE

CAMPDEN HILL ROAD

KENSINGTON CHURCH STREET

HOLLAND

KENSINGTON

ABBOTSBURY ROAD

HOLLAND PARK

HOLLAND ROAD

ADDISON ROAD

Leighton House

KENSINGTON

HIGH STREET

EARLS COURT ROAD

High Street Kensington

MAIN RD.

WARWICK GDNS.

PEMBROKE ROAD

ROAD

CROMWELL ROAD

EARLS COURT ROAD

WARWICK ROAD

EARLS COURT

Earl's Court

WARWICK ROAD

① 1

third of the population. From the exhibition was born the idea of the South Kensington cultural campus for public learning. Today, a monument to Prince Albert stands across the road from the Royal Albert Hall, completed in 1871. Royal colleges for art, organists, and music are nearby, together with the Royal Geographical Society, the Imperial College of Science and Technology, and the Goethe Institute. The area is also the home to three great museums: the Victoria & Albert, Science, and Natural History. ■

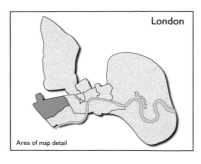

London

Area of map detail

KENSINGTON & SOUTH KENSINGTON

1 Linley Sambourne House
2 Royal College of Art 3 Royal College of Music 4 Imperial College 5 Serpentine Gallery
6 Royal Geographical Society
7 Goethe Institute

The south facade
of Kensington
Palace, home to
royalty since 1689

Kensington Palace

WITH ITS WARM REDBRICK EXTERIOR AND SMALL,
comfortable rooms, Kensington Palace instantly gives a feeling of
domesticity and informality that contrasts sharply with the formal
splendors of Hampton Court or Buckingham Palace. This family
mood was created by William and Mary. In 1689 they bought their
country mansion from Sir Heneage Finch, Duke of Nottingham, who
had remodeled the Jacobean house in 1661. That same year Sir
Christopher Wren and Nicholas Hawksmoor made essential changes
so the royal family could move in for Christmas. But work continued
for another seven years.

Kensington Palace

- Map p. 145
- Kensington Gardens, W8
- 0870 751 5170 www.hrp.org.uk
- $$$
- Tube: High Street Kensington

The best way to approach the
palace is from the south. The south
and east facades, with their fine
brickwork, are Wren's signature.
Leaving the statue of William III,
walk around the building, past the
State Rooms and the statue of
Queen Victoria by her daughter
Louise, and past the sunken garden
enclosed by pleached lime trees
(their branches entwined to form a
solid mass). On the right of the
entrance to the palace stands
Hawksmoor's Orangery, built in
1704–1705 and now a café where
customers can admire Grinling

Gibbons's elaborate carved pine
and pearwood festoons at either
end. The building adjoining the
back of the palace is home to some
members of the royal family. After
her separation from Prince Charles,
Princess Diana lived here; and it
was from Kensington Palace that
her funeral procession left for
Westminster Abbey.

William and Mary's monogram
is on the hood of the entrance
door. Inside, selected art from the
Queen's Royal Collection fills the
State Rooms. After the royal move
to Buckingham Palace they were

virtually abandoned, then opened to the public in 1899.

The plain oak Queen's Staircase rises to an intimate suite of Queen Mary's rooms. Her gallery has more Gibbons carvings on the overmantle mirror frames while the Dining Room retains its original paneling. Mary's Drawing Room has the Thomas Tompion barometer made for the palace around 1695 and a picture of Henry Wise, who first designed the gardens here. Mary's Bedchamber has the original elm floorboards and a bed, complete with hangings, used by James II.

The Privy Chamber marks the beginning of the high-ceilinged State Rooms designed by Colen Campbell for George I in 1718–1720. The rooms' gentle Palladian style is complemented by William Kent's ceiling decorations. The Privy Chamber decor shows Mars and Minerva, symbolizing the king's military prowess and the queen's patronage of the arts and sciences. Seventeenth-century Mortlake tapestries hang on the walls of this private audience chamber. From here Wren's Clock Court can be seen through a window. The public audience room, or Presence Chamber, is next. Here, Kent decorated the ceiling in cheerful Pompeiian colors, the first use in England of a style that was later used by the Adam brothers.

The King's Grand Staircase was designed by Wren, with ironwork by Jean Tijou. Kent's painting of the walls and ceiling is his most important decorative work: a Venetian-style view of a crowded gallery, inspired by Versailles and Blenheim (see p. 225). Courtiers and visitors to Kensington Palace would have climbed this appropriately grand staircase to the King's Gallery, built by Hawksmoor in 1695–96 and painted by Kent in 1725–26 with scenes from *The Odyssey*. The walls

of the gallery are now rehung with George II's paintings as he had them. Paintings in the spandrels depict the four continents known at the time.

A suite of rooms converted for the Duchess of Kent and her daughter, Victoria, follow. It was here that the teenage princess was awakened during the night of June 20, 1837, and informed by the Archbishop of Canterbury and the Lord Chamberlain that she was now Queen. Memorabilia include her own children's cot, David Roberts's views of the Great Exhibition, and Garrard's silver centerpiece, incorporating the queen's four dogs. But keep looking upward in these State Rooms. The King's Drawing Room has yet another splendid Kent ceiling. Wren and Kent together created the Cupola Room, next, where Victoria was baptized in 1819.

Finally, the **Royal Ceremonial Dress Collection** is all about royal fashion. Here is Queen Mary's wedding dress, a dozen of the present Queen's outfits, and much more. ∎

One of the rooms lived in by Queen Victoria before her accession to the throne

A walk around Kensington Gardens & South Kensington

A meander through Kensington Gardens is the prelude to a cornucopia of cultural feasts set in remarkable buildings.

William and Mary's creation of a Dutch garden on the 26 acres they bought with Kensington Palace were the humble origins of the 275-acre **Kensington Gardens.** Queen Anne anglicized and enlarged those gardens, and built the Orangery; she also laid out the promenade, Rotten Row. In 1728, George II's wife, Queen Caroline, and her gardener, Charles Bridgeman, fenced in more Hyde Park acres, dug the Round Pond, laid out the avenues radiating from it, and diverted the Westbourne stream to make the Long Water. With Victorian additions, the gardens fully opened to the public in 1851.

From the Lancaster Tube station, you enter the gardens at the **Italian Gardens,** added by Victoria and Albert in 1861. Follow the path beside the Long Water—perhaps spotting grebes and other waterfowl—to find George Frampton's 1912 statue of J. M. Barrie's fictional hero, Peter Pan. Through the trees to the right is George Frederick Watts's powerful 1904 bronze, "Physical Energy," and Queen Caroline's Round Pond. Back toward the Long Water, look for her Temple and the **Serpentine Gallery ❶** (Tel 7298 1515, www.serpentine-gallery.org), displaying contemporary art.

The **Flower Walk,** whose year-round blossoms attract birds and butterflies, leads to Sir George Gilbert Scott's flamboyant **Albert Memorial ❷** (Tel 7495 0916, guided tours on Sun.), created between 1864 and 1876. John Foley's statue has the seated prince holding the catalog of his Great Exhibition and looking down his lasting legacy, the South Kensington cultural compound that dominates the hillside.

This honeypot of institutions begins with the **Royal Albert Hall ❸** (Kensington Gore, tel 7589 8212, www.royalalberthall.org.uk) in front of the memorial. Designed by engineers inspired by Roman amphitheaters, the great oval hall is encircled with a frieze made by the Ladies' Mosaic Class of the Victoria & Albert Museum. The frieze depicts the Triumph of Arts and Letters. Inside, the iron-and-glass-

dome is an engineering triumph. The Henry Wood Promenade Concerts (www.bbc.co.uk/proms), an annual seven-week-long summer festival of nightly concerts known as the Proms, were transferred here in 1941, after being bombed out of Queen's Hall.

A cluster of small institutions surrounds the Hall. Upon leaving it, turn left (west) to find the **Royal College of Art** (Kensington Gore, tel 7590 4444, www.rca.ac.uk), founded in 1837, in H. T. Cadbury-Brown and Sir Hugh Casson's building (1962–1973). Farther along, F. W. Moody's multicolored graffito facade now fronts one of London's largest houses. Go behind the Royal Albert Hall to Prince Consort Road. On the left is the **Royal College of Music ❹** (Tel 7589 3643, www.rcm.ac.uk), founded in 1882, whose instrument collection includes Haydn's clavichord. Students perform in Sir Hugh Casson's Britten Opera Theatre.

Keep on to the end of Prince Consort Road to find Exhibition Road. The energetic can divert uphill to the **Royal Geographical Society ❺** (Kensington Gore, tel 7591 3000, www.rgs.org, closed Sat.–Sun.), founded in 1830 in Norman Shaw's Lowther Lodge (1873–75), and the **Polish Institute** (20 Princes Gate, tel 7589 9249) and its Sikorski Museum. This is the major Polish museum outside Poland because, after the German invasion in 1939, the government-in-exile came to London with 33,000 personnel.

The route downhill passes the **Goethe Institute ❻** (50 Prince's Gate, Exhibition Rd., tel 7596 4000, www.goethe.de/gr/lon, closed Fri. & Sun.) on the left and **Imperial College** on the right. The **Science Museum** (see p. 160) and the back entrance of the **Victoria & Albert Museum** (see p. 157) are beyond. Turn left into Prince's Gate Mews, then walk right, down past the mews cottages and through **Holy Trinity's garden ❼**. Go around the church and up the drive, then turn right to find the Oratory of St. Philip Neri.

Known as the **Brompton Oratory** ⑧ *(Brompton Road, tel 020-7589 4811)*, this branch of the oratory founded in Rome in 1575 was established by Father Faber in 1849. Inside the baroque church, Giuseppe Mazzuoli's exceptional "Twelve Apostles" from Siena Cathedral surround the huge nave.

Turn right out of the church along Brompton Road, past the V&A, then cross the road into Thurloe Place and Thurloe Square, built in the 1840s. On the corner of Exhibition Road, Sir Hugh Casson's **Ismaili Centre** ⑨ *(1 Cromwell Gardens, tel 7581 2071)* mounts exhibitions of Islamic art and culture. From here, the **Natural History Museum** (see p. 162) and South Kensington Tube station are each just a minute away. ∎

🅰	Inside front cover A4
▶	Lancaster Gate Tube station
↔	2.5 miles
🕐	2 hours
▶	South Kensington Tube station

NOT TO BE MISSED
- Albert Memorial
- Royal Albert Hall
- Royal Geographical Society
- Brompton Oratory

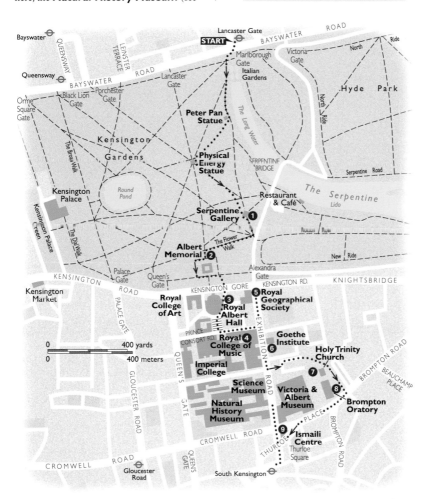

A WALK AROUND KENSINGTON GARDENS & SOUTH KENSINGTON

Holland Park
& Leighton House

HOLLAND PARK IS, CONFUSINGLY, THE NAME FOR BOTH the park surrounding Holland House and the two roads at the park's northwest corner, as well as for the whole area stretching from Kensington High Street to Holland Park Avenue.

Leighton House
- Map p. 144
- 12 Holland Park Road, W14
- 7602 3316
- www.rbkc.gov.uk
- Closed Tues.
- Tube: High Street Kensington or Holland Park, then walk through the park

Large and fashionable houses on the Holland Park estate date from 1866.

First, the house: **Holland Park,** now ruined, was built in 1606–1607 by Sir Walter Cope, minister to James I. It is the only Jacobean manor built to an E-shaped plan in London, and enough remains to enable us to imagine the grand life enjoyed by its owners. One was Henry Fox, created Baron Holland, who, using public funds for private speculation while paymaster-general in the government, bought it in 1768. The house became a center of Whig politics and literature, where Palmerston, Macaulay, Wordsworth, and Dickens made it a more significant court than the royal one. Later its fame came from partying rather than intelligent wit.

But after World War II bombs and social upheavals, the picturesque ruins are now a backdrop for summer theater. The Orangery holds art exhibitions and the garden ballroom is a restaurant. This ballroom was added by the 4th Baron, who also laid out the formal terraced gardens.

The 54 acres of **Holland Park,** opened to the public in 1950, begin with these terraces, shaded by magnificent horse chestnut trees. Newer additions include the Japanese Kyoto Garden, created in 1991. Cricket lawns to the south contrast with the wooded walks to the north. Wander through these and you might seem to be far from London. The rich woodland, with mature rhododendrons and azaleas, rose walks and spring daffodils gives an idea of what first lured the nobility to Kensington.

Next comes the **Holland Park estate,** lying outside the park's North Gate. An estate of 87 houses, it was built in 1866 by William and Francis Redford, after the 4th Baron's widow sold off a chunk of land to fund her lavish lifestyle. Elaborate ironwork and wide stairways accentuate the extremely grand facades of these houses.

All this is part of the present-day district of Holland Park. At the south end, a leafy residential enclave became home to wealthy artists and architects at the end of the 19th century, producing a crop of exotic houses. In Melbury Road, Pre-Raphaelite painter William

Lord Leighton
collected these
vividly colored
Arab tiles on his
travels.

Lord Leighton collected these vividly colored Arab tiles on his travels.

Linley Sambourne House

🅰 Map p. 144

✉ 18 Stafford Terrace, W8

☎ 7602 3316
www.rbkc.gov.uk

🕒 Open April–Oct. Sat. & Sun., & by arrangement with the Victorian Society, 1 Priory Gardens, W4

💲 $$

🚇 Tube: High Street Kensington

Holman Hunt lived at No. 18, while painter Luke Fildes lived in No. 31, designed by Norman Shaw, and William Burges designed his own Gothic Tower House at No. 29.

The most remarkable house in Holland Park is Frederick Lord Leighton's, designed by his friend George Aitchison in 1864–66. It is London's first full expression of the aesthetic movement. Leighton became established at the age of 25, when Queen Victoria bought one of his paintings at the Royal Academy exhibition of 1855. The interior of **Leighton House** is a bachelor's indulgence typified by the single bedroom with no space for guests. Red walls, ebonized wood, and gilt decorate the main rooms downstairs. Richly glazed tiles line the Arab Hall and staircase. ■

Linley Sambourne House

Behind its stuccoed, classical, Italianate facade in Kensington's Stafford Terrace, a perfect cameo of Edwardian London is lovingly preserved in its entirety by the Victorian Society. The political cartoonist Linley Sambourne, born in 1844, moved into his newly built house in 1874, and by his death in 1910 had filled it to capacity. Rooms decorated with William Morris wallpaper are hung with Sambourne's own cartoons for *Punch* magazine. Shelves are crammed with decorative china and the bathroom is hung with his early photographs. All this, plus the stained-glass windows heavily draped to keep the light dim, create an evocatively rich and somber mood. Do not miss Linley Sambourne's illustrations to Charles Kingsley's *Water Babies* in Roy Sambourne's bedroom upstairs. ■

London's markets

London has more than 340 markets of all sizes and themes, from Sunday's huge Petticoat Lane to little lunchtime Leadenhall.

Food

All the big wholesale markets need to be visited early. Smithfield Meat Market (see p. 66), the last wholesale fresh market remaining in central London, sells its bloody carcasses in the early weekday hours. Billingsgate fish market left the City and is now at West India Dock on the Isle of Dogs, and New Covent Garden Market still trades in fruit, flowers, and vegetables but has moved over the river to Nine Elms Lane in Vauxhall.

Clothes, antiques, & crafts

Other big markets thrive at more sociable hours, such as Portobello's on Saturdays and Camden's all weekend. The craft, clothes, souvenir, and antique markets that now fill Covent Garden's buildings daily, except Sunday, make up one of London's newest markets, established in the 1970s. The weekend market at Greenwich, which has echoes of the great market that was closed down last century, is down by the Thames on King William Walk and has an almost seaside feel to it. The whole atmosphere is fresh and lively, and stalls stocking clothes, antiques, books, and prints are complemented by the craft market in Bosun's Yard.

The best known large Sunday market is Petticoat Lane, where hundreds of stalls fill Middlesex and Wentworth Streets and the surrounding lanes to sell clothing of all kinds. Here, London's best East End street salesmen-entertainers run through their patter to gullible

For a really eclectic mix of goods, visit Portobello Road on a Saturday (left); go early to catch the best buys. Stands in the courtyard of St. James's Piccadilly (below) have eye-catching displays of silver and other small treasures.

crowds and skillfully sell useless gadgets and dubious perfumes with exotic French names.

Local markets

Dotted across London, little local markets vary their stock to suit their customers' tastes and traditions. Berwick Street's weekday market in Soho dates back to the 1840s when the area was an Italian and French quarter, and its quality vegetables, herbs, and flowers balance the supplies sold in nearby Italian food shops. Chapel Market in Islington has been lively for a century, serving the local population with no-nonsense food and basic household goods. Ridley Road market at Dalston is quite different: It has been thriving since the 1880s, but its injection of postwar Afro-Caribbean, Asian, and Turkish immigrants means such delicacies as live catfish are now on sale. Brixton Market is best for pure West Indian goods. Here, in the lanes around Brixton Underground station, you can find reggae and soul music

shops, fish such as goat fish, smoked angera, and blue runner, Nasseri African fabrics, and calves' hooves.

Specialist markets

For antiques, Camden Passage has a fine set of shops and stalls, with plenty of good restaurants nearby. Portobello has a similar mix. Bermondsey Market, held in Bermondsey Square on Fridays, has the largest and best value stalls, but means a 5 to 6 a.m. start for bargains, which are inspected by torchlight. Prices vary, and only the most knowledgeable will be able to compete with the dealers and the clients, who would be just as at home bidding in Sotheby's auction rooms. Safer to pick up a painting along Bayswater Road on Sunday, or a coin at the Collector's Fair on Villiers Street on Saturday. And there are markets in the courtyards of St. James's Piccadilly on Friday and Saturday, or St. Martin-in-the-Fields any day except Sunday. ■

Notting Hill & Portobello Road

Notting Hill & Portobello Road

Map p. 144

WHILE HOLLAND PARK LURED HIGH SOCIETY, THE AREA TO its north was developed with slightly lower aspirations to attract London's affluent Victorians. Farms, potteries, and piggeries were soon mere memory as pretty villas and terraces spread north. Today, Notting Hill is best known for its Portobello Road antiques market and the annual Caribbean carnival.

At the bottom of Notting Hill, Norlands Farm was transformed into the pretty, small-scale Norland Estate during the 1840s and '50s. Farther up, developer James Weller Ladbroke bought Notting Hill Farm, planning to create a utopian garden city of large villas with their own private gardens, which in turn opened onto communal gardens.

The antiques trade on Portobello Road attracts a variety of market stalls on Saturdays.

When the estate was finished in 1870 it was London's most spacious, and its architecture was of unusually high quality. Handsome Lansdowne Road and Crescent, Stanley Crescent, and Ladbroke Square illustrate the achievement.

PORTOBELLO ROAD

Portobello Road slips northward down the side of, and in contrast to, the grandeur of Ladbroke Grove. It was once the farm track leading down to Porto Bello Farm. By the 1870s gypsies were trading horses and herbs here and in the 1890s Saturday night markets were established, illuminated by flaming lamps. The antique dealers that now make the street famous began to arrive in 1948, when Caledonian Market near King's Cross closed.

Today, the **Portobello Road market** is one of Britain's longest and, when augmented by its Saturday stallholders, provides a daylong party of guaranteed fascination, noise, and color—and possibly a bargain or two.

At the end of Notting Hill, the established antique shops and stalls between Chepstow Villas and Lonsdale Road have quality, often rare, collectors items, with few bargains. The sharp-eyed and informed may have a better chance down the hill. Good food shops between Lonsdale and Lancaster Roads can restore strength. Beyond the Westway flyover, the imaginative hunter may find secondhand clothes and bric-a-brac to give individual character to an outfit or a room. Golborne Road has a fruit and vegetable market, and the shops between Aklam Road and Oxford Gardens sell the latest street fashion, worn by stylish Londoners sitting in the neighborhood bars. Beyond that, find secondhand bicycles, new clothes, and household goods. ■

Carnival

Every August Bank Holiday weekend, the streets of Notting Hill are one continuous Caribbean party. The Caribbean community grew here after World War II, when citizens of newly independent British Empire countries were also given British citizenship. The immigrants replaced Londoners who had left for a suburban life. They held the first African-Caribbean street festival in the 1960s, evoking the Trinidad Carnival that envelops the island for two days before Ash Wednesday. Today, it is Europe's largest street festival, drawing half a million people and filling the areas between Chepstow Road and Ladbroke Grove.

The action consists of music and parades and builds up over Saturday and Sunday. On Monday, dozens of bands play reggae, soul, and calypso in Powis Square, or tour the streets playing in open-back lorries. Trinidadian influence is in the steel bands—whose use of steel oil pans evolved in response to the colonial ban on playing drums—and the costume parades. These parades are spectacular, up to 200 people in each, all in fantastical costumes following themes such as African warriors, butterflies, and flowers; central characters may have costume extensions held up by wire frames. The best music and costumes win cash prizes. ∎

Notting Hill Carnival

Prince Albert's dream

South Kensington is the living legacy of one man, Prince Albert of Saxe-Coburg-Gotha. From the day of his marriage to Queen Victoria in 1840, he was her closest adviser and worked ceaselessly for his adopted country.

Albert's crowning achievement was the Great Exhibition of the World of Industry of All Nations, held in Hyde Park in 1851. It was a celebration of Victorian dynamism. Sir Joseph Paxton, once gardener to the Duke of Devonshire, designed a great cast-iron-and-

glass building, nicknamed the Crystal Palace. In it, 100,000 exhibits were shown by 13,937 exhibitors, half of whom were from Britain and its great empire. Conceived as a platform for and celebration of industrial enterprise worldwide, the exhibition ran from May 1 to October and was visited by six million British people, a third of the city's population.

The exhibition's success, and its substantial profits, inspired Albert to an even more ambitious dream: a cultural campus that would provide free learning for all people. It was to be a permanent showcase for the arts and for industry on the fields south of Hyde Park. The plan was to have an avenue of colleges for the arts and sciences leading to a huge national gallery, with museums and learned societies, concert halls, and a garden beyond.

Albert's devotion to his project, soon known as "Albertopolis," was unstinting. Tragically, he died of typhoid in 1861. While the Queen withdrew into seclusion, Prime Minister Benjamin Disraeli told a stunned public: "This German Prince has governed England for twenty-one years with a wisdom and energy such as none of our Kings have ever shown."

Nothing stopped Albert's dream, the biggest development for public use that London had yet seen. When the National Gallery refused to move, the Royal Albert Hall took its place in the scheme, and music and art colleges surrounded it. The Victoria & Albert Museum, which Albert hoped would be of practical help to students of commerce and industry, grew so fast that its art college became the separate Royal College of Art, and its science and educational collections became the Science Museum. Meanwhile, the British Museum's natural history departments overflowed and were given space here; more recently the Geological Museum arrived from St. James's in 1935, and was later absorbed by the Natural History Museum. ∎

The Albert Memorial (1876), Sir George Gilbert Scott's monument to Prince Albert, stands on Kensington Gardens' south side.

Victoria & Albert Museum (V&A)

At her last public engagement, Queen Victoria declared in 1899 that the museum be named after its mentor, Albert, and herself.

THE WORLD'S LARGEST MUSEUM OF DECORATIVE ARTS and design is encyclopedic. In fact, it is several museums in one. Primarily the national museum of art and design, it also includes the national collections of sculpture, watercolors, portrait miniatures, art photography, wallpaper, and posters, as well as the National Art Library. It has the best set of Italian sculpture outside Italy and the finest Indian decorative arts collection in the world.

The V&A began as a collection of plastercasts, engravings, and a few objects from the Great Exhibition. It was Prince Albert who, with art patron Henry Cole, conceived the idea of a museum of objects "representing the application of Fine Art to manufacture," to inspire British people. Cole, the first director, wanted a museum about design and craft in a commercial context, not craft for craft's sake. This is still the museum's philosophy today.

The humble museum with big ideas was first housed in wooden sheds, then in an engineer's iron-and-glass building known as the Brompton Boilers. It grew fast. While the keeper amassed quality objects for his students, gifts began to arrive: Sheepshanks's British paintings, the Bandinel Collection of pottery and porcelain, the Gherardini Collection of models for sculpture, and many more. Various rooms were built piecemeal to form the central quadrangle and the eastern courts, and Sir Aston Webb's slab of galleries was added to the front in 1899–1909. Whole departments later left to find space as V&A outposts or as independent museums—the Science Museum, the Bethnal Green Museum of

Victoria & Albert Museum

- Map p. 145
- Cromwell Road, SW7
- 7942 2000
- www.vam.ac.uk
- Charge for some exhibitions
- Tube: South Kensington

The Becket Cas

The Becket Casket, acquired by the V&A in 1997, is Limoges enamel made in 1180.

"Tipoo's Tiger," a mechanical marvel made circa 1790 to entertain Tipu Sultan, ruler of Mysore in India—the tiger's mechanisms simulate the groans of the dying British officer he savages.

Childhood, and the Theatre Museum. Late in the 20th century, the museum expanded into the adjacent Henry Cole Wing and there are plans to add Daniel Libeskind's Spiral, five self-supporting galleries designed with no core, clad in ivory ceramic tiles.

The best of past and contemporary design was bought by, or given to, the museum. Some pieces were tiny, such as the Canning Jewel; others were vast—the Raphael Cartoons, for instance, and whole rooms, including the Duke of Norfolk's Music Room and Frank Lloyd Wright's study. Today, most of the 2,000 or so annual acquisitions for the design, prints, and drawings departments are contemporary, and the museum regularly commissions silver, furniture, and other pieces. In addition, galleries are constantly being added; recent ones include ceramics, glass, and photography.

Just some of the museum's

4.5 million objects are exhibited in more than 170 galleries arranged on six levels around four courts. So confusing is it to visit that color-coded banners direct visitors: red for north; yellow, east; green, south; and blue, west.

Basically, there are two types of rooms: art and design galleries, such as Europe 1600–1700, where objects of a type are exhibited in their cultural context; and materials and techniques galleries, such as silver, where objects of one material or type are displayed to show their form, function, and technique.

For those who know what they want to see, a combination of the map, the list of galleries, and a keen sense of direction will be enough. For those who feel overwhelmed before they start, here are some interesting stops on an easy route (with room numbers indicated, as marked on the free museum maps available at the information desk).

THE TRAIL
From the entrance hall, turn right and go through Rooms 50A and B, Sculpture and Architecture. Then turn left into Rooms 46A and B, crowded with Victorian casts, where Trajan's Column and Michelangelo's "David" have inspired countless students; here, too, is the museum's collection of splendid fakes.

Past the Korean and Chinese art in Rooms 47G and F, turn right into the **Toshiba Gallery of Japanese Art.** One of the museum's best buys was 12,000 woodcuts in 1886. The **T. T. Tsui Gallery of Chinese Art** is next door, Room 44. Through it lies the **Medieval Treasury,** Room 43. The low-lit room contains masterpieces of intricate craftsmanship, using ivory, gold, and precious stones. From here, there is a good view of the Pirelli garden; the far side is the museum's original

facade. Down the steps, go left through Room 22 and left again to Room 41, the **Nehru Gallery of Indian Art,** where a tiny fraction of the Indian collection is on show, usually including some exquisite miniature paintings and some fine textiles. Indian objects fill the corridor Rooms 47A and B, too, which lead to the **hall of fashion,** Room 40, a feast of European costumes from the 16th century to today.

Across the corridor, stroll through the older rooms that surround the Pirelli garden, pausing in Rooms 11–20 to enjoy the collection of 15th-century Italian art. Now visit **Canon Photography Gallery** (Room 38). The display

has some of the museum's 300,000 photographs that date back to an 1839 daguerreotype of Trafalgar Square by M. De Ste. Croix.

Three more contrasting stops complete this introduction. The first is a wander through the stunning, renovated **British Galleries** upstairs, feasting your eyes on a jewel Francis Drake gave Elizabeth I, Huguenot silver, and whole rooms saved from Jacobean and Georgian London houses. The second is to go up the **Ceramic Staircase,** decorated with Minton tiles, to find the dazzling national collection of English silver. Finally, seek out the complete **Frank Lloyd Wright study** in Room 202 on the second floor of the Henry Cole wing. ■

The Gamble Room originally served as a dining room for the visiting public.

Science Museum

Science Museum

📍 Map p. 145

✉ Exhibition Rd., SW7

☎ 0870 870 4771

www.sciencemuseum
.org.uk

💲 Charge for special
sections

🚇 Tube: South
Kensington

THE MOST UNSCIENTIFIC PERSON WILL BE EXCITED BY Britain's National Museum of Science and Industry, where learning about an idea often demands more active participation than merely reading labels and looking at objects. In 1909 it became fully independent of its V&A mother, and in 1913 moved into Richard Allison's building. His department store format, with big windows and large, simple spaces, has been ideal. As the collection has grown, there is flexibility to display the full thrill of scientific discoveries through the ages, and it is easy to find one's way around.

Children love the Science Museum's hands-on approach to learning.

Today, some of the 200,000 items are displayed in 70 galleries on 7 floors covering 8 acres of floor space, telling stories of inventions and discoveries that have affected our lives, from the plastic bag and the telephone to the offshore oil rig and the airplane. And yet the

arrangement is straightforward: Lower galleries are geared to young people, and are often more crowded; upper ones are dedicated to a more sophisticated and detailed level of interest. This trail explores every floor, seeking out one or two highlights on each.

THE TRAIL

At the main entrance, there is information on the day's events and demonstrations, with a useful introduction to science on the mezzanine. Ground-floor galleries are **"Power"** (James Watt's steam engines to the earliest Rolls Royce, 1904), the **"Exploration of Space,"** and—a top favorite with all the family—the **"Science of Sport."** Here you can discover how the body works and how it can be trained, and test your skills against professional runners and other athletes. The basement's **"Things"** exhibition satisfies young children's natural curiosity.

Now go to the **Wellcome Wing,** where new state-of-the-art galleries include **"Who Am I?,"** the **IMAX cinema,** and **"Talking Points,"** which focuses on contemporary science issues.

On the first floor, gas, agriculture, meteorology, surveying, and time measurement are tackled at the back. **"Telecommunications"** and **"Launch Pad"** show how a

telephone works and how man first went to the moon, with plenty of hands-on equipment at the front. **"Challenge of Materials"** explores the world of materials using installations, audiovisual displays, and interactive computers.

Up on the second floor, you can see how the paper that fills our lives is made and how it was printed before computer typesetting confined metal type to museums. Other subjects, which need more scientific interest and application to appreciate, include chemistry, measuring, lighting, and nuclear physics and power. Sections on petroleum and computing lead to a large space devoted to navigation, marine engineering, docks, and diving—with lots of superb model ships. From here, steps lead up to the third floor. This end is all about flight: The **"Flight Lab"** has hands-on exhibits for testing the principles of flight, while a hangar full of aircraft includes Amy Johnson's *Jason*, in which she flew to Australia in 1930, and a model of the Wright brothers' flimsy plane in which they made the first power-assisted flight in 1903. The other end of this floor includes the Wellcome Institute's **"Health Matters"** area, where vaccinations are explained.

The smaller fourth and fifth floors cover medical history and tackle the **"Science and Art of Medicine."** Charming, if dated, dioramas tell the story of medical operations, dentistry, and open-heart surgery. Upstairs, the under-visited Wellcome Institute's gallery is a magpie hoard: an Egyptian mummified head, African fetish objects, George Washington's false teeth, Dr. Livingstone's medicine chest, Napoleon's silver-gilt toothbrush, and more, all helping to explain the history of science and medicine. ■

Space exploration is a popular theme at the Science Museum.

Natural History Museum

Natural History Museum

🅰 Map p. 145

✉ Cromwell Road, SW7; secondary entrance on Exhibition Road

☎ 7942 5000. Darwin Centre guided tours: 7942 6128 www.nhm.ac.uk

💲 Charge for some exhibitions

♿ Tube: South Kensington

BOTH THE COLLECTION—CONSISTING OF MORE THAN 68 million specimens and one million books and manuscripts—and the magnificent building could be daunting. But this museum has made its exhibits and knowledge highly accessible and exciting for the general public without sacrificing the prime job of informing and educating. The famous dinosaur exhibition explains what we can learn from these very ancient bones about the evolution of modern animals.

THE BUILDING

The building is as remarkable as its contents. First, the structure. When in 1862 the natural history collection of the British Museum (see p. 122), including pieces from Sir Hans Sloane's collection, came to the burgeoning South Kensington cultural campus, it needed a suitable home. This was realized in the cathedral-like proportions of Alfred Waterhouse's Romanesque building, whose towers, spires, arches, and columns look to the churches of the Rhineland. The iron-and-steel framework is covered with cream, blue, and honey-colored terra-cotta, which introduced color into dirty Victorian London and created an acid-free, easy-to-clean protective coat. Planned by the museum's first director, Sir Richard Owen, extant animals crawl over the west side, extinct ones over the east, reflecting the original gallery plans. At the end of the 20th century, the museum of specimens of living (or once-living) things formally amalgamated with the **Geological Museum** next door. The geological collection tells the story of the Earth itself, from a delicate 330-million-year-old fern fossil to the reenactment of an earthquake in Japan in 1995.

The **Life Galleries** housing the living things collection are reached from the main Cromwell Road entrance and connect to the geological section in the **Earth Galleries,** which can also be entered directly from Exhibition Road. Each display contains so much information that just one could fill a whole visit. Remember, 300 scientists and librarians are working behind the scenes here, and what you see is the result of a worldwide network of scientists striving to extend humankind's knowledge.

But for those who want an overview with some highlights pointed out, here is a suggestion for tackling this vast showcase.

The best way to see the new **Darwin Centre**'s zoological specimens is to sign up for a guided tour.

THE TRAIL

Pause in the vast **Central Hall** (Room 10), where Waterhouse's painted ceiling and zoo of terra-cotta animals, birds, flowers, and reptiles running up the columns and hiding in the arches is the setting for a single giant skeleton of a *Diplodocus.*

Turn left, westward, and follow **Waterhouse Way** to the dinosaurs in Room 21. Here are bones from creatures that roamed the Earth for 160 million years until their extinction 65 million years ago. They come in all varieties, and from these skeletons we

can understand their lifestyles—whether they lived alone, fought by charging like a ram, or hunted in packs, and how they developed defense mechanisms such as lashing tails, horns, and bony neck frills.

Farther along Waterhouse Way,

the **Human Biology Room** (No. 22) takes a closer look at a recent development, human beings. Models show how the memory works and the development of a baby from a single cell; optical illusions explain the relation between sight and knowledge.

Next door, Rooms 23 and 24 are devoted to mammals. A life-size model of a blue whale is complemented by tapes of whale songs and an explanation of why its enormous weight does not sink. Hands-on gadgets encourage the visitor to work out why horses can gallop and elephants cannot. Beyond Room 14, fish and reptiles fill Rooms 12 and 13. Here you can listen to the sea and wonder at the variety of marine life displayed in traditional cases—the bony soldier fish, slow-growing marine coral—overhung with a giant squid.

Back to Waterhouse Way, turn

Above: The museum's central hall was built as a cathedral to the wonders of creation and opened the year before Charles Darwin died.

Right: The mounted bones of an ichthyosaur, an extinct marine reptile

A model of a pterodactyl in flight shows the webs of skin, like those of bats, that enabled these now long-extinct reptiles to fly.

left and find fossils of marine reptiles on either side, from tiny ammonites found in Jurassic rocks in Dorset to sea dragons. To the left, Room 33 has creepy crawlers: Insects, spiders, crustaceans, and centipedes are highly adaptable and some have sophisticated social systems, and defense mechanisms, such as camouflage, armor, or weaponry. All this has helped them survive. To the right, through Room 31, devoted to British fossils, Room 32 explains our ecology: How we are linked to one another and how crucial air, soil, sunlight, energy, and water are to survival.

From here, stairs lead up to the first floor, where Room 105 tells the story of Charles Darwin's theory of natural selection. Other galleries are devoted to apes and monkeys, the place of humans in evolution, the many plants around the world, minerals, and meteorites.

At the end of Waterhouse Way, Room 40 has been left as it was when the museum opened in 1881.

Finally, Room 50 explains how animals grow and keep a record of their age in their bodies, even after death.

Room 60 is the big introduction to the **Earth Galleries,** focusing on the Earth itself. Displays of specimens line the gallery, including a piece of the moon and another of soft graphite, which is chemically identical to hard diamonds.

Then take the escalator on a journey through a vast iron, zinc, and copper globe. Upstairs, the subject is power and the restless surface of the Earth. Here, the constant changes in the Earth that continue today with alarming regularity are considered: Mount Pinatubo's 1991 volcanic eruption, Kobe's 1995 earthquake. To end, the visitor is reassuringly given the power to polish rocks, change the direction of rivers, and alter the Earth's climate. Do not miss the piece of rock that has somehow recorded all changes on the Earth's surface for millions of years. ∎

Containing the capital's largest tract of upscale housing, this area attracts international and moneyed residents. Two favorite London institutions are here: Harrods in Knightsbridge for shoppers, and Tate Britain in Pimlico for art devotees.

Chelsea, Belgravia, & Knightsbridge

A Chelsea pensioner, one of the veteran soldiers from the Royal Hospital

Chelsea, Belgravia, & Knightsbridge

IT WAS WHEN THE TRENDSETTING PRINCE REGENT BECAME GEORGE IV IN 1820 and began to remodel Buckingham Palace that developers recognized the promising possibilities of this area. London's 19th-century expansion from one to six million inhabitants included plenty of wealthy potential customers. Open fields and marshy but drainable land lay right next to the palace, Mayfair, and smart Hyde Park, and within easy reach of Westminster and St. James's Palace. The great manors of Chelsea gave it credibility; royals living in Kensington Palace were nearby. Soon, bargeloads of building materials were being unloaded along this stretch of the Thames. So began Belgravia. This, together with the Great Exhibition of 1851 and the development of South Kensington's museums and upmarket housing, stimulated the creation of Knightsbridge.

CHELSEA

The most interesting area is Chelsea, which had been a favorite aristocratic country retreat from London since Tudor times, when manor houses set in spacious orchards grew up around a fishing village. The Society of Apothecaries built its Physic Garden here in 1673, King William and Queen Mary chose Chelsea for their Royal Hospital in the next decade, and Sir Hans Sloane bought Chelsea Manor in 1712 and made it the repository for his collection (see p. 122). Chelsea linked the city to the aristocrats' country mansions upriver in two ways: The Thames was the safest and fastest way to travel, and King's Road was the private royal route between London, Hampton Court, and other royal idylls between 1660 and the 1830s.

Later, a less-smart 19th-century Chelsea attracted writers and artists, from Thomas Carlyle to Oscar Wilde. It was there that architects broke with the Georgians' stuccoed classicism to return to a more vernacular Queen Anne style using red brick. First adopted for houses along the Embankment, this style

was chosen by the Cadogan family when, in the 1870s, they laid out Cadogan Square and its surroundings. More recently, the King's Road, running from Sloane Square through the hearts of Chelsea and Fulham, was reborn in the 1960s as a public catwalk for the

avant garde, while the terraces off it, originally built as mass-produced housing for artisans, became the immaculate, if cramped, homes of successful City bankers and business people.

BELGRAVIA

Belgravia's story is shorter, but spectacular. With Mayfair and St. James's overflowing, this was the last London project to be developed by the rich (the Grosvenors) for the rich. Begun in 1824, the scheme centered on Belgrave Square, where the Regency style was taken to new heights. It was here that architect

Thomas Cubitt brought success and quality to a wobbling project; such success that the Grosvenors themselves have left Mayfair for Belgravia, and Belgrave Square accommodates a clutch of foreign missions. Cubitt then went on to develop Pimlico, starting in 1835.

KNIGHTSBRIDGE

Knightsbridge, meanwhile, was boosted not only by the Great Exhibition but by the building of Belgravia. The first village on the road that led west out of London from Mayfair was transformed from fields into a densely packed area whose heartbeat was, and is, retail commerce. Today, the heart of Knightsbridge is Harrods, whose international shoppers are content to feel they have visited London if they have shopped there. ■

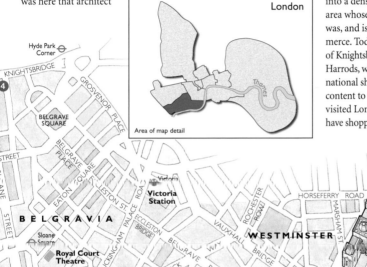

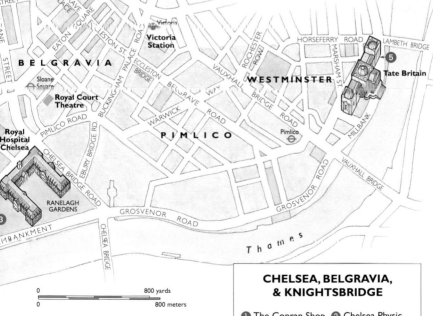

CHELSEA, BELGRAVIA, & KNIGHTSBRIDGE

❶ The Conran Shop ❷ Chelsea Physic Garden ❸ National Army Museum ❹ Harvey Nichols ❺ Clore Gallery

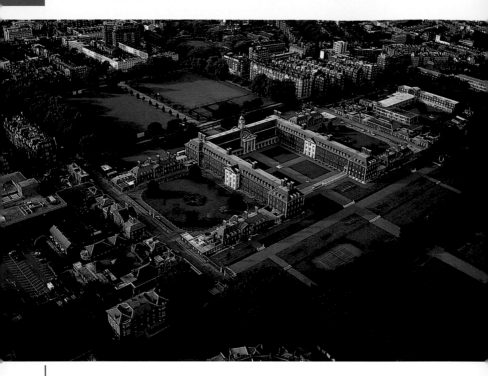

Chelsea

WHEN THE SCOTTISH HISTORIAN AND PHILOSOPHER Thomas Carlyle (1795–1881) chose to live in Chelsea in 1834, the lanes that are now so sought after were unfashionable.

ROYAL HOSPITAL CHELSEA

Royal Hospital Chelsea

- Map p. 167
- Royal Hospital Road, SW3
- 7730 5282
- Closed Sun. except for services and May–Sept. 2–4 p.m.
- Donation. Gardens: free.
- Sloane Square

First views of London buildings can be stunning. For the Royal Hospital, designed by Sir Christopher Wren for Charles II to house almost 500 army veterans and still home to red-coated Chelsea Pensioners today, there are two such views: from a leafless, winter-time Royal Avenue off King's Road, or from a boat on the river, looking up the lawns to the main river-facing facade.

Wren broke new ground with this, his first large-scale secular work. Inspired by Louis XIV's Les Invalides in Paris, it became a blue-print for institutional buildings in Europe and America: A central hall and chapel flanked by two side courts for the dormitories. The stables were added in 1814 by Sir John Soane, while he was Clerk of Works to the hospital.

On the garden facade, benches in Figure Court overlook Grinling Gibbons's bronze of Charles II and the formal gardens that once ended at the water. The more informal gardens to the left were, from 1742 to 1803, the infamous Ranelagh pleasure gardens.

Inside the hospital are three magnificent rooms. In the paneled Great Hall, today's pensioners dine

Chelsea Flower Show

Since 1913, the Royal Horti-cultural Society has held its annual competitive spectacular in and around huge marquees erected in the Royal Hospital's gardens. For a week in late May, Chelsea's streets are crowded with people more used to pruning and propagating than tackling London's Underground. Nurseries and plantsmen, garden designers, and manufacturers of gardening equipment exhibit their triumphs—a new rose, a complete garden, a wonder cure for slugs. Visitors come to admire, to glean ideas, or just to enjoy the show's profusion of perfect blooms. ■

beneath Verrio's painting of Charles II. In the chapel, they pray in box pews amid decoration that includes Sebastiano Ricci's "Resurrection" altarpiece. The Council Chamber, beyond, is even finer, hung with Van Dyck and Lely portraits.

CARLYLE'S HOUSE

Despite its then unfashionable location, Carlyle relished his "old-fashioned" street and his "most massive, roomy, sufficient old house" at 24 Cheyne Row.

Today, like so many house-museums, the personality of its owner still pervades it. Carlyle would wander the house and garden in his dressing gown, straw hat, and pipe; all three props are still intact. Here the intellectual, famous after his account of the French Revolution was published, and his witty wife would receive John Stuart Mill in the drawing room, Dickens and Browning in the parlor, and Darwin or Thackeray in the back dining room. Carlyle lived here for 47 years, and in the garden his ghost seems to haunt the walnut tree and the vine.

CHELSEA PHYSIC GARDEN

Carlyle undoubtedly visited this walled garden a mere two minutes' walk from his house. Founded in 1673 by the Society of Apothecaries to grow plants for medical study, the 4-acre garden was stocked with many specimens cultivated for the first time in England. One early curator, Philip Miller (1722–1770), author of *The Gardener's Dictionary,* sent cotton seeds to Georgia in the U.S. to establish the staple crop in the new colony. Today, with its herbs and exotic trees, the garden remains a place of serious study as well as a peaceful haunt for visitors. ■

Chelsea Flower Show
☎ Ticket hotline 0870-906 3781
$ $$$–$$$$$. Reservations required

Carlyle's House
△ Map p. 166
✉ 24 Cheyne Row, SW3
☎ 7352 7087
www.nationaltrust.org.uk
🕐 Closed Mon.–Tues. & Nov.–March
$ $$
🚇 Tube: Sloane Square, then any bus down King's Road to Oakley Street (on left). Walk down Oakley Street, then turn right into Cheyne Row

Chelsea Physic Garden
△ Map p. 166
✉ 66 Royal Hospital Road, SW3; entrance on Swan Walk
☎ 7352 5646
www.chelseaphysic garden.co.uk
🕐 Open April–Oct. p.m. Wed. & Sun., & during Chelsea Flower Show
$ $$
🚇 Tube: Sloane Square, then any bus down King's Road to Flood Street (on left). Walk down to Chelsea Embankment, turn left, then first left on to Swan Walk

Belgravia & Pimlico

WITH BRITAIN ENJOYING AN ECONOMIC BOOM AND George IV rebuilding Buckingham Palace, the 2nd Earl of Grosvenor focused on his 400 undeveloped acres south of Hyde Park. Over this marshy scrubland, notorious for its highwaymen, duels, and duck shoots, he created a 200-acre estate that stole the limelight from his 100-acre Mayfair estate. Georgian brick, simplicity, and modest scale gave way to high Regency stucco. Thus Belgravia was born, a suburb for the very grand. Soon society moved west to take up residence there, Knightsbridge and South Kensington moved upscale to meet it, and Chelsea was linked to the continuous London sprawl.

The master plan had a traditional square (Belgrave) surrounded by a network of streets, Georgian in concept but Regency in scale. Three big developers took on the site. Two went bankrupt; the third, Thomas Cubitt (see box p. 171), made a fortune. Work began in 1824 and continued for 30 years.

To appreciate Belgravia's magnificence, take a walk around these awe-inspiring streets and squares. From Sloane Street, walk east on Pont Street and Chesham Street, past Cadogan Place's stucco. Turn left into Belgrave Mews, once the stables for the grand houses in the square in front and now converted into attractive (and pricey) little houses, to find Halkin Place leading into the grandeur of Belgrave Square. Turn left and walk the sweep of Wilton Crescent, which will bring you back to Belgrave Square. On the opposite side, Upper Belgrave Street leads to magnificent Eaton Square.

Today, foreign embassies and high-flying international entrepreneurs fill Belgravia houses and streets, along with a sprinkling of old British aristocrats. The dry, formal atmosphere is different from Pimlico's, where Londoners step out of less opulent houses to join their lively community in Tachbrook Street's market and Warwick Way's restaurants.

Grosvenor Crescent, Belgravia, where gleaming facades of stucco plaster enhance the brick-framed buildings

Cubitt, backed by three Swiss bankers, took the lease on Belgrave Square and employed George Basevi as architect. The square was an instant social success: Dukes and duchesses moved into the palatial mansions and held glittering parties in their first-floor ballrooms. Work continued. Soon Cubitt had added Upper Belgrave Street, Chester Square, and Eaton Place (where he had his offices).

Pimlico was Cubitt's own project. After years of negotiation, Cubitt persuaded the Grosvenors to lease him the land south of the canal, today cut off by Victoria Station. On this, he laid out two squares, Eccleston and Warwick, set on terraced streets of houses. ■

Thomas Cubitt

London's most successful developer in the early 19th century was Thomas Cubitt. Born in 1788 near Norwich, he revolutionized the building industry and, with a mixture of commercial acuteness and bold imagination, oversaw a series of large construction projects across London.

As a young man, he worked as a ship's joiner on a voyage to India, making enough money to start his own business on his return. By 1815, the 25-year-old Cubitt had recognized that contracting each building trade as needed was not the most efficient way to work. So at his Gray's Inn Road workshops he employed a full set of laborers and craftsmen on a permanent wage, creating London's first modern building firm. The need to keep these workers busy

encouraged his hugely successful career as a speculative builder.

Cubitt's London work took off in Bloomsbury, where he laid out Gordon Square, Endsleigh Place, and Tavistock Square. When the Grosvenor family developed Belgravia, he moved into the big time. He crowned his career with Pimlico, a daring piece of speculation. In Belgravia, Pimlico, and the government project that created Battersea Park, Cubitt raised the low-lying land and firmed up the clay by using the earth that was being excavated from the great docks in the East End, in which he was heavily involved. Meanwhile, he baked his bricks on site. This rags-to-riches builder also fought for the improvement of London's drainage system and the creation of open spaces for public use. ∎

Curving Wilton Street shows off the best of Belgravia.

Harrods & the Knightsbridge shops

THE MOST DEVOTED SHOPPER CAN NO MORE "DO" Harrods than the most curious art lover can "do" the British Museum. The world's most famous shop is enormous. Its 300 departments on seven floors spread over 20 acres. Every day, 4,000 staff serve 35,000 customers and take in around £1.5 ($2.5) million.

It all started when Charles Henry Harrod, a tea merchant, opened a grocery shop in the hamlet of Knightsbridge in 1849, bringing in about £20 (equivalent to around $30 today) a week. Two years later, the Great Exhibition brought plenty of trade and, as Knightsbridge began to expand and move up the social scale, business boomed. Charles's son, another Charles, took over in 1861, rebuilt, and soon quintupled his takings. After a devastating fire in 1883, he simply informed his customers that their deliveries would be delayed "a day or two." Harrods' service was established. When Richard Burbidge took over the shop in 1894, he created the slogan "Harrods serves the world." In addition, he installed London's first escalator in 1898.

Burbidge also rebuilt. The pink, domed Edwardian building we know today was designed by Stephens and Munt, and built between 1901 and 1905. Louis de Blanc added the back extension in the 1920s. The Food Halls were decorated with W. J. Neatby's mosaic friezes and tiles. Burbidge's store has always been a royal favorite: George V made him a baron for his service.

Many visitors to London feel their trip is incomplete without a Harrods' session, and most are not content merely to window-shop at the 80 displays or gaze at the 11,000 light bulbs illuminating the building; 40 percent of all sales go

abroad, packed in the now famous moss-green bags with gold lettering. Londoners may try to say they can do without Harrods, but many go there for something—perhaps the patient children's hairdresser, or the health juice bar, or the massive greeting card department, and almost always their route will go via the Food Halls to pick up some perfectly ripened cheeses, fine patisserie, or delicious terrine.

To go inside Harrods is truly to enter the ultimate self-contained retail city. It has everything a dedicated shopper needs to survive the day, or several days. Most entrances have an information desk, which supplies events information and the essential free map of the store. Bars and restaurants are scattered throughout the store. Departments range from beauty parlor, pet shop, and bridal gowns to London's best toy department, Harrods own-brand shop, a sweet-smelling Perfume Hall, a ticket agency that can get tickets for almost anything officially sold out, a choice of more than 150 whiskeys, and the irresistible Food Halls.

Naturally, other retailers hoping to benefit from Harrods' shoppers set up nearby. Using profits from the Great Exhibition's visitors, Benjamin Harvey's daughter brought an experienced silk buyer, Colonel Nichols, to the family drapery business. The long-term result, **Harvey Nichols,** is a paradise for women: floors of designer

clothes and accessories topped by the Fifth Floor, a stylish food hall, bar, and restaurants designed by Wickham & Associates. Opposite Harrods, the Gardiner brothers arrived from Glasgow in 1830 to open the now landmark **Scotch House,** which still stocks tweeds and tartans.

The Harvey Nichols store stands at the corner of Sloane Street, site of a solid string of international designer clothing stores that rivals New and Old Bond Streets. Other recent designer shop arrivals fill Brompton Road. A honeypot of home furnishing and fashion shops surround the **Conran Shop** in the decorated Michelin building at Brompton Cross, where Brompton Road meets Walton Street and Fulham Road.

None of the competition has a building to compare with Harrods, but several flatter their discerning fashion victims with inspired modern structures. Eva Jiricna's signature staircase, cable balustrades, and polished white plaster walls are in the remodeled **Joseph** chain of shops, including 16 and 26 Sloane Street. Architect Stanton Williams remodeled the **Issey Miyake** store at 270 Brompton Road. ■

The magic of Harrods on a winter night, its silhouette outlined in lights

Harrods

- 🅼 Map p. 166
- ✉ 87–135 Brompton Road, SW1
- ☎ 7730 1234
  www.harrods.com
- 🕓 Closed Sun.
- Ⓣ Tube: Knightsbridge

Tate Britain

Tate Britain

🅰 Map p. 167

✉ Millbank, SW1;
secondary entrance
on Atterbury Street.
The Clore Gallery
has own entrance.

☎ 7887 8000.
Information:
7887 8008
www.tate.org.uk

💲 Charge for
temporary
exhibitions

🚇 Tube: Pimlico

A CENTURY AFTER IT OPENED IN 1897, THE TATE SPLIT IN two. Its superb national collection of British art from 1500 to the present day—the foremost collection of its kind—fills the renovated and expanded buildings here on the north bank of the Thames. Its modern international collection is now housed in the separate Tate Modern at Bankside in Southwark on the south bank (see p. 216). Shuttle buses and water taxis ply between the two. The Tate has two outposts: one in Liverpool and the other in St. Ives, Cornwall.

THE SITE & THE BUILDING

The story of the Tate begins with controversy. Henry Tate, the 18th-century sugar millionaire, led a public movement demanding a showcase for British art. Tate himself offered the nation his collection of Victorian paintings, and some money to pay for housing it. The government dithered before grudgingly accepting Tate's offer. There was then a wide debate on its location: South Kensington, Blackfriars, or Millbank, whose land became available first. Tate's money paid for Sidney Smith's building. The new gallery replaced the octagonal Millbank Prison, an

enlightened building proposed by Jeremy Bentham, designed by Robert Smirke, and built between 1812 and 1821.

Smith's neoclassic facade, entrance hall, and rotunda were completed for the opening. Many additions followed. The most significant were nine galleries added in 1899 and the central cupola and sculpture galleries given by the art dealer Joseph Duveen and his son in 1937. One small but delightful addition in 1983 was the Whistler Restaurant, where Rex Whistler's landscape mural called "Expedition in Pursuit of Rare Meats" (1926–27) keeps art and food in harmony.

A school group in one of the Tate's galleries

Stirling and Wilford's Clore Gallery opened in 1987 to house the Turner Bequest. The artist left some 300 paintings, 20,000 drawings, and nearly 300 sketchbooks to the nation. Through the apple-green door of the Clore Gallery, the eight top-lit galleries admit natural light without damaging Turner's fragile watercolors.

The Centenary Development increased gallery space by a third, enlarged exhibition space, and renewed Henry Tate's vision of a showcase for British art. The foundation collection had grown quickly since 1916, when the Tate was given the additional responsibility of forming the national collection of international modern art (which is now at Bankside). Galleries are equipped with much improved facilities and online access to images in the collection. There is more space for items in the permanent collection to be hung, and regular rehangs enable visitors to see a changing selection of works.

THE COLLECTION

There are nearly 3,500 paintings, plus prints—including those belonging to the Turner Bequest—and sculptures. New works are added every year.

The naive formality of Tudor and Stuart portraiture is exemplified in "The Cholmondeley Sisters" (1600–1610), two sisters born, married, and brought to death on the same days, and in Hans Eworth's "Portrait of a Lady" (1565–68). Another 17th-century work is Edward Collier's extraordinary "Trompe l'Oeil of Newspapers…" (circa 1695–1700).

The 18th century saw British painters responding to the Enlightenment. William Hogarth's paintings include the series of his servants (circa 1750–55). Here is Stubbs's "Horse Devoured by a Lion" (circa 1760s) and his "Reapers and Haymakers" (1785), Reynolds's "Three Ladies Adorning a Term of Hymen" (1774), and several Gainsboroughs, including the delightful "Rev. John Chafy Playing

The Millbank site of the Tate Britain houses the national collection of British art.

John Singer Sargent's "Carnation, Lily, Lily, Rose," painted in 1885–86

the Violoncello in a Landscape" (1750–52) and the later, ravishing "Giovanna Baccelli" (circa 1782).

Nineteenth-century British painting developed in several directions, and the Tate has examples of each. The great visionary poet and painter William Blake is represented by his illustrations for Milton's *Paradise Lost*, and many others. Several paintings by John Constable include the well-loved "Flatford Mill" (1816–17) and "The Opening of Waterloo Bridge" (1832). Turner's great collection of light-drenched oils and watercolors fills the Clore Gallery. Pre-Raphaelite paintings include many of the best-known: Arthur Hughes's "April Love" (1855–56), Sir John Millais's "Ophelia" (1851–52), William Frith's "Derby Day" (1856–1868), and William Holman Hunt's "The Awakening Conscience" (1853).

This diversity and originality continued into the 20th century. Stanley Spencer's mystical paintings include "Swan Upper at Cookham" (1914–19). Works by Francis Bacon are equally powerful.

More recently, the Tate's remit to buy contemporary British art has, inevitably, generated controversy given the nature of some such work (bricks, sliced-up animals, and so on). Much of the art now accepted as representative of its period was openly questioned when the gallery acquired it. Looking at works by Anthony Caro, Richard Hamilton, and David Hockney, now classics, it is hard to understand the fuss. The same is true of Edouardo Paolozzi, Frank Auerbach, Lucian Freud, and Richard Long, as well as Bridget Riley's black-and-white geometry and Howard Hodgkin's pure color. Future visitors must judge purchases of the still-controversial Damien Hirst.

In addition to modern art, the Tate's collection of works on paper ranges from 18th-century watercolors to postwar prints. There are also good examples of Britain's preeminent achievement in sculpture in the 20th century, notably by Henry Moore and Barbara Hepworth.

The curators have a clear idea of how their new space will be used. The new gallery will have four self-contained sections. Certain British artists, such as Hogarth, Constable, the Pre-Raphaelites, and Bacon, will always have works on display; others will rotate. There will be more displays of works on paper; sculpture will be placed in the Duveen Galleries, as well as in the main display areas. New basement galleries will house temporary exhibitions, also drawn from the collection. Among them, there will almost always be paintings of London—perhaps the American Kitaj's "Cecil Court, London WC2," or Samuel Scott's "An Arch of Westminster Bridge." ■

West of London lie elegant Adam houses and their parks, Kew's botanical gardens, and Hampton Court Palace, all as seductive to today's city-dweller as they were to the sovereigns and aristocrats who built them centuries ago.

West London

Royal insignia on the main gates to Kew's gardens

West London

FROM TUDOR TIMES UNTIL THE 20TH CENTURY, THE THAMES WAS THE principal highway for escaping the city. Roads were potholed, slow, and fraught with dangers. Kings, queens, aristocrats, and successful merchants wound their way up the river accompanied by musicians, gliding past the fishing villages, market gardens, and boatbuilders to reach their country estates. More modest Londoners boarded pleasure boats for day trips upstream to the taverns strung along the waterside at Chiswick, Kew, and Richmond. Most of the splendid buildings and gardens were built alongside the Thames, or within easy reach of it. Even today, by far the most pleasant way to reach them is by boat (see p. 53).

Though now surrounded by urban sprawl, these one-time rural estates have preserved pockets of green space for Londoners to escape to.

As the Thames begins to turn southward (see map p. 46), large patches of parkland, some wild, some tamed, lie on either bank. Inside the curve, there are the wide open spaces of Barnes Common and the adjoining Putney Lower Common comprising oak trees, blackberry bushes, elder trees, and a riverside strip that runs along to Putney Bridge. Together, Wimbledon Common and Putney Heath make up London's largest common, 1,060 protected acres of rough grassland, with heather and gorse bushes, oak and birch woodland, wildflowers, and many bird species. Farther upstream, the 2,358 acres of Richmond Park make it the largest of London's royal parks and one of southern England's important nature reserves. Its mixture of grass, woods, lakes, marsh, and managed

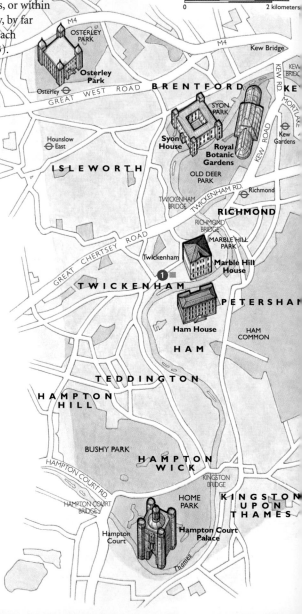

forest includes more than 200,000 trees, many of them descendants of the ancient oak, elm, and lime forest once surrounding London. Highlights here include the herds of dappled fallow and red deer, Isabella Plantation's azaleas and rhododendrons, and magical views through the trees over the Thames.

Down beside the river lie the intricately planted Royal Botanic Gardens at Kew, with their remarkable glasshouses, and the evoca-

tive 17th-century Ham House at Twickenham. The diarist John Evelyn compared its garden with the finest Italian gardens. Remarkably, with the help of the original plans and surviving plants, part of that garden has been reconstructed. Enjoy the square lawns, a wilderness with hornbeam hedges and field maple trees, and a cherry garden planted with yew hedges and herbs.

Outside the Thames's curve, the grounds surrounding Chiswick House, Osterley Park, Syon House, and Marble Hill House were all tamed in the 18th century. This was when aristocrats, inspired by the Enlightenment, built their pleasure villas. Richmond's royal connections made this a favorite spot, as did the fashionable prospects from Richmond Hill. Indeed, ideally a villa needed its own view, and both Syon and Marble Hill Houses overlook the Thames.

Another aim of the designer was to control and improve nature. Royal gardener Charles Bridgeman and poet Alexander Pope designed Marble Hill's garden, and both they and William Kent worked with Lord Burlington at Chiswick. For Syon House, the Northumberland family brought in Capability Brown, who created lakes and a formal rose garden, and planted specimen trees such as swamp cypresses and sessile oaks. At Osterley, banker Francis Child improved his flat, viewless estate with garden follies and generous planting of trees—including the impressive dark, spreading cedars between the house and the lake. The lake now attracts great crested grebes, corn buntings, kestrels, kingfishers, and other birds.

As the map shows, the river twists back northwest again at Kingston. The whole bowl contained within is filled with Hampton Court Palace, whose gardens include the restored Dutch garden, the deer park, and the deliciously wild Bushy Park. This, then, is the setting for some of London's most special treats—royal and aristocratic country houses. ∎

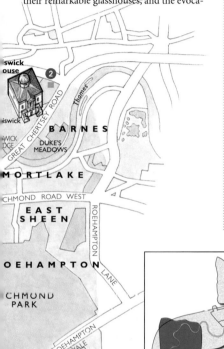

London

Thames

Area of map detail

WEST LONDON

❶ Orleans House Gallery
❷ Hogarth's House

Royal Botanic Gardens, Kew

Opposite: Spiral stairs in the Victorian Palm House
Below: The giant tropical water lilies at Kew

THIS IS LONDON'S LIVING MUSEUM OF PLANTS, LANDSCAPES, buildings, and statuary. The 300-acre garden of perfect specimen trees and plants is part of an institute of botanical research. Visitors gasp at some of the 50,000 species of plants and explore glasshouses full of lilies and orchids. Meanwhile, behind the scenes, for more than a century this has been a major center for the identification and distribution of plants from around the world.

Royal Botanic Gardens

- Map p. 178
- Kew, Richmond, Surrey
- 8332 5655. Information: 8940 1171 www.kew.org
- Check occasional area closures. Queen Charlotte's Cottage: closed Mon.–Fri. & Oct.–March
- $$
- Train or tube to Kew Gardens, then walk; Riverboat (see p. 53)

However, you need no botanical knowledge to revel in the sheer beauty of the gardens. They began as two very different estates. The part on the west, bordering the river, belonged to George II and Queen Caroline's country house, White Lodge on the Richmond Estate. Capability Brown created the original lake and the dell, now planted with rhododendrons. The eastern part was the nine-acre Kew estate, where Prince Frederick's widow, Princess Augusta, lived in Kew Palace. Kew was built in 1631 by a London merchant of Dutch descent (hence the Dutch gables). In 1759 the princess took up

gardening. Her head gardener was William Aiton, her botanist Lord Bute, and her builder Sir William Chambers. In 1761 Chambers designed the Orangery, now the Tea House, and the Pagoda, Kew's ten-story landmark. Inspired by Chambers's visit to China, the pagoda once had dragons fixed to the corners of its balustrades.

George III, who came to the throne in 1760, inherited both estates from his mother, Princess Augusta, and his grandfather, George II. George III stayed in tiny Kew Palace and soon employed Sir Joseph Banks to enlarge and replant both gardens, now

joined. Banks had collected specimens on his travels with Captain Cook, and he sent gardeners off to find additional plants.

More acres were added, and in 1841 the gardens were given to the state, with Sir William Hooker as director. It was Hooker who founded the Department of Economic Botany, the museums, the Herbarium, and the Library. And in 1844 the first of Kew's custom-designed glasshouses was built (see box this page). Later, W.A. Nesfield, who also worked at Regent's Park, laid out the four great vistas—Pagoda Vista, Broad Walk, Holly Walk, and Cedar Vista. He also designed the lake and pond. His son, W. E. Nesfield, designed the delightful Temperate House Lodge in 1866–67, one of London's first Queen Anne Revival buildings. Note the fine detailing of the tall, central chimneys.

Whatever the season, Kew has something glorious for you to see. The Orangery is a good place to start. Then, the magic of a perfect garden is yours to explore. In spring, there are the daffodils, crocuses, tulips, and bluebells, especially surrounding Queen Charlotte's Cottage. Early summer shrubs and trees include azaleas, magnolias, rhododendrons, and

flowering cherries—there is a fine view across to Syon House from the end of the azalea walk. After the autumn color, there are winter-flowering prunus, the Heath Garden by the pagoda, and the glasshouses. At all times, Nesfield's great vistas are impressive, as are the groves of tree collections including willow, beech, and birch. Each tree is identified by its country of origin. ■

Opposite: Crocuses herald the arrival of spring.

The pagoda at Kew introduced Chinese taste to 18th-century London.

Kew's glasshouses

Kew's seven glasshouses possibly look for inspiration to Syon's huge Great Conservatory (see p. 185), built in the 1820s by Charles Fowler. The gardens' first glasshouse was the Aroid House, designed by Nash in 1836 as a garden pavilion for Buckingham Palace. The Palm House, though, was specially designed in 1844–48 by Decimus Burton and Richard Turner. Its slender cast-ironwork makes it the finest glass-and-iron structure in England. The Palm House predates Paxton's Crystal Palace by three years. The Water Lily House (1852) was followed by Burton's Temperate House, built between 1860 and 1898 as the world's largest glasshouse. More recently, the Princess of Wales Conservatory, completed in 1987, contains ten climatic zones and replaces 26 old glasshouses. ■

Eighteenth-century country retreats

Marble Hill House

- Map p. 178
- Richmond Road, Twickenham
- 8892 5115
- www.english-heritage.org.uk
- Closed Nov.–March
- $$
- Tube: Richmond, then walk over the bridge.

Marble Hill House, built for Henrietta Howard, one of George II's mistresses

WITH A NEW APPRECIATION FOR THE PICTURESQUE sweeping the country, and in particular for fine prospects, the pretty stretch of the riverside that included Chiswick, Richmond, and Twickenham villages became the favorite choice for aristocratic country houses. It also had royal associations and was accessible by the river, the preferred method of travel.

TWICKENHAM

Several 18th-century country idylls survive, with settings that evoke the elegance of their period. **Marble Hill House** is an early one, built between 1723 and 1729 for George II's mistress, Henrietta Howard,

Chiswick House

- Map p. 179
- Burlington Lane, Chiswick, W4
- 8995 0508
- www.english-heritage.org.uk
- House closed Oct.–March
- House: $. Gardens: free.
- Train to Chiswick, then walk along Burlington Lane.

Countess of Suffolk. This restored, white Palladian villa overlooks the Thames between Twickenham and Richmond. Both house and park were inspired by the classical idea of an earthly Elysium, as revived in the 16th-century villas of the Italian Veneto. Nature was tamed to produce good views down to the river and, just as important, up from the river for arriving guests. On the north of the park, Montpelier Row, dating from about 1720, is one of Twickenham's gracious early terraces. Follow the riverside path through the woods to James Gibbs's octagonal 1720 **Orleans House** *(Riverside, tel 8892 0221, www.rich mond.gov.uk/orleanshouse, closed*

Mon.); just enough survives to hint at its former grandeur. Bell, Water, and Church Lanes have more old houses, and the ferry to **Ham House** runs from here.

CHISWICK

Downriver from Twickenham, Richard Boyle, 3rd Earl of Burlington and a connoisseur of great refinement, built his perfect Palladian temple to the arts, **Chiswick House,** in 1725–29. Burlington's town house, the inner part of what is today the Royal Academy, had already broken with Wren's English baroque for Palladio's light, Italian style. Here, at Chiswick, the earl went further. Inspired by Palladio's Villa Capra near Vicenza, he built an exquisite Palladian villa and garden in which to display his art and entertain his friends, rather than a house to live in. William Kent added ideas on decoration and greatly influenced the design of the garden, one of London's most interesting. Like the house, the garden breaks away from the geometric designs of English baroque. Its design moves toward the freer, although equally contrived, curves of Capability Brown, which evolved into later English landscape garden concepts. Thus, while the layout is still essentially geometrical, with radiating paths, it is given informality through the use of statuary, garden buildings, and unevenly planted trees.

SYON & OSTERLEY

The mansions of Syon and Osterley are grand indeed. Sumptuous and magnificent **Syon House** is a 16th-century stone building, totally remodeled in 1761 by Robert Adam for Sir Hugh Smithson, 1st Duke of Northumberland. Adam controlled the whole project, from the building and fine plasterwork to the gilding, carpets, ceiling designs, furniture, and even the doorknobs. Most of it survives in perfection: the Matthew Boulton fireplaces, the Wedgwood pottery, the Spitalfields silks. Later, in 1827, Charles Fowler's magnificent Great Conservatory was added, linking the house to its gardens landscaped by Capability Brown in 1767–1773. These gardens were first opened to the public in 1837. Do not miss the Great Conservatory, the **London Butterfly House** *(Tel 8560 0378, www.butterflies.org.uk)*, and the 6-acre Rose Garden, which blooms from June to September.

Adam created another masterpiece nearby, **Osterley Park** *(Tel 8232 5050, www.nationaltrust .org.uk)*. Again, he took a 16th-century house—this one of red brick—and transformed it into a Palladian mansion suitable for City bankers Francis and Robert Child. Today, Adam's great portico leads to a string of State rooms furnished with Gobelin tapestries. ■

Syon House

- Map p. 178
- Brentford, Middlesex
- 8560 0881 or 8560 0883
- www.syonpark.co.uk
- Closed Mon., Tues., & Sat.; and Nov.–March
- $$. Gardens only: $.
- Train or tube to Kew Bridge station, then bus 237 or 267

Syon House's Anteroom

Furniture from the V&A Museum enhances Ham House's grand 17th-century rooms.

Ham House

THIS IS ONE OF LONDON'S EARLIEST AND LOVELIEST grand houses. Scrupulously run by the National Trust since 1949, it is furnished with pieces lent by the V&A. Built in 1610 for Sir Thomas Vavasour, Knight Marshal to James I, it was dramatically remodeled in 1673–75 by William Samwell for Elizabeth, Countess of Dysart, and her husband, John Maitland, Duke of Lauderdale, who was the virtual ruler of Scotland for some time after the Restoration. Together, they created a flamboyantly palatial baroque home. Using house records and plans, the Trust has fully restored both house and gardens, so that it gives a more accurate and extensive idea of grand domestic 17th-century life than any other house in England.

Ham House

- 🅰 Map p. 178
- ✉ Richmond, Surrey
- ☎ 8940 1950
  www.nationaltrust
  .org.uk
- 🕐 House open
  April–Oct.
  Sat.–Wed. p.m.
  Gardens open all
  year
- 💲 $$
- 🚇 Train or tube to
  Richmond, then bus
  65 or 71

Start by looking at the facade of the house: three simple stories of brick with stone dressings. The busts in the oval niches, however, give a taste of what is to come.

Inside, the double-story, galleried Great Hall has a pre-refurbishment ceiling by Joseph Kinsman dating from 1637–38. Here, too, is Reynolds's portrait of Elizabeth, Countess of Dysart, painted in 1775. Several ground floor rooms have ceilings painted by Neapolitan artist Antonio Verrio, the Dining Room has leather wall hangings, and the Duchess's Private Closet has its original japanned furniture. Up the great staircase, two early Constables hang in Lady Maynard's Dressing Room. The Cabinet of Miniatures has works by Hilliard and Cooper, and the North Drawing Room is hung with English tapestries depicting the months of the year, probably woven in Soho around 1700. The Long Gallery, decorated in 1639, has a remarkable set of 17th-century portraits in contemporary gilded frames. The Queen's Closet, the richest room of all, has a Verrio ceiling, marbled flat surfaces, early examples of scagliola decoration around the fireplace, and full baroque carving on the wainscoting. Go back through these State Rooms and visit the garden. It should not be missed (see p. 179). ■

Hampton Court Palace

OF ALL LONDON'S ROYAL PALACES, HAMPTON COURT HAS the most to offer the visitor, including two sets of regal rooms (intimate Tudor and grand Wren), numerous gardens (Tudor, Dutch, the Maze, and more), and two great parks (Home and Bushy). In all, more than 500 years of tip-top royal patronage is now conserved by a huge team of specialists.

Choices will have to be made, and the first is whether to whisk out there by train to enjoy the rooms relatively empty in the morning, possibly returning to London by riverboat; or to glide up by riverboat, find busier rooms, and spend a summer's afternoon and early evening in the gardens and parks.

HISTORY

The palace began as a 12th-century moated estate office. By 1514, it was a courtyard house. That year, Thomas, Cardinal Wolsey, Henry VIII's chief minister, leased it as his country house. Wolsey built grandly and copiously. He added most of the Tudor buildings that stand today: 44 lodgings for his guests in Base Court; three stories of rooms expressly to honor Henry VIII's visit in 1525; a long gallery; and a magnificent chapel.

When Wolsey fell from favor in 1528, Henry VIII took over this ready-made country palace. He immediately extended the kitchens, and in 1532–35 added the Great Hall. His daughter, Elizabeth, added more kitchens and laid out formal gardens. Of the Tudor sovereigns' 60 residences, Hampton Court was one of the few capable of housing

Hampton Court Palace

- Map p. 178
- East Molesey, Surrey
- 8781 9500
- www.hrp.org.uk
- Palace & gardens: $$$. Gardens only: $$. Parks: free
- Train to Hampton Court, then walk over bridge. Riverboats from Westminster pier in summer (see p. 53)
- Note: The palace offers an extensive program of tours, talks, & special events.

Wolsey built so grandly at Hampton Court that Henry VIII took the palace for himself when Wolsey fell from favor.

the entire 1,000-strong court. Yet it was not the service rooms that impressed visitors so much as the royal apartments; most are gone now, and only the Great Watching Chamber, the chapel, and the Wolsey Closet remain.

William and Mary, after their accession in 1689, made dramatic changes. They brought in Sir Christopher Wren to create a new baroque palace. Wren began by replacing Henry's royal apartments. The queen's room overlooked Charles II's garden and his Long Water. The king's overlooked his Privy Garden, newly created in the Dutch style, and the Thames. After Mary caught smallpox and died in 1694, building stopped for four years. The work was completed in 1700 and William moved in, but died two years later. The remaining Tudor buildings were safe.

Queen Anne redecorated the chapel and the Queen's Drawing Room, employing the Neapolitan artist Antonio Verrio, who had worked at Kensington Palace, Ham House, and elsewhere, and who died here in 1707. George I and II resided in Hampton Court. After Queen Caroline's death, the Court ceased to stay here. Gradually, the rooms became "grace and favor" apartments for retired servants of the Crown. The royals continued to care for Hampton Court. Queen

Victoria added the Great Hall's stained glass, "improved" the Palace's Tudor style by adding most of the tall, brick chimneys, and, in 1838, opened it to the public. The railway station opened in 1849, making the palace easily accessible. After a fire in 1986, the King's Apartments were painstakingly restored.

HAMPTON COURT ROUTES

Because the palace is so vast, its curators have devised six routes, each exploring a theme. Guides can be booked for routes and plans are available for self-guidance. Here are two approaches, one Tudor, the other William and Mary.

Trail 1: The Tudors

This visit takes in routes one, six, and then five. The Tudor visit begins with the "King's Beasts" at the palace entrance, although these are 20th-century replacements. Henry VIII's State Apartments are

Left: The sun revolves around the Earth in Hampton Court's 1540 astronomical clock.

Great Gatehouse

Right: The bed in the Queen's Bedchamber was made for Queen Caroline.

found through Wolsey's Great Gatehouse in Base Court. The Great Hall (1532–35), with its painted hammerbeam roof, is hung with Henry's 1520s Flemish tapestries. Through the Great Watching Chamber, a gallery leads to the chapel, whose Tudor ceiling is the most sumptuous of its kind.

From here, visit the Tudor kitchens, entered between the Clock and Base Courts. They occupied 50 rooms, and 200 staff fed Henry's 1,000-strong court. Ten rooms are open, including the Beer Cellar, Boiling House, and Wine Cellar— where some of the 600,000 gallons of ale drunk annually were stored.

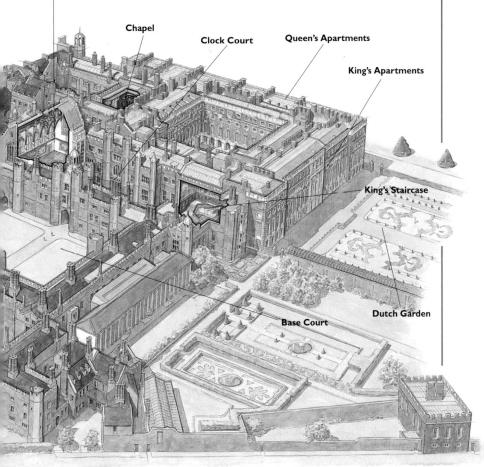

Great Hall (Kitchens below)

Chapel

Clock Court

Queen's Apartments

King's Apartments

King's Staircase

Dutch Garden

Base Court

Blind alleys and dead-ends make the Maze a proper puzzle.

Trail 2: William & Mary

To see the two grand suites of royal baroque rooms, begin in Fountain Court and go up a grand staircase painted by William Kent in 1735. The Queen's Presence Chamber leads to the grandest rooms: the Public Dining Room and then the Queen's Audience Chamber (with throne canopy). Next, the Drawing Room, the Bedchamber (whose bed was made for Queen Caroline in 1715), the Gallery, and the Closet.

Go down the back staircase and return to Clock Court to visit the King's Apartments. Up the monumental King's Staircase, decorated with Verrio's allegory of William III's good government, find the Guard Chamber, which stored 3,000 weapons. The Presence Chamber has its original throne to which courtiers would bow, even if empty; Sir Godfrey Kneller's equestrian portrait of the king; and tapestries made for Henry VIII's Whitehall Palace. Ahead you'll come to the grand King's Eating Room, Privy Chamber, Withdrawing Room, Great Bedchamber, and Closet. The King's more private apartments continue downstairs. ■

Go across Clock Court and upstairs to find the Wolsey Rooms and the Renaissance Picture Gallery. Here, in rooms built by Wolsey in 1515–1526, are displayed some of the finest Renaissance pieces from the Queen's collection. They include the great panorama of the "Field of the Cloth of Gold," recording Henry VIII's meeting with Francis I of France in 1520.

Hampton Court Gardens

Tudor, baroque, and Victorian gardens are minutely tended by a bevy of 41 gardeners. Of Henry VIII's grand layout, little survives. The secluded Knot and Pond Gardens give a flavor—Henry's Pond Garden (1536) had ornamental fishponds stocked with edible fish for the kitchens. The Great Vine is grown from a cutting taken in 1768 from the original vine. The nearby Mantegna Gallery is where the painter's stage designs "Triumphs of Caesar" (circa 1486–1494) are on display. William's 3-acre Privy Garden is now restored to its 1702 state, complete with authentic flowers, shrubs, and 33,000 box plants. Wren designed the riverside Banqueting House, and Jean Tijou the ironwork gates. Other parts to enjoy include the Maze, first planted in 1690, and the Wilderness, planted with a million bulbs. Beyond Charles's Long Water, Home Park's 300 fallow deer are descended from Henry VIII's herd. This is where the annual Royal Horticultural Society Hampton Court Palace Flower Show, the largest of its kind in Europe, is held in July. ■

East of the City, the Tower of London, Georgian Spitalfields, and the jolly East End markets lead to the new merchant powerhouse, the reborn Docklands; then on to the Millennium Dome and maritime Greenwich.

East London

Contemporary sculpture in London's revived Docklands setting

East London

HERE IS THE FLIPSIDE TO STUCCOED BELGRAVIA AND THE ART DEALERS OF St. James's. The medieval Tower of London still slams its doors shut against the London mob each night. Downstream, the palatial splendors of Royal Greenwich Palace and Park are matched by its maritime museum and ships. In between, the East End throbs once more with a vitality that first exploded into life when the enclosed docks were built in response to the vast increase in trade that followed the 18th-century industrial revolution.

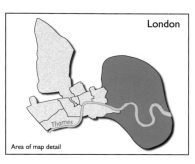

London

Area of map detail

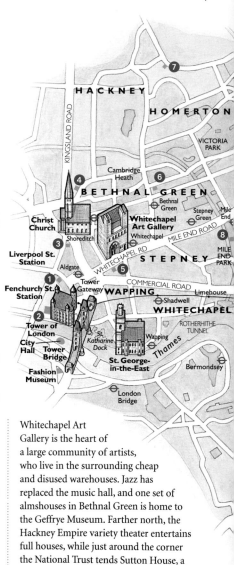

The romance of the overcrowded, poor, but spirited East End—of Cockney rhyming slang, pearly kings, and music halls—was born in the 19th century. Older areas, such as Spitalfields and Whitechapel, and the East End villages of Hackney and Limehouse, were swallowed into the giant Victorian sprawl of housing for British workers from rural areas and migrants from other countries. Men and women worked on the docks and in their related trades—shipbuilding, engineering, furniture-making, and, at the Whitechapel Bell Foundry, making bells for London's many Victorian churches. They brewed beer, ran the street markets, and entertained great crowds in the music halls. Here Charlie Chaplin made his stage debut at the Royal Cambridge music hall. Meanwhile, the government created a "green lung," Victoria Park, and well-wishers and missionaries started such homes as the Ragged School.

Today, having slumped after the docks were closed, the heart of the East End beats again. The map is once again dotted with interesting places to visit.

Spitalfields, focused on Christ Church, mixes new gentility with the rag trade, restaurants, and the mosques of the Bangladeshis.

Whitechapel Art Gallery is the heart of a large community of artists, who live in the surrounding cheap and disused warehouses. Jazz has replaced the music hall, and one set of almshouses in Bethnal Green is home to the Geffrye Museum. Farther north, the Hackney Empire variety theater entertains full houses, while just around the corner the National Trust tends Sutton House, a rare surviving 16th-century merchant's home. Most surprising of all, a few streets southwest of Victoria Park, the V&A has its easternmost outpost: the Bethnal Green Museum of Childhood.

Down by the Thames, the revival of the 13-mile strip of once-disused docks began in 1981 with massive government help. It is now established and self-reliant; as evident in the success of St. Katharine Dock, London City Airport, Cascades apartments, and the soaring beauty of Canary Wharf towers.

The interior of Dennis Savers's House reveals the comfortable life of a middle-class 18th-century merchant.

Docklands' building continues, and new projects should further enliven several parts of this massive chunk of London. On the Isle of Dogs, the offices and apartments that dominated the first two decades of building have the Museum in Docklands and a host of restaurants at West India Docks. Farther east, Royal Victoria Docks has Excel, the London International Exhibition Centre. Still farther east, Royal Albert Dock has the Royal Albert Dock Regatta Centre. At Greenwich, the *Cutty Sark* is restored, and refurbished Ranger's House has reopened, while the Millennium Dome, where the new millennium officially began, is the world's largest dome. ■

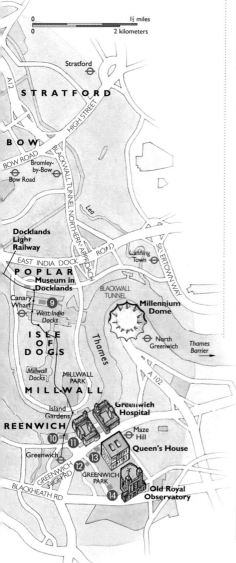

EAST LONDON

❶ Spanish & Portuguese Synagogue
❷ All Hallows by the Tower ❸ Dennis
Savers's House ❹ Geffrye Museum
❺ Whitechapel Bell Foundry ❻ Bethnal
Green Museum of Childhood ❼ Sutton
House ❽ Ragged School Museum
❾ Canary Wharf Tower ❿ *Gypsy Moth IV*
⓫ *Cutty Sark* ⓬ Fan Museum
⓭ National Maritime Museum
⓮ Ranger's House

Tower of London

Tower of London

- 🅰 Map p. 192
- ☎ 0870 756 6060
  www.hrp.org.uk
- 💲 $$$
- 🚇 Tube: Tower Hill; or, to get an idea of its setting, Monument, then walk to it through the City

All Hallows by the Tower

- 🅰 Map. p. 192
- ✉ Byward Street, EC3
- ☎ 7481 2928
  www.allhallowsbythe tower.org.uk
- 💲 Donation
- 🚇 Tube: Tower Hill

BRITAIN'S MOST PERFECT SURVIVING MEDIEVAL FORT IS tucked behind the sleek City towers, forgotten by most Londoners but ever popular with visitors. In fact, the Tower is not just a fort; it contains a palace, prisons, an execution site, chapels, and museums. Since William the Conqueror began building it soon after his 1066 conquest, it has served the sovereign. Today, covering 18 acres, it is London's smallest village, with a population of 18 families.

The story of the Tower is as much about people as about buildings. Following its story is a good way of familiarizing yourself with the kings of England.

The Tower began as a temporary fort, constructed by William to keep watch on untrustworthy City merchants. He built it between their Saxon walls and the high surviving Roman ones. Later, he built what is now the central White Tower, completed by William II and Henry I. Constructed of stone from Caen in France, this keep had walls 90 feet high and 15 feet thick, with room inside for three wells, a banqueting hall, a council chamber, and even the tiny St. John's Chapel, plus a prison and dungeon. Henry I also built the Tower's second church, St. Peter ad Vincula. The last Norman king, Stephen, was the first to live in the Tower.

The Plantagenet kings used the Tower well. Henry II added kitchens, a bakery, and a jail. William of Longchamp, loyal servant of

H.M.S. *Belfast*

☎ 7940 6300

www.iwm.org.uk

🚇 Tube/rail: London
Bridge

⛴ Ferry from Tower
Pier

💲 $$

From street level, the walls of the Tower mount up: Outer walls, inner wall, and then the turrets of the White Tower.

Richard II, added more wall, the Bell Tower, Wardrobe Towers, and the ditch while the King was at the Crusades—to no avail, however. Prince John besieged it, became king, and further strengthened the walls. Henry III began the inner wall, the moat, his own watergate, and the royal palace. He white-washed the White Tower and began a zoo—the King of Norway gave him a polar bear that went fishing in the Thames on a leash. Edward I completed the western inner wall and the Outer Wall including Byward Tower and Traitors' Gate. He moved the mint and Crown Jewels here from Westminster.

Since then, the Tower has changed little. Such extras as the Tower's 14th-century cupolas, Henry VIII's half-timbered houses and two circular bastions on Tower Green, and the barracks of 1840 are minor additions.

The Tower witnessed great joys and great horrors. Henry IV initiated the Ceremony of the Bath here in 1399. Under Henry VI, the Duke of Exeter introduced the rack for torture and Edmund Campion, the English Jesuit martyr (1540–1581), was stretched on it three times. The Yorkist Edward IV picnicked and played on the Tower lawns. But when Richard III went off to be crowned in 1483, his two prince nephews were murdered in the Bloody Tower. Then came the Tudors: Henry VIII may have built houses on Tower Green, but he also had two of his wives executed there, Anne Boleyn and Catherine Howard. In fact, they were comparatively lucky; Thomas Cromwell, Archbishop Laud, and others ending with Lord Lovat in 1747, provided public spectacle when they were beheaded up on Tower Hill. Princess Elizabeth first arrived through Traitors' Gate, but later

began her coronation procession in a golden chariot from here. Then the Stuarts: James I, the last king to live in the Tower, watched his lions and bears fighting from the Lion Tower. Charles I sent six Members of Parliament to the Tower for insulting his favorite, the Duke of Buckingham. The restored Charles II held the Tower's last pageant in 1661, extravagant spring festivities that included an entire new set of Crown Jewels, as Cromwell's men had stolen the previous ones.

VISITING THE TOWER

The Tower is very popular. Early arrivals can rush to the Crown Jewels and see them in relative peace. However, the most exciting way to arrive is by riverboat (see p. 53), which means arriving too late for this. There is much to see; reentry tickets allow for a lunch break on Tower Wharf or at nearby St. Katharine Dock. If the lines are horrendous, consider visiting the nearby fascinating church of All Hallows by the Tower, Tower Bridge (see p. 198), and St. Katharine Dock, or taking the ferry from Tower Pier to H.M.S. *Belfast* (see p. 209); then return to the Tower later.

THE TRAIL

Arrival by river means going under London Bridge, where prisoners such as Princess Elizabeth would have gazed up at the severed heads of previous inmates, exhibited on spikes. Arrival on foot from the City allows a visit to All Hallows and a first view of the Tower, with the Victorian Tower Bridge beyond.

You enter the Tower of London through the Byward Tower, at the southwest corner, not far from Tower Pier. You can walk around on your own, or join a tour led by one of the Yeoman Warders, or Beefeaters, who have guarded the Tower since 1485.

It is best to visit the Crown Jewels, housed in the Waterloo Barracks, first. To get there, go straight ahead and find Traitors' Gate on the right; turn left, go up the stairs past Tower Green and straight on. The Crown Jewels exhibition begins with a succession of picture collages; the actual jewels are minimally identified, but if you want to see them again you can often go around the exhibit twice. There are plenty of sparkling, egg-size diamonds to note: the First Star of Africa (530 carats), in Charles II's scepter; the 2,800 diamonds in the Imperial State Crown worn for the State Opening of Parliament; and the Koh-I-Noor diamond from India, in the Queen Consort crown. Also exhibited are the ampulla and spoon for anointing the sovereign, made in 1399, and the beautifully ornate baroque plate made for Charles II.

From here, return to Tower Green to see St. Peter ad Vincula Church, the execution site, and, in Bloody Tower, the rooms where Elizabeth I's favorite, explorer Sir Walter Raleigh, spent 13 years. Then proceed to the original keep, the White Tower, whose most magical room is the tiny St. John's Chapel on the second floor. Beside this, a chunk of Roman wall leads down to the home of the eight Tower ravens, who have their own Raven Master.

Alternatively, Martin Tower in the northeast marks the start of the Wall Walk through Henry III's towers and walls, down to Salt Tower. To finish, see

The Raven Master with one of his charges

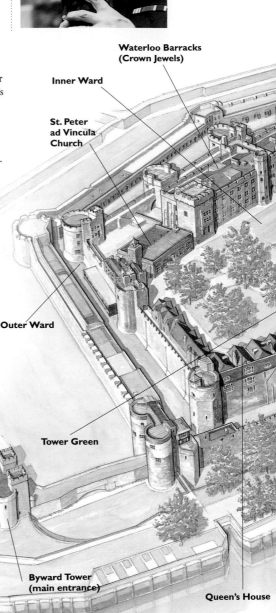

Waterloo Barracks (Crown Jewels)

Inner Ward

St. Peter ad Vincula Church

Outer Ward

Tower Green

Byward Tower (main entrance)

Queen's House

some of the Tower's best rooms, in the medieval palace. Strung along the south side, overlooking the river, they include St. Thomas's and Wakefield Towers, sensitively restored to give an idea of their structure, possible decoration, and probable use during the reign of Edward I. ■

Round-headed arches in the St. John's Chapel reveal the Tower's Norman origins.

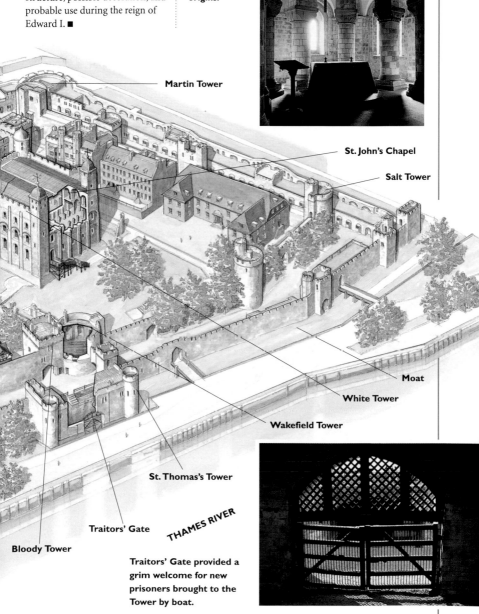

Martin Tower

St. John's Chapel

Salt Tower

Moat

White Tower

Wakefield Tower

St. Thomas's Tower

Traitors' Gate

THAMES RIVER

Bloody Tower

Traitors' Gate provided a grim welcome for new prisoners brought to the Tower by boat.

Panorama of
Tower Bridge
and the modern
Docklands
redevelopment

Tower Bridge

Tower Bridge

⬛ Map p. 192
☎ 7403 3761
www.towerbridge
.org.uk
💲 $$
Ⓣ Tube: Tower Hill
Tube/rail: London
Bridge

THIS IS THE CAPITAL'S ONLY BRIDGE DOWNRIVER OF
London Bridge and, begun in 1886, it is also one of its newest. It was
designed to relieve congestion on the other City bridges, while still
enabling large vessels to enter the Upper Pool of London's port.

A special Act of Parliament in 1885
authorized the construction of a
double drawbridge. It stipulated a
Gothic-style bridge to sympathize
with the neighboring Tower of
London and an opening span width
of 200 feet and 135 feet headroom.

The Prince of Wales opened the
bridge in 1894. It was 800 feet long
and cost the huge sum, for the time,
of £800,000 ($1.2 million). The ele-
vators now take visitors to the
Tower Bridge Experience.
Here there is an exhibition about
the bridge and the Engine Room,
whose coal-fired boilers drove the
hydraulic system until electrifica-
tion in 1976. ■

Tower Bridge mechanics

Despite its Gothic design,
Tower Bridge was extremely
modern. The bridge's two towers
have a steel frame covered in stone
to house the hydraulic machinery
and to support the 1,000-ton
weight of each bascule; they also
contain the elevators to the foot-
bridge. The two side-spans are on
the suspension principle, the decks
being hung from curved girders.

It takes just 90 seconds to raise
the bridge. In its heyday, it was
opened up to 50 times a day. Today,
with the wharves closed, the bridge
opens about 500 times a year (up
to 15 times a day in summer).
Sometimes the openings are for
ceremonial occasions, such as the
arrival of the royal yacht *Britannia*
for the 50th anniversary celebra-
tions of the end of World War II. ■

East End & Spitalfields

A DAY SPENT IN THIS UNCOMPROMISING, UNGLAMOROUS area is rewarding for its local flavor and lack of tourists. Plan your schedule carefully to be sure the places that interest you are open.

Whitechapel Art Gallery, a ten-minute walk from the Tower, was founded as a permanent showcase for the visual arts in the East End. C. H. Townsend's art nouveau building of 1897–99 is still that, and local artists can be located through the gallery. A more unusual stop is **Whitechapel Bell Foundry** (*Tel 7247 2599, www.whitechapel bellfoundry.co.uk*), where descendants of the men who made Big Ben still practice their skills. Aldgate has the sumptuous **Spanish and Portuguese Synagogue** (*Tel 7626 1274*), built in 1701 by a Quaker, Joseph Avis, for Jewish refugees.

Spitalfields, east of Liverpool Street station, has a rare concentration of fine houses. By the end of the 18th century, 12,000 silk looms built by immigrant French Huguenots thundered in the Georgian lanes. Many houses have been restored, including **Dennis Severs's House** (*Tel 7247 4013, www.dennissevershouse.co.uk*). Nicholas Hawksmoor's **Christ Church** (1720), with its tall spire, should not be missed. Beside Commercial Road, the former **Spitalfields Market,** dating from 1893, is liveliest on Sundays.

North of Spitalfields lie three small museums. The **Geffrye Museum** has furniture and woodwork arranged chronologically in 14 almshouses, built in 1715, plus contemporary locally made pieces, and a good restaurant. The V&A's dollhouses, teddy bears, a model of a circus, and much more fill the **Bethnal Green Museum of Childhood** (*Tel 8983 5200, www. museumofchildhood.org.uk*). **Sutton House** (*8986 2264, www.national trust.org.uk*) is a Tudor merchant's house, now a community scheme with café and art gallery. ∎

Whitechapel Art Gallery
- Map p. 192
- Whitechapel High Street, E1
- 7522 7888
  www.whitechapel.org
- Closed Mon.
- Tube: Aldgate East

Geffrye Museum
- Map p. 192
- Kingsland Road, E2
- 7739 8543
  www.geffrye-museum.org.uk
- Closed Mon.
- Donation
- Liverpool Street/Old Street, then bus/taxi

Christ Church
- Map p. 192
- Commercial Street, E1
- 7247 0165
- Aldgate East/ Liverpool Street

Docklands

THE SAVING GRACE OF THIS FORTHRIGHT EXAMPLE OF free-market inner-city redevelopment is its setting. For this was a renovation scheme that both flew in the face of the great conservation movement and passed up the opportunity to create something that would be a British 20th-century city of architectural significance. Use the Docklands Light Railway (DLR) to enjoy a spectacular overview of one section, from the Tower down to Island Gardens.

Docklands

Ⓜ Map p. 193

Opened in 1987, the DLR is London's Light Rail Transit system serving the Docklands area. It connects into the Tube system at Bank and Tower Hill stations. (Docklands also connects to the South Bank and Westminster on the new, fast Jubilee Tube line.) Each two-car train is run by computer through unmanned stations.

Board your DLR train at Bank Tube station. First stop is Tower Gateway. Here, **St. Katharine Dock** is now a yacht haven where expensive boats slide in and out of the lock gates. Next is Shadwell, the stop for Hawksmoor's handsome church of **St. George-in-the-East** (1714–1729). It is also the location for News

Docklands Light Railway with Canary Wharf behind

International, Europe's largest newspaper plant. Limehouse station is near another magnificent Hawksmoor church, **St. Anne's** (1714–1730), and Narrow Street's pretty houses and pub.

The line then turns southward after Westferry station, and the dock views begin. West India Quay is the station for the excellent new **Museum in Docklands** (see p. 201), Canary Wharf for the three soaring **Canary Wharf** towers, the first to be clad in stainless steel. Heron Quays hovers between two strips of dock. Look left to see Greenwich Peninsula's **Millennium Dome.** Island Gardens has the best views of Greenwich—reach it by a pedestrian tunnel under the Thames. ∎

Museum in Docklands

HOUSED IN A GEORGIAN WAREHOUSE ACROSS THE DOCK
waters from Canary Wharf's gleaming high rises, this is the ideal spot
to explore the turbulent story of the Thames and London's great port.
You can get to grips with 2,000 action-packed years, from Roman
times to the river's heyday as the entrepot for a world-
encircling empire, from wartime years to its revival as a modern landscape for living and working.

The museum shares many of its
objects with the Museum of
London. And more are found almost
daily by archaeologists working on
the city's many building sites such as
the Jubilee Tube line or No. l Poultry.
Here, though, the museum itself is
an object: a handsome, three-story
brick building that once stored
exotic spices, rum, and cotton.

Starting on the top floor, the
chronological arrangement of galleries makes London's story about as
clear as possible. But it is never dull.

After the intriguing sections on
the early Londons—Londinium,
Lundenwic, and Lundenburh, each
in a slightly different location—the
medieval highlights include two
large models of Old London Bridge
covered in houses, each of a different historical period. Later, as
Tudor explorers leave London in
search of riches, there is a splendid
interactive story of a voyage on an
East Indiaman.

As London's wealth grew, so did
its quays, and by 1794 some 3,663
layden ships arrived and departed
annually. Hence the enclosed docks
that surround the museum. Their
complexity and atmosphere are
captured in the full-scale models of
ship's chandlers, alleys, taverns, and
shops. Goods of all kinds arrived,
from tobacco and sugar to rum and
timber; some 14 million tons of tea
alone were being unloaded annually in the 1930s.

There is a gallery of boats, the
full story of the 1889 Great Dock
Strike, and the "Black Saturday" film
about the 1940s Blitz. The final
chapter, "Revitalization," looks at the
Docklands today, after which you
long to go out and explore them. ∎

Greenwich
Map p. 193

**Painted Hall
& Chapel**

✉ Old Royal Naval
College, King
William Walk, SE10

☎ 8269 4747
www.greenwich
foundation.org.uk

🚉 DLR: Cutty Sark
DLR/rail: Greenwich

**GETTING TO
GREENWICH**

There are several
ways to reach the
Greenwich sites: by
Underground on the
Jubilee Line; by
Docklands Light
Railway to Island
Gardens, then walk
through the tunnel;
by riverboat
(see p. 53); or by
railway from
London Bridge
station. ■

Greenwich

THE ELEGANT BUILDINGS AND EXCELLENT MUSEUMS IN and around the expansive Greenwich park and the delightful town of Greenwich are a peaceful refuge from the resurging Docklands and Greenwich Peninsula, its neighbors.

The view of Greenwich from the riverside is one of London's finest. It is best to arrive by river, or by Docklands Light Railway at Island Gardens. Otherwise, go along King William Walk, and then along a path beside the college railings, called Five Foot Walk. It was here that George I landed on September 18, 1714, to succeed to the throne.

The fabulous setting was created piecemeal in the 17th and 18th centuries, yet Greenwich's true heyday was during the 16th century, under the Tudors. Henry V's brother, the Duke of Gloucester, built the riverside Bella Court in 1427, and six years later enclosed 200 acres to make Greenwich Park. The Tudor king Henry VII remodeled it as the Palace of Placentia in 1500, then Henry VIII, born at Greenwich, adopted it as his favorite palace during his rule. He added copious buildings, including

a banqueting hall, armories, and a tiltyard for staging jousting tournaments. In the park, he hunted deer and went hawking. His daughters, Mary and Elizabeth I, were born here, as was his son, Edward VI. Most importantly, from here he could watch his ships arriving with exotic cargoes, and he could oversee his navy. In 1512 he built a royal dockyard at Woolwich, and the next year he built a second at Deptford.

Little remains of this period. In the distance, what we see today is the central building. Anne of Denmark, James I's queen, initiated the changes, and introduced an entirely new style of architecture from the Continent. Sweeping away some of the vernacular timber palace buildings, she employed Inigo Jones to start building the Queen's House in 1616. This Palladian villa was England's first

Renaissance building, and Jones's earliest surviving English work. Another queen, Charles I's Henrietta Maria, completed and decorated it, and Jones's son-in-law, John Webb, then enlarged it, building bridges to overcome the problem of the main London–Dover road running through the grounds. During the Commonwealth, Cromwell's men turned the Queen's House into a biscuit factory. All the while it stood amid the remaining Tudor buildings.

Then Charles II, who spent his exile in France and dreamed of creating an English Versailles here, returned and began by building a riverside wing in 1664. He also brought in Louis XIV's Versailles gardener, André Le Nôtre, to design a plan for the park, with avenues spreading out from the Queen's House up the hill. When William and Mary came to the throne, their extensive building projects also included Greenwich. They invited Sir Christopher Wren to create a hospital for retired sailors, following the success of Royal Hospital Chelsea, his hospital for soldiers (see p. 168). Between 1696 and 1702, he created the breathtaking

sight we see today. Demolishing the last of the Tudor buildings, he added a mirror wing to Charles's, with a great staircase between them. The two U-shaped buildings face each other, with the Queen's House the main focus between them.

KING WILLIAM WALK
To visit the grand public rooms of Wren's baroque hospital, once home to 2,710 sailors, find the entrance on King William Walk. The walk's gateposts are topped with symbolic celestial and terrestrial domes. The hospital, now the **University of Greenwich,** is mostly closed to visitors, but the **Painted Hall** and **Chapel** can be visited. The Painted Hall was designed as the sailors' dining room but rarely used. Wren's design, Hawksmoor's architectural decoration, and James Thornhill's paintwork make this England's grandest secular interior of the period. Thornhill's ceiling, painted between 1707 and 1726, shows William and Mary handing down Peace and Liberty to Europe, and a crushed Louis XIV holding a broken sword below them. When the chapel burned down in 1779, James Stuart

The Queen's House framed by the buildings of Charles II's palace and Wren's hospital

The Painted Hall, designed as a dining room for the veteran sailors, was rarely used.

Cutty Sark

- Map p. 193
- King William Walk, SE10
- 8858 3445
  www.cuttysark
  .org.uk
- $$
- DLR: Cutty Sark
  DLR/rail: Greenwich

designed its coolly classical replacement. Stuart's assistant, William Newton, controlled the refined decoration, some of London's, even England's, finest. See especially the doorway between the chapel and the octagonal vestibule.

From the Palace, walk east along the towpath to reach the **Trafalgar Tavern** (1873), next to the **Trinity Hospital,** founded in 1613; and then the 17th century Cutty Sark pub on Ballast Quay, with splendid views of the lazy, widening Thames.

Back past the pier toward the tunnel opening, there are two boats on the quay. The **Cutty Sark** tea-clipper, built at Clydeside in Scotland in 1869, is the only survivor from a brief period when the fastest ships then available raced between the Far East and London with their high-value cargoes. The *Cutty Sark* sailed from China to England in 99 days and then, as a wool carrier, zipped from Australia to London in just 72. Nearby, tiny **Gypsy Moth IV** *(Tel 8858 3445),* a 54-foot-long ketch, was the boat in which Sir Francis Chichester sailed around the world alone in 1966–67.

Now is a good moment to see a bit of Greenwich town, which has an enjoyable weekend market (see p. 152). Behind elegant Nelson Road and College Approach, the Victorian covered market survives near Hawksmoor's much-restored **St. Alfege Church** (1714). Walk up Croom's Hill to the **Fan Museum** (*Tel 8305 1441, www.fan-*

museum.org), where the social history and delicate craft of the fan is laid out in two Georgian town houses. The exhibit includes the 2,000-piece collection showcasing the beauty, quality, and range of designs.

NATIONAL MARITIME MUSEUM

Tracing the story of Britain and the sea, this is the world's largest nautical museum. It is also one of the most beautiful museum complexes in Britain. The collection ranges from porcelain and glass to royal barges, and fills the Queen's House, Royal Hospital School, and the Old Royal Observatory in Greenwich Park on the hill.

The museum was founded in 1934. Its recent renovation includes a stunning glass-roofed courtyard designed by Rick Mather, plus state-of-the-art themed galleries with plenty of visitor participation.

The collection looks at Britain's navy, merchants, explorers, and their related trades. It considers explorations to the Arctic, mapping the British Empire, the great migration to North America, Cook's travels, and Nelson's battle triumphs. There are especially fine collections of ship models, paintings, medals, uniforms, navigational instruments, and boats.

Here are 10 treats to look for: finds from Henry VIII's flagship, the *Mary Rose*, which sank off Portsmouth in 1547; a decorative painting of the defeat of the Spanish Armada in 1588; Van Wieringen's superb battle painting "Heemskerk's Defeat of the Spaniards at Gibralter, 25 April, 1607"; a 1669 model of the ship *St. Michael*; Kneller's 1689 portrait of Samuel Pepys, the diarist, who was a top naval administrator; the gilded state barge designed by William Kent for Frederick, Prince of Wales, in 1732; a collection of 40 ship

models including the 1719 *Royal William*; Canaletto's painting "Greenwich Hospital from the North Bank of the Thames" (1747–1750); Captain Cook's reindeer-hide sleeping bag; Paul Storr's silver-gilt table centerpiece of 1817; the steam paddle tug *Reliant* (1907); and the huge collection devoted to Admiral Lord Nelson, including silver, swords, and uniform.

Do not miss the interior of the **Queen's House.** The hall is a perfect 40-foot cube and has Nicholas Stone's black-and-white floor laid in 1638, a Tulip Staircase, and a boldly cantilevered balcony. On the ceiling, Gentileschi's paintings, now in Marlborough House, were re-created by computer when the room was restored. Upstairs, the

National Maritime Museum

🅐 Map p. 193

✉ Romney Road, SE10

☎ 8858 4422.
Information:
8312 6565
www.nmm.co.uk

💲 $$. Tickets include the Queen's House & Old Royal Observatory

🚇 DLR: Cutty Sark
DLR/rail: Greenwich

The *Cutty Sark,* one of the big Victorian sailing ships called clippers

The Greenwich meridian line at the Old Royal Observatory

Old Royal Observatory
- 🗺 Map p. 193
- ✉ Greenwich Park, SE10
- ☎ 8312 6565
- www.rog.nmm.co.uk
- 🚇 DLR: Cutty Sark
  DLR/rail: Greenwich

Ranger's House
- 🗺 Map p. 193
- ✉ Chesterfield Walk, SE10
- ☎ 8853 0035
- www.english-heritage.org.uk
- 🕐 Closed Mon.–Tues. Nov.–March
- 💲 $$
- 🚇 DLR/rail: Greenwich
  Rail: Blackheath

State Apartments have the King's on the east side, furnished as they would have been when he was not in residence. On the west side, the Queen's Apartments are fully furnished as they would have been when she was in residence.

Up in the park, the **Old Royal Observatory** consists of several buildings with a spectacular view over London. **Flamsteed House** was built by Wren in 1675 for John Flamsteed, the first Astronomer Royal, and used by his successors until 1948. Flamsteed found his project for Charles II very dull as it involved more than 30,000 observations, studying the stars and producing accurate navigational maps. Timekeepers tick-tock in the rooms, and since 1833 the Time Ball on the eastern turret drops at 1 p.m., so passing sailors can check their clocks. In 1884 an international convention agreed that Greenwich would mark zero degrees longitude. The Greenwich Meridian passes through the courtyard, dividing the western and eastern hemispheres. The world's time is dictated by

Greenwich Mean Time. Flamsteed House and Observatory and the Meridian Buildings house the museum's astronomical collection.

GREENWICH PARK & RANGER'S HOUSE

This 200-acre park has many fine trees dating back to Le Nôtre's landscaping for Charles II. Along the formal avenues, there are gnarled and twisted sweet chestnut, old cypress, paper birch, and prickly castor-oil trees, as well as specimens such as Indian bean, tulip, single-leaved ash, Chinese yellow wood, pride of India, and red oak. From Great Cross Avenue, below the bandstand, the panoramic view of the East End, the City, and Westminster is spectacular. There is a rose garden near the **Ranger's House.** This refurnished, pretty, 18th-century redbrick villa is the setting for the eclectic but high-quality collection amassed by Julius Weinher. The German-born millionaire spent his money made from South African diamond mines on everything from Italian majolica to medieval ivories and Memlinc paintings. ■

For 2,000 years, London has focused its serious activity on the north bank of the Thames. The great draw of the South Bank has been entertainment and it still is today: Museums, concert halls, theaters, restaurants cluster here.

South Bank

Globe Theatre gate

South Bank

THE SERIOUS CORE OF LONDON—WESTMINSTER AND THE CITY—SITS ON the north bank of the Thames; the south bank is a solid strip of entertainment. Here, museums for design, modern art, war, and underwater life are interspersed with theaters, concert halls, restaurants, and a fine cathedral. The seeds for development were sown when Puritan City government banned theaters from the City in 1574. They went over the river, where such simple pleasures as cherry gardens, taverns, bearbaiting, and dancing made Southwark the refuge for actor-managers. Later, 18th-century ideas for a national theater eventually materialized in a custom-designed triple-stage theater in the South Bank Centre. Today, bridges old and new, plus the new Jubilee Tube line running along the South Bank, make access to this vibrant area easy.

This stretch of the Thames between Tower and Westminster Bridges sits directly opposite the City and Westminster, filling the space inside the river's broad curve. Here, Southwark developed early as a dormitory town for Roman London directly opposite, linked by the one bridge across the tidal Thames. Over the centuries, as London expanded, the south bank developed—and the bridges multiplied to six for road traffic, three for rail, and one for pedestrians. A revival of the south bank is now close to completion. A nearly continuous river walkway provides stunning views of City and Westminster landmarks.

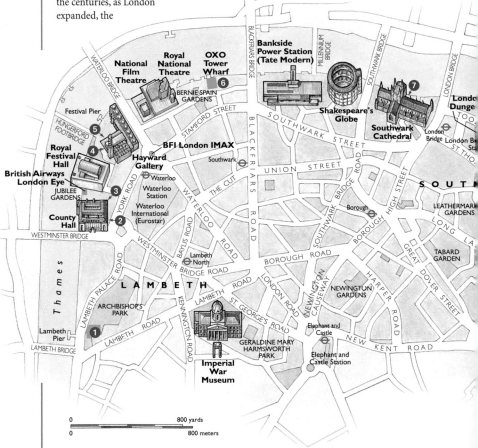

The Jubilee Line extension, which runs along the south bank from Westminster to the Dome, is London's newest section of Tube. Its Bermondsey station is a short walk from Cherry Garden Pier. Today, Edward III's moated manor to the east at the corner of Bermondsey Wall Street and Cathay Street has been partially excavated. Nearby, The Angel pub is where Captain Cook planned his trips and James McNeill Whistler painted London views. In the 18th and 19th centuries, massive warehouses here storing up to three-quarters of London's imported provisions were nicknamed London's Larder. In the 1960s, the inability of the narrow canal lanes to accommodate container trucks, and of the Thames to take the container ships, quickly led to almost total dereliction.

Moving westward to St. Saviour's Dock, Mill Street is where Andrew Wadsworth, then aged 23, bought New Concordia Wharf in 1980 and made the Docklands' first residential conversion. It became a model project that showed meticulous respect for the building while developing it for a variety of uses. Here, too, is Piers Gough's dramatic China Wharf and Michael Squire Associates' Vogan's Mill. Beyond Butler's Wharf and Tower Bridge is London Bridge City. Here, medieval inns and gardens gave way to warehouses, where Goodhart-Rendel's striking art deco St. Olaf's House and Hay's Wharf have been restored. H.M.S. *Belfast* (see p. 195), moored in the River Thames nearby, is a World War II cruiser, fully equipped with sailors' rooms, weapons, and lots of ladder stairways.

Southwark fills the area between London and Blackfriars Bridges. Its great cathedral is almost smothered by railway lines. In contrast the riverside beyond is open, a fine setting for the rebuilt Globe Theatre and its Museum, which evoke memories of Tudor entertainment. Here, too, is Tate Modern at Bankside.

West of Blackfriars Bridge and the Oxo Tower, the South Bank Arts Complex now fills the riverside. The project was kickstarted by the 1951 Festival of Britain. In the heart of this major entertainment area is Nicholas Grimshaw's heroic, 400-yard-long, curved and glazed Waterloo International Terminal (1991–93). This is where visitors from the Continent arrive by Eurostar, the Channel Tunnel rail link. Finally, the London Aquarium fills the basement of the County Hall building. Beyond it, steps lead onto Westminster Bridge, one of the best viewpoints for the Houses of Parliament across the river. ■

Area of map detail

SOUTH BANK

1. Lambeth Palace 2. London Aquarium
3. Saatchi Gallery 4. Purcell Room
5. Queen Elizabeth Hall 6. OXO Tower
7. Clink Exhibition 8. Hays Galleria
9. H.M.S. *Belfast* 10. City Hall
11. Bramah Tea and Coffee Museum
12. Design Museum

South Bank Arts Complex

BUILT FOR THE 1951 FESTIVAL OF BRITAIN, THIS IS NOW Western Europe's largest arts complex. Events run from morning until late at night, and range from informal jazz to highest Shakespearean tragedy. From the north bank the buildings are best reached along the splendidly wide river walk, a pleasant stroll in summer after crossing Waterloo or Westminster Bridges, or the elegant new pedestrian section of Hungerford Bridge.

The 1951 Festival of Britain, a government-sponsored extravaganza, was held to cheer up the British people during postwar austerity. It was also a showcase for the better world Londoners had fought for. A new generation of architects built a miniature wonderland showing off Britain's modern achievements in science, art, and sociology. Its uncompromising modern designs and ideas doesn't seem to bother the millions who have flocked to enjoy it. There was a Dome of Discovery, itself destined to inspire the Millennium Dome, and the Skylon, a futuristic aluminum shaft that appeared to float midair. There were sculptures by Reg Butler and Henry Moore, and the Festival Hall.

Now called the **Royal Festival Hall** (*www.rfh.org.uk*), this concert hall built in 1951 by Robert Matthew and J. L. Martin was extended in 1962 and is the only building to survive from the festival. The 2,600-seat hall replaced Queen's Hall, which had been bombed during the war, and superseded Albert Hall's unreliable acoustics. With its Le Corbusier inspiration, its clean lines, and its egglike auditorium nestling in a forest of columns and glazed galleries, this was London's first modern public building.

In 1964–67, the **Queen Elizabeth Hall** and the **Purcell Room,** smaller concert halls, were built, together with the now refur-

bished **Hayward Gallery** (*www.hayward-gallery.org.uk*), whose rooftop neon sculpture changes with the wind. The upper level, often windy walkways, the anonymous entrances, and the blank concrete walls are not inviting —but compensation is found in the glorious music and art inside.

The **National Film Theatre** (1956–58) is tucked beneath Waterloo Bridge, where second-hand bookstalls are set up daily on the towpath beneath the bridge arches. The NFT's huge program ranges from old classics to the latest avant-garde foreign films. It is notable for its special themed seasons, and also runs the huge annual London Film Festival.

Sir Denys Lasdun's **Royal National Theatre,** known by Londoners as the "National" or the "NT," was the culmination of an old dream. Back in the 18th century, actor-manager David Garrick, who brought Shakespeare back into vogue, suggested a national theater. The campaign was taken up by H. Granville-Barker, George Bernard Shaw, Laurence Olivier, and others,

and the theater finally opened in 1977. It has three auditoriums. The Olivier's open stage lends itself to epic productions; the smaller Lyttelton has a conventional layout; and the flexible little Cottesloe has a shell that can be made into any shape at all. Foyer spaces are also used for music, the theaters for pre-performance talks, and the back-stage tour is one of London's best. The nighttime panorama from the terraces is breathtaking—stretching from St. Paul's to Westminster.

The distinctive circular **BFI London Imax Cinema** (*Tel 7902 1234, www.bfi.org.uk/showing/imax*) shows 2D and 3D films on the largest screen in Britain. Digital sound and larger-than-life images offer fun for the whole family.

British Airways London Eye opened in 2000 opposite the Houses of Parliament and quickly established itself as one of the capital's best run, high-quality attractions. Passengers ride a complete circle in one of 32 enclosed capsules. Breathtaking views are enjoyed morning to late evening, weather permitting. Behind, the **Saatchi Gallery** (*Tel 7823 2363, www.saatchi-gallery.co.uk*) fills some magnificent County Hall rooms with conversation-stimulating contemporary art. ∎

Fashion shoot at the British Airways London Eye

Royal National Theatre
- 🅰 Map p. 208
- ✉ South Bank, SE1
- ☎ Information & backstage tours: 7452 3400. Box office: 7452 3000 www.nt-online.org
- 🕐 Closed Sun.
- 💲 Free–$$$ depending on the event
- 🚇 Same as South Bank Centre

British Airways London Eye
- ✉ South Bank, SE1
- ☎ 0870 5000 600 www.ba-londoneye .com
- 💲 Book a timed ticket in advance to beat the lines
- 🚇 Waterloo, Westminster

Left: The South Bank's Royal Festival Hall

London Aquarium

London Aquarium

▲ Map p. 208

✉ County Hall,
Riverside Building,
Westminster Bridge
Road, SE1

☎ 7967 8000
www.londonaquarium
.co.uk

💲 $$$

🚇 Tube: Westminster,
Waterloo

DOWN IN THE BOWELS OF COUNTY HALL LURKS THE
capital's biggest, darkest, and most fascinating maze; for its glass walls
are windows onto softly lit underwater habitats from around the
world. Thousands of fish live here, from shoals of tiny, turquoise
fish, zipping along in formation, to smoothhound sharks. In our
world of increasing curiosity about our surroundings, where there is
a growing interest in caring for our fragile planet, aquariums are a
fairly new kind of "living museum"—and London's is one of the best.
After a visit here, the desire to slow down the destruction and
pollution of the world's waters takes on a new urgency.

**Once home
to London's
government, County
Hall now houses
an aquarium.**

Water covers almost three-quarters
of our globe, from clear sparkling
streams to deep oceans. The aquari-
um's tanks are arranged along these
themes, with sound effects, a touch-
pool, "newsplash" (eggs and newly
born residents), and plenty of clear
descriptions about the contents of
each tank. What is needed is time:
To stand watching one tank for sev-
eral minutes is much more reward-
ing than rushing from one to
another. Free talks by the resident
aquarists add to the fascination, but
do allow time to find their meeting
place in the maze. One of several
films shows how an octopus attacks
the crabs on which it feeds.

The first display traces the
journey of a stream from its fast-
moving, turbulent upper reaches
to the lazy wash of its estuary,
showing how fish and other water
creatures live in the moving waters
and stiller ponds and canals.
Moving on, temperate waters
are explained in a fishing harbor
where octopus, cuttlefish, moon
jellies, and pipefish live. The
Atlantic Ocean is a vast three-story
tank whose dark depths are inhab-
ited by stingrays, conger eels, cow-
nosed rays, and sharks. The Indian
Ocean is shown as home to design-
er lionfish, blue spot rays,
anemones, and tasselled carpet
sharks. There are also seahorses
and clownfish of coral reefs, the
ancient lungfish of tropical fresh-
waters, and the archerfish of
mangroves, which shoots flies
with deadly marksmanship. ■

Imperial War Museum

BRITAIN'S NATIONAL MUSEUM OF 20TH-CENTURY WAR IS
not only about tanks and guns. In fact, they form just a tiny fraction of
a large and fascinating collection that covers every aspect of war, civil
or military, allied or enemy, military or political, social or cultural.

**Imperial War
Museum**
- Map p. 208
- Lambeth Road, SE1
- 020-7416 5000 or
  0900-160 0140
  www.iwm.org.uk
- $$
- Tube: Lambeth
  North, then
  5-minute walk

The museum opened in 1920 in
the former Bedlam Asylum, built in
1812–15, where Charlie Chaplin's
mother lived for some time. In
addition to the wide-ranging
displays, special exhibitions draw
on the museum's 10,000 or so
quality posters and paintings. The
museum continues to send official
war artists to places of conflict
around the world.

Fighter planes and a giant V2
rocket stand in the hall, contrast-
ing with the displays that graphi-
cally demonstrate the human
damage of war such as an impres-
sive but extremely harrowing
account of the liberation of Belsen
in 1945. This is part of the
permanent exhibition (recom-
mended for people over 14 years
old) devoted to the Holocaust,
which examines the persecution
and murder of European Jews and
other groups from 1933 to 1945.
It is housed in Arup Associates'
extension, along with an
exhibition on the impact of
20th-century war on civilians, and
personal study galleries.

The **Secret War Gallery,**
upstairs, justifies the money and
expertise spent on government spy-
ing, artificial intelligence, and
undercover espionage, with
accounts of Special Air Services
(SAS) operations in the Gulf War.
Other galleries contain Arthur
Hardon's Douglas Doll, which
entertained the troops, and German
straw overboots for protection
against the Soviet Union's cold.

The gallery focusing on con-
flicts since 1945 has a slice of the

Berlin Wall and General
Schwarzkopf's Gulf War uniform.
The walk-through of World War I
trenches and the Blitz Experience,
portraying London's bomb-strewn
streets, are especially evocative,
and don't miss trying out the flight
simulator named Operation
Jericho. A recently opened gallery
is devoted to Britain's postwar
economic and social recovery from
austerity to affluence. ■

**Machines of
war under the
glass atrium of
the museum's
main hall**

Southwark Cathedral

Southwark Cathedral

📍 Map p. 208

✉️ Southwark Cathedral, SE1

☎️ 7367 6700. Tours: 7367 6734 www.dswark.org/cathedral

💲 Donation

🚇 Tube/rail: London Bridge

MEDIEVAL SOUTHWARK'S LIBERAL REPUTATION WAS encouraged by its priory church, St. Mary Overie, which belonged to the diocese of Winchester, in Hampshire. Prostitutes, known as Winchester Geese, were rife, and assorted rough entertainment included bull- and bearbaiting, cockfighting, and gambling. The arrival of the theaters sealed the area's position as the Tudor and Stuart entertainment center. All this is evoked in the little Clink Exhibition, on the site of Clink Prison, which began as a dungeon beneath the bishop's palace for his disobedient clerics. See also the surviving, beautiful 14th-century rose window nearby.

Effigy of John Gower, Chaucer's friend, his head resting on his literary works

Today, after new warehouses, railways, and a new bridge have destroyed much of the Southwark of the 19th century, devoted renovation work has restored the cathe-

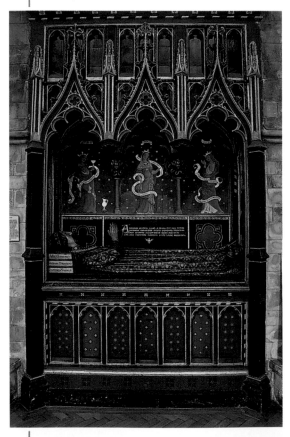

dral and its surrounding cobbled streets and old warehouses.

The restored and cleaned cathedral began as the Augustinian Priory of St. Mary Overie, founded in 1106. In 1212 the whole priory burned down; of the Gothic church, only the choir and retrochoir survived. The choir was then renovated (a fine Tudor stone screen was added), but after the Reformation it was used as a bakery and pigsty. In the 19th century, it lost its east end chapel to the London Bridge approach, and was substantially restored—the tower and retrochoir in 1822, the nave in 1838, and again in 1890 by Sir Arthur Blomfield. In 1905 the church of St. Mary was made a cathedral.

You need sharp eyes to pick out the mixture of French and English Gothic style, to see the English chancel, plain capitals, and clerestory in contrast to the more ebullient French arcaded first-floor wall passage and vaulting. Attentive eyes may note the 14th-century crossing tower with its later (1689) pinnacles, the Norman north transept and 19th-century south transept window, and the Harvard Memorial Chapel's 12th-century walls and 1907 interior. The cathedral's interesting memorials include the brightly painted tomb of poet John Gower, a contemporary of Chaucer. ∎

Shakespeare's Globe Theatre

WHEN AMERICAN ACTOR SAM WANAMAKER CAME TO London in 1949, he began searching for the site of the original Globe Theatre, first built in 1599, closed in 1642, and later destroyed. In 1970 Wanamaker began to re-create what he believed was the most important public theater ever built. Although he died in 1993, and the theater's architect, Theo Crosby, in the following year, the project to reconstruct the Elizabethan theater continued to completion.

Shakespeare's Globe Theatre

- Map p. 208
- New Globe Walk, Bankside, SE1
- Theater: 7902 1400.
  Exhibition:
  7902 1500
  www.shakespeares-globe.org
- Closed Oct.–April
- Exhibition: $$
- Tube: Southwark, London Bridge
  Tube/rail: London Bridge

The site of the theater, 200 yards from the original location, was cleared in 1987. Pentagram Design used contemporary illustrations and archaeological evidence, together with traditional materials and techniques, to re-create the Tudor theater: a polygonal building of 20 three-story wooden bays. Audience capacity is 1,401, including 500 standing places. In 1994 the theater's walls were constructed as Britain's largest lime plastering project, and thatching began of the first new thatched building in central London since the Great Fire of 1666. On May 27, 1997, the theater opened for its first season of 17th-century plays with Shakespeare's *Henry V* and *The Winter's Tale*, Middleton's *A Chaste Maid in Cheapside*, and Beaumont & Fletcher's *The Maid's Tragedy*. It has all been hugely successful, apart from the difficulty of hearing if it is raining. Actors report experiencing a new closeness with their audience, one that must have been important to Shakespeare.

Each season has brought the acting company more acclaim. Shakespeare addicts should reserve time for the hands-on challenges in the exhibition, too. ∎

Tate Modern

**Bankside Power
Station brought
back to life by
the imaginative
conversion of
Herzog &
de Meuron**

AS IF TO PUT THE FINAL STAMP OF APPROVAL ON THE
revived South Bank, the Tate's collection of international modern art
opened in May 2000 in the Sir Giles Gilbert Scott's Bankside Power
Station. Now a major London landmark, the Tate Modern is revital-
izing its surroundings, and has generated the first new Thames bridge
in a century—the Millennium Bridge, which opened in June 2000.

Both building and site are sensa-
tional. Scott's cathedral-like, brick
power station stands on a wide
riverside terrace looking across to
St. Paul's Cathedral. Wren lived
nearby, and the favorite view of his
masterpiece was from here. Completed in 1963 to replace an older
power station on the same site, the
Bankside structure's most valuable
asset is the Turbine Hall, about 100
feet high and 500 feet long, running
the full width of the building.

Herzog & de Meuron, a Swiss
architectural firm, won the international competition (there were 148
entries) to make the transformation.
They have been praised for their
use of space and light and for their
originality. Visitors enter the building on a ramp and descend into the
Turbine Hall, which is a "covered
street." They then proceed through
a series of top- and side-lit galleries
into the other areas of the building.
There are activity spaces, an
information center, an auditorium,
shops, and education programs.
There are four eating areas, with
pleasant garden and riverside out-

look; one rooftop bar-restaurant has spectacular views over London. Indeed, much has been made of the views throughout the building. The ground-floor café opens for breakfast.

THE COLLECTION

In 1916 the Tate was given the responsibility of forming a collection of international modern art, encompassing painting and sculpture from 1900 and after. The recent growth of the collection, together with a huge increase in its popularity, meant the Millbank site was too small. Tate outposts opened in Liverpool in 1987, and St. Ives in Cornwall in 1993. Then, due to popular demand, the modern collection has its own vast space.

As the number of works has doubled since 1950, the collection is now acknowledged as one of the world's four most important collections of modern art, competing with New York's MoMA and Solomon R. Guggenheim Museum, and Paris's Musée National d'Art Moderne. Tate curators know precisely where their voids are, and have compiled a list of particular paintings or sculptures that would complete a truly representative collection of important artists.

Movements especially well represented include surrealism, abstract expressionism, pop art, minimalism, and conceptual art. Many masterpieces by influential European and American artists seen only rarely until now are regularly rotated among the three suites of permanent galleries. These include Constantin Brancusi's "Maiastra" (1911), Salvador Dali's "The Metamorphosis of Narcissus" (1937), Henri Matisse's "The Snail" (1953), Pablo Picasso's "The Three Dancers" (1925), and Andy Warhol's "Marilyn Diptych" (1967). The same is true for major

British artists. There is more opportunity to see great works such as Francis Bacon's "Three Studies for Figures at the Base of the Crucifixion," Sir Anthony Caro's "Early One Morning," David Hockney's "Mr & Mrs Clark and Percy," Henry Moore's "Recumbent Figure," and Stanley Spencer's "The Resurrection, Cookham."

In addition, a special suite of galleries holds three major loan exhibitions a year, one of them a single-artist exhibition. These exhibitions, which may include architecture or design, are chosen to complement the permanent collection. ■

Amedeo Modigliani's "Portrait of a Girl" (ca 1917)

Butler's Wharf

Design Museum

- Map p. 209
- Butler's Wharf, Shad Thames, SE1
- 7403 6933 www.design museum.org
- $$
- Tube: Bermondsey, or Tower Hill then walk across the river Tube/rail: London Bridge

The Design Museum was born of the beliefs of its founder, Sir Terence Conran.

LONDON'S PRINCIPAL WHARVES WERE THE "LEGAL QUAYS" on the north bank, while the south bank's "suffrance wharves" eased the volume of 19th-century shipping. After the docks closed, Londoners treated these testimonies to their city's wealth in different ways. Two vistas reveal the dramatic differences. One is from Butler's Wharf to the unforgiving Tower Thistle Hotel, out of sympathy with St. Katharine Dock and the riverside in scale, shape, and materials. The other is of Butler's Wharf from the north bank. Here, the sensitive mixture of renovated warehouse building and interesting, well-proportioned new structures maintains London's riverside history while equipping it to be a lively neighborhood for the 21st century.

The hero of Butler's Wharf is Sir Terence Conran. As a small boy, he came here with his father, a dealer in gum copal resin, and watched the freighters unloading. He saw Bermondsey's decline, then boldly stepped in to revive this spot. In 1984, his company, Conran Roche, acquired the site and its 17 historic buildings. The flour, grain, and rice warehouses had closed, as had those for rubber, tapioca, tea, and coffee.

Conran opened up the quayside and converted the central, massive Butler's Wharf Building (1871–73) into apartments, shops, and a string of restaurants. His pet project was the newly built **Design Museum,** opened in 1989 to display provocative and classic examples and thus stimulate design awareness. Its restaurant offers panoramic views.

Inland from Butler's Wharf, look for newer buildings such as Julyan Wickham's Horsleydown Square (1989), CZWG's The Circle (1987–89), Panter Hudspith's Camera Press (1993), and Michael Hopkins's David Mellor Building (1990).

Designer Zandra Rhodes is the energy behind the **Fashion & Textile Museum** *(83 Bermondsey St., tel 7403, 0222, www .ftmlondon.org),* which displays temporary exhibitions by contemporary designers.

As if to confirm Conran's revival, the first Mayor of London, Ken Livingstone, has chosen this area, just west of Tower Bridge, for **City Hall** *(The Queen's Walk, SE1, www.london.gov.uk),* his egg-shaped headquarters designed by Foster and Partners. ∎

When London begins to stifle, escape is easy: Hop on a train and glide out of the city to the comparative calm of Windsor Castle, Oxford, the Cotswolds, Brighton, or York Minster.

Excursions

St. Thomas à Becket, depicted in a stained-glass window in Canterbury Cathedral

Excursions

LONDON CAN SOMETIMES BE SIMPLY TOO STIMULATING, TOO OVER-whelmingly urban and noisy, and relentlessly busy. It is comforting to know that this is a very easy city to leave. Yet the story of London until the 20th century was one of people arriving rather than leaving. England's great 19th-century railway system was built to bring people, trade, and supplies into London, the giant city that since medieval times has been so much bigger than any other on this small island.

Today, while the congested roads discourage some potential travelers, the railway system has become a vital tool for escaping the city. London's grand Victorian stations invite you to dip into the clean air of England's lush countryside. Travel by train is easy and bargain ticket deals abound. Reservations can be made by telephone, as can car rental for your destination (*National rail inquiries, tel 08457-484950*).

For ideas on where to go, the British Tourist Authority information desk (*1 Regent Street, W1*) has details on monuments, historic houses, gardens, music festivals, and accommodations. The National Trust owns and cares for a large number of properties; the *National Trust Handbook* lists and explains the houses and gardens under its care. Membership brings unlimited free entry to their properties (*Tel 020-8315 1111*). English Heritage membership also offers free entry to their properties (*Tel 020-7973 3000*). For garden enthusiasts, the National Gardens Scheme's annual list of gardens open in England is essential, as is the National Trust's guide to 200 gardens. In addition to hotels, there are plenty of characterful places to stay. For instance, the Landmark Trust (*Tel 01628-825925*) has more than 150 buildings to rent, ranging from temples and towers to cottages and follies. Distinctly Different (*Tel 01225-866648*) offers a group of unusual places to stay, including castles, windmills, and lighthouses. Wolsey Lodges (upscale B & B, *Tel 01473-822058*), much loved by discerning visitors in Britain, has a thick brochure.

A 40-minute train ride westward from Waterloo station brings you to Windsor, a delightful outing. In addition to the castle, there are the twin towns of Windsor and Eton to explore, the Great Park, boat trips on the Thames, and Legoland. Trains from Waterloo go southwest to Salisbury, with its magnificent cathedral and close. The ancient monumental stones of Stonehenge stand a few miles to the north on Salisbury Plain, while Inigo Jones's Wilton House and the classic landscape gardens of Stourhead are to the west.

Eurostar trains depart from Waterloo International station for the three-hour journey to central Paris, a real daytrip or weekend opportunity. Lille (2 hours) and Brussels (2 hours, 40 minutes) are even closer (*Eurostar inquiries, tel 0990-186186*).

From Paddington station, trains snake out westward to Oxford's dreamy college spires. The unashamedly grandiose Blenheim Palace is at nearby Woodstock. Beyond them, Kemble's pretty, honey-colored stone railway station signals your arrival in the Cotswolds. Kemble lies outside the central Cotswold market town of Cirencester, surrounded by rolling, sheep-dotted hills and picturesque villages. Another line from Paddington leads to Shakespeare's birthplace, Stratford-upon-Avon, and the well-known towns of Broadway and Moreton-in-Marsh, best avoided in the crowded summer months. A third Paddington rail service brings you to the elegant Georgian crescents of honey-stoned Bath.

Trains leaving from Charing Cross, Victoria, and Waterloo stations go to the county of Kent in the southeast. Here Canterbury's magnificent cathedral dominates the city, where medieval streets and a Norman keep survive. The station for romantic Leeds Castle, bought by Queen Eleanor in 1278, is Bearstead, near Maidstone, with bus connections. Trains from Victoria also speed down to Lewes for summer opera at Glyndebourne and to Brighton for seaside promenading, antique shops, and the Prince Regent's Pavilion.

Trains from Liverpool Street and King's Cross go north to Cambridge's colleges and cloisters, with Ely's and Peterborough's magical cathedrals nearby.

Farther afield, but perfectly manageable on a long daytrip or for a weekend, are York and Leeds. York has its fine Minster, Jorvik Viking Centre, and ancient city walls to explore, while handsome Leeds sits amid the rolling Yorkshire hills so vividly brought to life in the Brontë novels, with the North Yorkshire Moors National Park nearby. ■

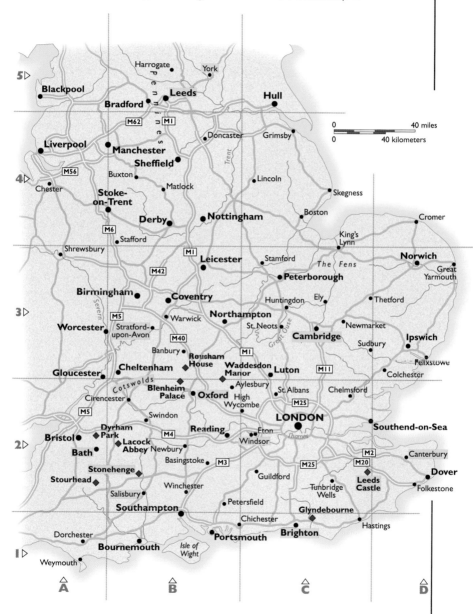

Windsor

Windsor

🗺 Map p. 221 C2

Visitor information

✉ 24 High St.

☎ 01753-743900.
Accommodations:
01753-743907
www.windsor.gov.uk

SET BESIDE THE THAMES 20 MILES WEST OF CENTRAL London, Windsor is quick and easy to reach. The castle is magnificent, and is complemented by other things to see and do. A string of annual events includes the Royal Windsor Horse Show in May; the Windsor Carnival in June; the Royal Windsor Rose Show and polo matches in July; and the Windsor Festival in September. All are very jolly, friendly occasions.

Windsor Castle

☎ 01753 831118 or
(020) 7766 7304

🕐 Open daily except
during state
occasions & official
engagements.
Chapels: Worshipers
only Sun. services
at 10:45 & 11:45
a.m. & 5:15 p.m.
Changing of the
Guard ceremony
daily May—early
Aug.; alternate days
rest of year.

💲 $$$

Everyone will enjoy visiting **Windsor Castle,** which stands on a hill in the town center, its fairy-tale towers silhouetted against the sky. It was William the Conqueror who, in about 1080, threw up this defense as part of his ring of fortifications around London. The Norman castle was converted into a Gothic palace by Edward II. He founded the College of St. George in the Lower Ward and rebuilt the Upper Ward, while Edward IV built **St. George's Chapel** and Henry VIII added the grand gate in the Lower Ward. For Charles II, who wanted to make

Windsor his principal palace outside London, architect Hugh May created England's grandest suite of baroque **State Apartments,** decorated by woodcarver Grinling Gibbons, painter Antonio Verrio, and others. Later, George III brought in James Wyatt to enhance the castle's romantic character; but it was George IV who employed Jeffrey Wyatville to raise Henry II's famous **Round Tower** to its present height of 215 feet and improve the castle's medieval silhouette with extra towers. Wyatville also lavishly refurbished the State Rooms and completed the park's **Long Walk,** begun by Charles II.

Queen Victoria made Windsor her principal palace, so it was natural that when her consort, Prince Albert, died in the castle in 1861 she chose to create his marble and mosaic memorial chapel here.

After a devastating fire on November 20, 1992, the Grand Reception Room, State Dining Room, Crimson Drawing Room, and other casualties were meticulously restored. The work took five years, and was partly funded by income raised when Buckingham Palace opened to the public in 1993. Those parts of the castle beyond restoration were rebuilt by the Sidell Gibson Partnership. They created a modern Gothic style whose craft and design traditions stretch back to the Middle Ages. This style can be seen especially in the **Lantern Lobby.**

The State Apartments, embellished with art from the Queen's unmatched collection, may be the central showpiece of the castle, but do not miss other special things. There is the exquisite **Queen Mary's Dolls' House,** designed by Sir Edwin Lutyens for the Queen in 1924 to a scale of 1:12; the **China Museum,** whose display cabinets contain Sèvres, Worcester, Meissen, and more; **St. George's Chapel,** built 1475–1528; and the **Albert Memorial Chapel,** created by Sir George Gilbert Scott.

At the foot of Windsor town, past the **Theatre Royal** (*Thames Street, tel 01753-853888)* and the house where Sir Christopher Wren lived, lies the Thames. Towpath walks are beautiful, and riverboats make gentle journeys up- and down-river. Over the bridge lies **Eton,** whose college buildings were the haunt of such schoolboys as the Duke of Wellington, the 18th-century author Henry Fielding, and a string of prime ministers.

The town is bounded in the south and east by **Windsor Great Park,** whose 4,800 acres contain many trees more than 500 years old. Just to the south, **Legoland** lives up to expectations. ■

Henry II's Round Tower later romanticized by Wyatville (above). The grand way to leave Windsor Castle (left).

Legoland
☎ 08705-040404
💲 $$$$

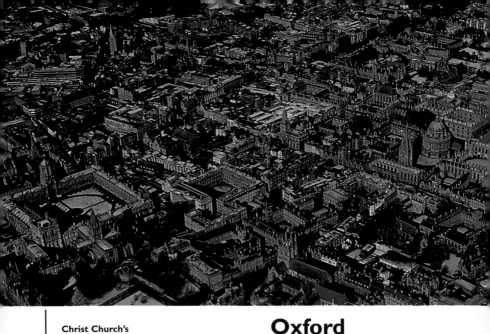

Christ Church's Tom Quad, with Sir Christopher Wren's "Tom Tower," shows left; the dome of the Radcliffe Camera, right.

Oxford

LYING BETWEEN THE RIVERS CHERWELL AND THAMES (called the Isis here), the honey-colored walls and spires of Oxford's ancient university buildings give the center of this busy city a timeless tranquility. By joining a guided walk, visitors can see colleges that are little changed in their layout and traditions since their medieval or Tudor foundation.

Oxford

- Map p. 221 B2
- Train takes 1 hour from Paddington station; National Express coach service takes about 90 minutes from Victoria Coach Station
- Information: 08705-808080

Visitor information

- Broad Street, near The Oxford Story, Oxford
- 01865-726871. Information & maps, plus guided walks and tours: www.oxfordcity.co.uk

Among the oldest colleges is **Merton** (*Merton St., tel 01865-276310*), founded in 1264. Its 14th-century Mob Quad contains the oldest library in England still in use. **Balliol** (*Broad St., tel 01865-277777*) has nurtured more politicians than any other college. Poet Percy Bysshe Shelley was "rusticated" (sent away for a term) for writing subversive pamphlets from **University College** on High Street, called The High (*Tel 01865-276602*). Former President Bill Clinton was a Rhodes Scholar here.

Magdalen (pronounced "Maudlin") (*The High, tel 01865-276000*) was built at the end of the 15th century and has a lovely deer park behind it. The largest college, **Christ Church** (*St. Aldate's, tel 01865-276150*), was founded by

Cardinal Wolsey in 1525. Its chapel is also Britain's smallest cathedral, built in the 12th century as a priory church. In summer, a towpath stroll might go across **Christ Church Meadow** to Britain's oldest **Botanic Gardens,** whose most exotic plants are kept in riverside greenhouses.

To join undergraduates in a traditional Oxford pastime, test your skills by hiring a punt on the Cherwell (pronounced "Charwell") from beside Magdalen Bridge or on the Isis from Folly Bridge near Christ Church, where boat trips depart, too. Summer events include Eights Week rowing competitions at the end of May.

Out at Garsington village, operas are staged at **Garsington Manor** (*Tel 01865-361636*) in June, when the audience picnics in the gardens in their fine clothes to create a *fête champêtre* atmosphere.

Oxford's impressive museums are open all year. The **Ashmolean** *(Beaumont St., tel 01865-278000, closed Mon.)*, founded in 1683 and Britain's oldest public museum, houses Egyptian, classical, Oriental, and European art, plus silver and ceramics. The city's own story is told in the **Museum of Oxford** *(St. Aldate's, tel 01865-252761)*; the university's is explained in the **Oxford Story** *(Broad St., tel 01865-790055)*; and that of the universe is explored in the glorious building of the **University Museum of Natural History,** complete with dodo remains *(Parks Road, tel 01865-272950)*. The **Pitt Rivers Museum** *(Parks Road, tel 01865-270927)* is devoted to archaeology and anthropology. Other Oxford buildings to seek out include the **Bodleian Library,** founded in 1598, and the round **Sheldonian Theatre,** both on Broad Street; the domed **Radcliffe Camera,** part of the Bodleian Library, is next to the Sheldonian.

AROUND OXFORD

There are three interesting country houses to visit in the vicinity of Oxford, each with a fine garden.

The Duke of Marlborough's **Blenheim Palace** stands outside the charming village of Woodstock, 8 miles northwest of Oxford on the A44. Built as the nation's grateful gift to the duke after his victory over the French and Bavarians at the Battle of Blenheim in 1704, John Vanbrugh's huge Italianate palace is surrounded by a very English park landscaped by Capability Brown. Sir Winston Churchill was born here in 1874, amid the tapestries, paintings, and fine furniture that still fill the gilded State Rooms and Long Library. The rolling acres of park include a narrow-gauge railway, a lake, and the Marlborough Maze.

Another grand house near Oxford is **Waddesdon Manor,** a French Renaissance château built by Baron Ferdinand de Rothschild between 1874 and 1889. Approximately 20 miles northeast of Oxford, the house now belongs to the National Trust. French furniture and porcelain gleam in the gilded salons, and the French-influenced gardens are clipped to perfection.

Less grand **Rousham,** 12 miles north of Oxford on the A4260, is a 17th-century house standing in a garden little changed since it was landscaped by William Kent in the 18th century. ■

Blenheim Palace
- Map p. 221 B2
- Woodstock, Oxfordshire
- 01993-811325
- Closed late Oct.–mid-March
- $$: includes park & most attractions. Supplement for Marlborough Maze and rowboat rentals

Waddesdon Manor
- Map p. 221 B3
- Waddesdon, near Aylesbury, Buckinghamshire
- Booking line: 01296-651226. Recorded information: 01296-653211
- House: closed Mon.–Tues., also Wed. April–June & Sept.–Oct., & all Nov.–March Grounds: closed Mon.–Tues. & Jan.–Feb.
- $$$. Tickets issued for a timed entry

Rousham House & Garden
- Map p. 221 B3
- Rousham, Oxfordshire
- 01869-347110
- House: open Wed. & Sun. April–Sept., & Bank Holiday Mon. p.m. Gardens open all year. No children
- $$

Find peace in a rowboat or punt on Oxford's rivers.

Salisbury & Stonehenge

Salisbury

🗺 Map p. 221 B2

Visitor information

✉ Fish Row, Salisbury

☎ 01722-334956

www.visitsalisbury
.com

**Salisbury
Cathedral**

✉ The Close, Salisbury

☎ 01722-555120

🕐 Open daily.
Evensong 5:30 p.m.

💲 Donation. Various
tours: $

**Mompesson
House**

✉ The Close, Salisbury

☎ 01722-335659

🕐 Closed Mon.–Tues.
& Nov.–March

💲 $

SOUTH WILTSHIRE IS BEST KNOWN FOR TWO TRULY magnificent sites: the soaring elegance of Salisbury Cathedral, set in its magnificent close, and Stonehenge's standing stones on the open grasslands of Salisbury Plain. This is ideal country for walking, horseback riding, cycling, and exploring unspoiled villages.

SALISBURY

The Avon, Wylye, and Bourne Rivers twist their way through the chalk valleys to meet at New Sarum, or Salisbury. A good place to start exploring this city, however, is at **Old Sarum,** just north of the city. Here mounds, ditches, and walls tell the silent story of an Iron Age fort, a Roman settlement, a fortified Saxon town, and a Norman castle *(Castle Road, tel 01722-335398)* and **Cathedral.**

It was Bishop Richard Poore who moved Old Sarum's cathedral

Gothic statues in the niches above Salisbury Cathedral's doors

to its present site. In 1220 he began the only medieval cathedral in England to be built in a single, unified style throughout. Completed in 1258, its 400-foot-tall spire was added a generation later. While the exterior is rich in traceried windows and ornate friezes, the interior's simple symmetry is emphasized by a lack of furnishings and by medieval stained glass. There are some grand tombs, however, such as that of Bishop Giles de Bridport (1260). The Chapter House, in the cloisters, exhibits one of the four surviving copies of the Magna Carta.

Salisbury's **Cathedral Close** is the finest and largest of its kind in the country. Once the precinct of the ecclesiastical community serving the cathedral, it is now a peaceful square overlooked by elegant houses. Pierced by three strong gateways, its walls were built around 1330. The gates are still locked each night.

Several buildings in the close can be visited. **Mompesson House,** run by the National Trust,

was built for Charles Mompesson in 1711 and later decorated by Charles Longeville with fine plasterwork and a carved oak staircase. The Wardrobe dates from 1254, when it was built to store the bishop's clothing; today it houses the **Royal Gloucestershire, Berkshire, & Wiltshire Regimental Museum** *(Tel 01722-414536)*. Sit beneath the magnificent roof of the **Medieval Hall** *(Tel 01722-412472)* to see a 30-minute show recounting Salisbury's history. For information on Stonehenge and related sites, visit the **Salisbury & South Wiltshire Museum.**

AROUND SALISBURY

Another elegant building, just west of the city, is **Wilton House,** home of the Herbert family since 1544. Its magnificent rooms are matched by a romantic park. In the village of Wilton, known for its carpets since French weavers introduced the craft early in the 18th century, the **Wilton Carpet Factory** offers tours of its original weaving sheds. For garden lovers, **Heale Garden** *(Middle Woodford, tel 01722-782504)* is a pretty 5-mile drive north through the Wiltshire countryside, and **Houghton Lodge Gardens and Hydroponicum** *(near Stockbridge, tel 01264-810177)* are 15 miles east, beside the River Test in Hampshire.

STONEHENGE

One of the most significant prehistoric sites stands on the rolling chalklands of Salisbury Plain. This mystical, enigmatic, and surely symbolic circle of giant standing stones may have marked the center of an ancient administrative, cultural, and social territory that was important as long ago as 3000 B.C. It stands near the sites of five prehistoric communities, marked by the remains of ceremonial and domestic structures, including barrows—the burial mounds of Neolithic and Bronze Age peoples—and the rectangular markings of Celtic farms and fields.

The original function of the stone circle has been discussed endlessly: Perhaps it was the center for a religious celebration of the winter and summer solstices, aligned to moon and sun; perhaps a gigantic astronomical stone calendar. At a later date, a 2-mile-long avenue to the River Avon was added to mark the line of Midsummer's Day sunrise, and about 80 blue stones, some weighing 2 tons, were transported 240 miles from the Preseli Hills of South Wales. Later still, trilithons were added at the heart of the complex. Stonehenge is a center for revived Druid ceremonies; several thousand people attend the summer solstice. Visitors may walk around the circle close to the stones. ∎

Stonehenge retains its mystery and strength.

Salisbury & South Wiltshire Museum
- ✉ The King's House, The Close, Salisbury
- ☎ 01722-332151
- 🕐 Closed Sun. Sept.–June
- 💲 $$

Wilton House
- ✉ Wilton, Salisbury
- ☎ 01722-746729
- 🕐 Closed Nov.–March
- 💲 $$$

Wilton Carpet Factory
- ✉ King Street, Wilton, Salisbury
- ☎ 01722-744919
- 💲 $

Stonehenge
- 🅰 Map p. 221 B2
- ✉ Jct. of the A303 & A360
- ☎ 01980-624715
- www.english-heritage.org.uk/stonehenge
- 💲 $$ (includes excellent audioguide)

Bath

STRADDLING THE RIVER AVON IN A GREAT BOWL OF SOFTLY curving hills, Bath was the Roman spa Aquae Sulis, popular from the first to the fifth centuries. The mineral-rich waters and natural hot spring have ensured the city's prosperity through the ages.

Stone gorgon's head from the museum in the Roman Baths

Bath
🅰 Map p. 221 A2
Visitor information
✉ Abbey Church Yard, Abbey Chambers, Bath
☎ 870 444 6442 (outside U.K.) or 0906 7112000 (inside U.K.)
www.visitbath.co.uk

Roman Baths & Museum
✉ Pump Room, Stall Street
☎ 01225-477785
💲 $$$

Thermal Bath Spa
☎ 01225-477051
www.thermalbathspa.com

After speeding along high above the Avon Valley, the train from London slows down for a magnificent panorama of the city, with **Bath Abbey's** *(Abbey Courtyard, tel 01225-422462)* pinnacled tower rising above Georgian terraces and crescents. The abbey is a good place to start a visit. It is the last complete monastic church to be built in England before the 16th-century Dissolution of the Monasteries. With its huge windows, the interior seems like an enormous lantern roofed with a vast, spreading fan vault, much rebuilt by Sir George Gilbert Scott in 1864. Do not miss the intriguing monuments to those for whom Bath's curative waters did not work. Nearby, the **Roman Baths** complex, with temple, baths, and a museum of sculptures, coins, and other remains, constitutes one of Europe's best Roman sites. Adjoining them, the Pump Room was the social center of 18th-century Bath, whose fashionable visitors included the Prince of Wales, later George IV, and the budding society painter, Thomas Gainsborough. Architect Nicholas Grimshaw has incorporated some of the complex into Britain's only natural thermal spa.

It was during the 18th century that much of Bath was built, the mellow, local stone creating an elegant Georgian town that is now highly valued and lovingly preserved. Great Pulteney Street is particularly fine, reached across Robert Adam's Pulteney Bridge, built in 1770. Other remarkable buildings to seek out include **Guildhall,** on the

High Street next to the old covered market, the beautiful **Theatre Royal,** on Milsom Street, and the **Octagon** building lying off it. The **Circus** and **Royal Crescent** are two superb architectural compositions created by Bath's chief architects, John Wood the Elder and his son, John Wood the Younger. **No. 1 Royal Crescent,** designed for the younger John Wood's father-in-law, has been meticulously restored and furnished and is open to the public. It is worth comparing with the home of astronomer and scientist **William Herschel** on New King Street.

Bath abounds in museums, many celebrating its history. The **Building of Bath Museum** *(The Vineyards, tel 01225-333895)* tells the story of Georgian Bath, while the **Georgian Garden** at No. 4, The Circus, perfectly re-creates an 18th-century town garden. The **Book Museum** celebrates the craft of bookbinding and Bath's place in English literature; Mr. Bowler's business tells the story of a century of one small Bath firm at the **Museum of Bath at Work** *(Julian Road, tel 01225-318348).* **Bath Postal Museum** *(8 Broad Street, tel 01225-460333)* reminds visitors that the first Penny Black, the world's first stamp, was posted from Bath on May 2, 1840. The **Bath Boating Station** is a living museum of skiffs, punts, and canoes for rental.

Another museum worth visiting is the **Holburne Museum and Crafts Study Centre,** Sir William Holburne's collection of silver, porcelain, paintings, and

The weir below
Pulteney Bridge

**American Museum
in Britain**
✉ Claverton Manor,
Bath
☎ 01225-460503
🕐 Closed Mon.
& Nov.—Feb.
$ $$

**Bradford-on-Avon
Visitor information**
✉ 34 Silver Street
☎ 01225-865797

Dyrham Park
🅰 Map p. 221 A2
✉ Near Chipping
Sodbury, Wiltshire
☎ 01179-372501
🕐 House: closed
Wed.—Thurs.
& Nov.—March
$ $$

Lacock Abbey
🅰 Map p. 221 B2
✉ Lacock, near
Chippenham,
Wiltshire
☎ 01249-730227
🕐 Abbey: closed Tues.
& Nov.—March
Cloisters & grounds:
open daily
$ $$

Stourhead
🅰 Map p. 221 A2
✉ Stourton, Wiltshire
☎ 01747-841152.
Recorded
information: 0900-
133 5205
🕐 House: closed
Thur.—Fri. &
Nov.—March
Gardens: open daily
$ $$

more, housed in the 18th-century Sydney Hotel, together with a celebration of British craft that includes works by Arts and Crafts architect-designer Ernest Gimson and potter Bernard Leach. In the basement of the grand 18th-century Assembly Rooms, the **Museum of Costume** *(Bennett Street, tel 01225-477789)* has an excellent collection covering Tudor times to the present.

If your feet get tired, take a ride on an open-topped bus, a horse-drawn carriage, or a pleasure boat on the Avon.

AROUND BATH
On the southeastern outskirts of the city, the **American Museum in Britain** displays its quality collection in 18 re created period rooms of the 17th to 19th centuries. **Bradford-on-Avon** is a delightful stonebuilt, riverside town located about 8 miles southeast of Bath on the A363. Farther afield, but still easily reached, the National Trust runs three magnificent sights: **Dyrham Park,** 8 miles north on the A46, an early 18th-century house with deer park; **Lacock Abbey,** 12 miles east of Bath, just off the A350, a country house founded as an abbey in the 13th century and now home to a museum commemorating Henry Fox Talbot, father of photography; and **Stourhead,** 20 miles south of Bath off the B3092, a beautiful example of an 18th-century English landscape garden. ■

Stratford & the Cotswolds

THE TOWN WHERE THE POET, ACTOR, AND PLAYWRIGHT William Shakespeare was born is now so bound up with its renowned citizen that avoiding crowds of fellow visitors is a problem. The same applies to the surrounding countryside and the Cotswolds that stretch southward from here. Try the off season; and always reserve tickets in advance for the Royal Shakespeare Theatre *(Tel 0870 6091110)*.

Ann Hathaway's farmhouse

Stratford-upon-Avon
📍 Map p. 221 B3
Visitor information
✉ Bridgefoot
☎ 01789-293127
www.shakespeare-country.co.uk

Other information centers
✉ Corn Hall, Market Place, Cirencester
☎ 01285-654180
✉ 77 Promenade, Cheltenham
☎ 01242-522878

For Shakespeare pilgrims, there are five key sites to see. In Stratford, **Shakespeare's Birthplace** on Henley Street *(Tel 01789-204016);* **Nash's House and New Place** *(Tel 01789-204016)* on Chapel Street, home of Shakespeare's granddaughter and site of his retirement house, where an Elizabethan knot garden has been planted; and the Tudor **Hall's Croft** *(Tel 01789-204016),* where his daughter and son-in-law, Dr. John Hall, lived, furnished in period style. Outside the town, you can visit his wife **Anne Hathaway's Cottage** *(Tel 01789-204016),* a thatched Tudor farmhouse at Shottery; and his mother Mary Arden's half-timbered house at **Wilmcote.**

Aside from Shakespeare, the town has John Harvard's ornate Elizabethan mansion, where the founder of Harvard University was born in 1607. River cruises run along the Avon.

Ten miles north of Stratford on the A46, **Warwick Castle** *(Tel 01926-406600)* is one of England's finest, having grown from a wooden motte and bailey built by William the Conqueror in 1068 into the huge towered complex seen today. A few miles north again, the ruins of **Kenilworth Castle** *(Tel 01926-852078)* include a Norman keep, the Great Hall, and restored Tudor gardens. Elizabeth I was entertained by Robert Dudley here, and it was he who built the fine soldiers' retirement home in Warwick. **Ragley Hall** and its 400-acre park *(8 miles west of Stratford, tel 01789-762090)* is matched by several smaller houses and gardens in the surrounding area, including **Snowshill Manor** with its hoard of collectibles, and the remarkable **Hidcote Manor Gardens.**

THE COTSWOLDS

South of Stratford, sheep grazing the rolling hills of the Cotswolds brought prosperity that can be seen today in handsome stone-built market towns. **Cirencester** is the grandest, **Burford** has an impressive main street, and **Charlbury** is set in the timeless Evenlode Valley. **Tetbury** and **Chipping Norton** both testify to wool wealth. However, there may be too many visitors to enjoy the beauty of such towns as Bourton-on-the-Water, Moreton-in-Marsh, and Stow-on-the-Wold. ■

Canterbury & Leeds Castle

CANTERBURY CATHEDRAL, FOUNDED IN A.D. 597, IS THE
Mother Church of the Anglican Communion and the Seat of the
Archbishop of Canterbury. As such, it is not only full of interest
inside; it also dominates the city's history. To explore the streets and
sights, you can walk alone or take a guided tour, gaze at the city from
a punt, or ride through in a horse and carriage.

**Leeds Castle
surrounded by
its lake**

The present **Cathedral** building
(*Tel 01227-762862*), started in
1070, displays more than four centuries of architectural progress
from the Norman of the choir and
crypt to the high Gothic nave. The
landmark Bell Harry Tower, 235
feet high, built in 1495 is also
Gothic. Archbishop Thomas à
Becket was murdered in the northwest transept in 1170 by Henry II's
knights, because he had dared to
criticize the king. The golden shrine
to the saint became one of the
major medieval pilgrimage objec-
tives. Geoffrey Chaucer's fictional
pilgrims in the Canterbury Tales
were following the many real pilgrims. The shrine itself was pillaged
by Henry VIII, but candles still
burn on the site in the Trinity
Chapel at the Cathedral's East End.

In the town, walk through the
streets of half-timbered medieval
buildings from the cathedral to **St.
Augustine's Abbey** (*Longport,
tel 01227-767345*), the **Roman
Museum** (*Longmarket, tel 01227-
785575*), and **The Canterbury
Tales** (*St. Margaret's Street, tel
01227-479227*) where Chaucer's pilgrims' tales are reenacted.

Just east of Maidstone, **Leeds
Castle** was one of Henry VIII's
palaces. Built in the middle of a lake
and surrounded by 500 acres of
parkland, this is the epitome of the
romantic medieval castle. ∎

Canterbury
🅰 Map p. 221 D2
Visitor information
✉ 12/13 Sun St.,
 The Buttermarket
 (opposite Cathedral
 entrance)
☎ 01227-378100
 www.canterbury
 .co.uk
🕐 Closed Sun. Nov.–
 Easter

Leeds Castle
🅰 Map p. 221 C2
✉ Broomfield, Maidstone
☎ 01622-765400.
 Recorded info.:
 0870-600 8880
 www.leeds-castle.com
💲 $$$

The Prince Regent's Royal Pavilion

Brighton & Hove

THE PRINCE REGENT PUT BRIGHTON ON THE MAP WHEN he built his Royal Pavilion, an India-inspired palace. Ever since, Brighton has welcomed visitors and offered them entertainment.

Brighton
🅰 Map p. 221 C1
Visitor Information
✉ Bartholomew Square
☎ 0906 7112255
www.brighton.co.uk

Glyndebourne
🅰 Map p. 221 C1
Festival Opera
✉ Glyndebourne, Lewes, East Sussex
☎ 01273-812321
www.glyndebourne.com
🕐 Performances late May–end Aug.

Visit the Royal Pavilion to catch a glimpse of Regency high life. Nearby, you can get lost in the maze of lanes crammed with antiques shops, while a walk along the seafront passes Regency terraces and Palace Pier. Brighton also has an excellent **Museum & Art Gallery** (Church St., tel 01273-290900), haunting Victorian memorials in **Lewes Road Cemeteries,** the **Booth Museum of Natural History** (194 Dyke Road, tel 01273-292777), and the **Brighton Fishing Museum** (201 Lower Kings Road Arches, tel 01273-723064), as well as a delightful theater and a calendar of arts festivals and fairs. North of the city center, there is Edwardian **Preston Manor** (Tel 01273-290900). In neighboring **Hove,** the

Regency Town House (13 Brunswick Square, tel 01273-206306) has been restored and is open to the public, while on the outskirts the camera obscura of **Foredown Tower** (Foredown Road, Portslade, tel 01273-292092), a converted Edwardian water tower, gives views over the Sussex Downs.

Walks on the downs can be combined with visits to pretty Alfriston or Firle, villages within a few miles of each other. They lie about 15 miles east of Brighton, near **Charleston Farm House,** associated with the Bloomsbury Group. Opera enthusiasts can enjoy world-class opera in Michael Hopkins's theater at **Glyndebourne,** taking picnic supper on the lawns in their formal evening dress in the interval. ■

Cambridge

SET IN A LOOP OF THE CAM RIVER IN FLAT COUNTRYSIDE, Cambridge is an idyllic, tranquil university city, quite different from bustling, hectic Oxford.

Punting down the Cam River past the Colleges, with the "Backs" on the right

The oldest college is **Peterhouse,** founded in 1284. Each one that followed was a superb example of its particular period of English architecture. The most beautiful is **King's College** *(Tel 01223-331417)*, best seen from a boat on the River Cam or from the secluded walks of the "Backs," meadows across the river from the colleges edged with weeping willows and spring daffodils. King's College Chapel is probably Britain's finest example of Perpendicular Gothic architecture.

Queens' *(Tel 01223-335511)* has wonderful Tudor courts and the Mathematical Bridge built in 1749 without nails or bolts (but subsequent repair work has added them). **Trinity** *(Tel 01223-338400)* has a Wren-designed library by

the river. Undergraduates try to race around Great Court while the clock strikes twelve. Other Colleges not to miss are **Clare, Magdalene, St. John's, Jesus,** and **Emmanuel.** Visitors may walk into their courtyards and chapels, and sometimes their gardens, or take a guided tour. (Access may be restricted at certain times.)

ELY & PETERBOROUGH

Both these cities in the flat fenlands north of Cambridge have magnificent Norman cathedrals. Ely's is famous for its lantern tower and stained glass, Peterborough's for its West Front and painted ceiling. Ely is an unspoilt market town on the Great Ouse River about 15 miles north of Cambridge, Peterborough lies 25 miles northwest of Ely. ■

Cambridge
▲ Map p. 221 C3
Visitor information
✉ Wheeler Street
☎ 0906-5862526
www.tourism
cambridge.com

Ely
▲ Map p. 221 C3
Visitor information
✉ Oliver Cromwell's
House, 29 St. Mary's
St.
☎ 01353-662062

Peterborough
▲ Map p. 221 C3
Visitor information
✉ 45 Bridge Street
☎ 01733-452336

York & Leeds

York
Map p. 221 B5
Visitor information
✉ Exhibition Square
☎ 01904-621756

**The towers of
York Minster**

A THREE-HOUR TRAIN JOURNEY FROM LONDON REACHES the wild moors of Yorkshire in northern England. Here Romans, Saxons, Vikings, and Normans have all left their mark on York.

Visitors can walk the city walls, first built by the Romans, and explore the **Jorvik Viking Centre** *(Coppergate, tel 01904 -*

643211), where they travel back through the centuries in "time-cars." But it is **York Minster** that dominates the narrow streets. Begun in the 13th century, it is England's largest Gothic church and has remarkable stained glass. Other attractions include the **York Castle Museum** *(The Eye of York, tel 01904-653611)* with its re-created period rooms, the huge **National Railway Museum** *(Leeman Road, tel 01904-621261),* **Merchant Adventurers' Hall,** built by York's powerful medieval guilds, and the **City Art Gallery** *(Exhibition Square, tel 01904-551861)* with paintings spanning 600 years and an excellent collection of studio pottery.

LEEDS

Across the moors lies **Leeds** *(Visitor information, City Station, tel 0113-242 5242, www.leeds.gov.uk),* a handsome city whose markets and public buildings testify to centuries of wealth derived from wool and, later, industry. In town, museums include the **City Art Gallery** *(The Headrow, tel 0113-247 8248),* notable for its 20th-century works, and the **Royal Armouries Museum** *(The Waterfront, tel (0870-510 6666),* where you can watch live displays of jousting and swordsmanship. The **Henry Moore Institute** *(The Headrow, tel 0113-234 3158)*—the sculptor studied in Leeds—puts on a variety of exhibitions. Three of Britain's national parks are within reach: the Yorkshire Dales, the North Yorks Moors, and the Peak District, all glorious places for walking. ■

Travelwise

A Trafalgar Square lion

TRAVELWISE INFORMATION

PLANNING YOUR TRIP

WHEN TO GO

London is what you make of it. There are, however, seasons that are particularly good for certain interests, such as traditional events, gardens, or church music.

January, February, and March are good months for getting into popular plays and operas and enjoying museums in relative peace. Even the top restaurants are easier to book; and shoppers can take advantage of the sales. On the last Sunday of January, the beheading of Charles I is commemorated; February traditions include Chinese New Year celebrations in Soho.

Easter, which may fall in March or April, brings exceptional music when the Easter Passions are sung in the cathedrals, churches, and concert halls. At this time of year, there is plenty of horse racing, and the Oxford versus Cambridge boat race takes place between Putney Bridge and Hammersmith. In the parks, daffodils carpet the lawns while trees burst into leaf. Hyde Park is the setting for the Easter Parade and the Harness Horse Parade.

April and May mark an increase in cultural events. Arts festivals, houses that open only for the summer months, and fashionable sports such as polo at Ascot and the Windsor Horse Trials swing into action. A string of antiques fairs begins. There are flower shows at the Royal Horticultural Society's halls in Pimlico, culminating in the Chelsea Flower Show. The Queen spends most of this time at Windsor, so the State Apartments may be closed. Watch for special events on the first and last Mondays of May, both public holidays.

June brings hope for good weather. Arts festivals include Greenwich, Spitalfields, and the summer-long season of open-air concerts at Kenwood House and Marble Hill House. Tra-ditional sporting events include The Derby at Epsom, Ascot Week, Henley Royal Regatta, the Stella Artois tournament at Queen's, and the All England Lawn Tennis championships at Wimbledon—all need advance reservations for good tickets. Traditional events peak, too, with Beating the Retreat, the Garter Ceremony at Windsor, and Trooping the Colour. Again, the Queen is often at Windsor, when State Apartments close.

July and August are months when offices go quiet and many Londoners leave town. But museums and theaters fill up with visitors. To June's arts festivals add the City of London Festival and the nightly Henry Wood Promenade concerts at the Royal Albert Hall. With Londoners back from the summer break, September and October mix festivals on the Thames and in Covent Garden with major art shows, operas, and plays. In the parks, summer blooms give way to fall color.

November and December are strong on tradition: the State Opening of Parliament (October or November), Guy Fawkes' Day, the Lord Mayor's Show, and then the Christmas festivities. Shops and streets are decorated, theater tickets need to be re-served in advance, and an abun-dance of Christian church music is performed in cathedrals, churches, and concert halls.

CLIMATE

British weather is a daily surprise for every British person. Anything can happen on this island at the mercy of its surrounding seas, Gulf Stream, and prevailing winds: hot sun in April, sleet in August. This has two results in London: Weather is a constant topic of conversation; and, since anything can happen, few people carry umbrellas or raincoats. In theory, London enjoys defined seasons. Winter (November–March), when it should be cold with frosts and sometimes snow; spring (April––May), when it should warm up; summer (June–August), when it can be warm enough to eat outside for dinner and even become humid and sticky; and fall (September–October), when chilly mornings can become sunny days.

For visitors, the motto is "be prepared." Ignore Londoners' laid-back approach to equipment and carry a fold-up umbrella, wear a waterproof coat, and consider waterproof shoes. Finally, any day planned outside needs a fallback indoor plan in case it rains, or worse.

PASSPORTS & VISAS

Nationals of the United States, Canada, Australia, and New Zealand can enter the United Kingdom with just a passport (no visa is required).

HOW TO GET TO CENTRAL LONDON

FROM THE AIRPORTS

Gatwick (Tel 0870 000 2468, www.baa.co.uk/gatwick) The airport lies 30 miles south of central London, so rail is faster and more reliable. There are two routes: Gatwick Express to Victoria, a 30- to 35-minute ride, runs every 15 minutes by day and less frequently by night. Connex South Central's trains on the same route take longer as they are not non-stop. Thameslink trains stop at London Bridge, Blackfriars, City Thameslink, Farringdon, and King's Cross Thameslink. By road, the Airbus A5 (Tel 08705-747777) bus takes 80 minutes and departs about once an hour, 5 a.m. to 8 p.m. A taxi costs more than £50 ($75).

Heathrow
(Tel 0870 0000 123)
London's main airport is 15 miles west of central London, so rail and road are options. Rail is more dependable during rush hours. By rail, the Heathrow Express to Paddington, a 20-minute ride, runs every 15 minutes between 5:07 a.m. and 11:52 p.m. By Tube train, the Piccadilly line trains, a 40- to 60-minute ride, run regularly 5:30 a.m. to 11:30 p.m. through central London, with many stops including Knights-bridge (30 minutes), Piccadilly Circus, and Oxford Street. By road, Airbus A2 (Tel 08705-747777) takes 60 to 90 minutes, with several stops in central London. A taxi costs £25 to £45 ($37.50–$70), depending upon destination, congestion, and resulting trip time.

London City Airport
(Tel 7646 0000, www. londoncityairport.com)
This small airport lies on the Isle of Dogs in Docklands, 9 miles east of central London. An Airbus service runs to Canary Wharf Station, where the Docklands Light Railway goes to Bank. The whole journey takes 20 minutes, and connects with the Tube system. The Airbus continues to Liverpool Street Station (25 minutes), and runs every 10 minutes when the airport is open. A taxi takes 20 to 40 minutes and costs £15 to £20 ($22.50–$30).

Stansted
(Tel 0870 0000 303, www.baa .co.uk/stansted)
London's newest airport is 35 miles northeast of central London, so rail is much faster than road. Stansted Express to Liverpool Street Station takes 42 minutes, and runs every 30 minutes between 6 a.m. and 11:59 p.m. By road, a taxi costs more than £50 ($75).

BY TRAIN OR BUS

Eurostar trains (Tel 0870 160 6600, www.eurostar.com) arrive at Waterloo International from Paris, Disneyland Paris, Brussels, and Lille.

National trains (Tel 08457-484950, www.virgintrains.co.uk, www.nationalrail.co.uk) arrive at Charing Cross, Euston, King's Cross, Liverpool Street, Paddington, Victoria, and Waterloo Stations.

Long-distance bus services arrive at Victoria Coach Station (Tel 0870 580 8080, www.go-by-coach.com). National Express (Tel 0990-808080) is Britain's biggest company, Eurolines (Tel 01582-404511) travels to the Continent.

GETTING AROUND

PUBLIC TRANSPORTATION

Learning to enjoy London's public transportation system is the first step to enjoying exploring the capital. Taxis, although fun, are just one transportation experience, and when the traffic snarls the bills mount up very quickly. Taking an Underground train or a bus, as all Londoners do, saves time and can be great fun; and just ask if you are in doubt.

BY TAXI
There are two kinds of taxi: the "black cab" and the minicab. Black cabs (some painted other colors) are a distinct shape and are restricted in numbers, and their drivers have all passed the tough "The Knowledge" exams and know their city extremely well. They also have full insurance and are reliable to use to deliver parcels. To use one, either go to a taxi stand, phone a company such as Radio Taxis (Tel 7272 0272) or Dial a Cab (Tel 7253 5000), or hail one on the street that is displaying an illuminated yellow "For Hire" sign on top. The fare rises according to distance and time;

charges rise evenings and weekends. The driver is obliged to use the straightest route to your destination unless you instruct him to do otherwise. To complain, call the Public Carriage Office (Tel 7230 1631).

Minicabs often have untrained drivers and uninsured cars. Legally they may only be booked by phone and may not be picked up on the street—it is extremely unwise to do so. A minicab company should only be used by personal recommendation. An exception is Lady Cabs (Tel 020-7254 3501), which employs only women drivers and is preferred by some single women.

BY BUS & THE TUBE
London Transport runs the Underground (also known as the tube, or subway) and most of the buses. Fares for both methods of transportation are structured according to six concentric zones—zones 1 and 2 cover most of central London. Tickets can be bought individually for each trip, but the easiest, quickest, and most economic way to buy tickets is to choose a Travelcard. A Travelcard can be used on the Underground and bus system, plus the DLR and some rail services. There are various kinds of Travelcards, including one-day (valid before 9:30 a.m.), one-day (valid after 9:30 a.m.), one-week, weekend, and family cards. Each card can be bought for some or all of the zones. Once bought, you simply use it or show it on demand.

London's bus system
There is nothing quite like rumbling through London on the upstairs front seat of a red double-deck bus, looking at the people, buildings, advertisements, and street art. To catch a bus, first find a bus stop, indicated by a pole with a red sign. This will list the bus numbers that stop there, together with their routes. On one-man buses, the ticket is bought or Travelcard shown on

GETTING AROUND/PRACTICAL ADVICE

entry. On others, the conductor comes to the passenger to sell the ticket or inspect the card.

The Tube (Underground)
This huge system of a dozen lines with about 300 stations snakes all over London and carries 2.5 million people a day. London's Tube (subway) is well lit, easy to use, and safe. First, plot your route on the Tube map. Then, buy a one-day Travelcard. Use the ticket to pass through the automatic barriers, get on the right color-coded line, and ensure you are traveling in the right direction. To change lines, follow the signs to the connecting line on the platform. Use your ticket to exit through the barriers, then keep it flat for the next journey. When in doubt, ask; Londoners get lost, too.

Docklands Light Railway (the DLR)
(Tel 7376 9700, www.dlr .co.uk)
This high-level railway runs from Bank to Tower Gateway Stations, both connected to the Tube network, and on through Docklands.

ORGANIZED SIGHTSEEING

Even the most independent traveler may find it helpful to take a tour sometimes. Bus tours give an overview of the city; walking tours open your eyes to a street's history and monuments; river tours provide a new perspective on London; and some tours simply get you into places usually closed to the public. Here is a selection; local tourist information centers will carry information on others and *Time Out* lists several in their *"Around Town"* section. Most telephone numbers provide detailed recorded information.

BUS TOURS
Big Bus Company (Tel 0800 169 1365, www.bigbus.co.uk); Original London Sightseeing Tour (Tel 8877 1722, www.the originaltour.com).

RIVER TOURS
Westminster Passenger Services Association (Tel 7930 2062) has information, as does www. tfl.gov.uk. See also pp. 52–3.

WALKING TOURS
Citisights (Tel 8806 4325, www. chr.org.uk); Historical Tours (Tel 8668 4019, www.historicalwalks oflondon.com); Original London Walks (Tel 7624 3978, www. walks.com).

TAILOR–MADE TOURS
To employ a guide with the highest qualifications, the Blue Badge, contact Tour Guides (Tel 7495 5504, www.tourguides .co.uk).

TOURS FROM THE AIR
Adventure Balloons (Tel 01252 844222, www.adventureballoons .co.uk); Cabair Helicopters (Tel 020-8953 4411).

SPECIALIST TOURS
The many available include Super Tours of Westminster Abbey and St. Paul's Cathedral, tours of the Royal National Theatre, tours of special houses such as Linley Sambourne House or Dennis Severs's House

THE LONDON PASS
A bargain way of visiting several fee-paying attractions (Tel 0870 242 9988, www.londonpass.com).

PRACTICAL ADVICE

ELECTRICITY

The supply is 230V, with a permitted range of 216.2–253V, and 50 cycles per second (kHz). Plugs are three-pin. U.S. appliances need a voltage transformer and an adapter.

MONEY MATTERS

Sterling currency is used throughout Britain: 100 pence make 1 pound. Coins are in denominations of 1p, 2p, 5p, 10p, 20p, 50p, £1, and £2. Notes are in £5, £10, £20 and £50.

WHAT'S GOING ON?

Time Out (www.timeout.com), published on Tuesdays, provides exhaustive lists of London activities, together with reliable reviews and previews. Quality newspapers include *The Times, The Financial Times, Daily Telegraph, Independent, Guardian;* London's only evening paper is the *Evening Standard,* daily Monday to Friday. It has a large entertainment section. See also websites, p. 263.

OPENING HOURS

Major attractions are open seven days a week, though some open late on Sunday. Shops are open six days a week, with some open on Sunday. Late night shopping takes place on Wednesday (Knightsbridge) and Thursday (Oxford Street, Regent Street, and Covent Garden). Banks are open Monday to Friday from 9:30 a.m. to 5 p.m. Some branches also open 9:30 a.m. to 3.30 p.m. on Saturday. Twenty-four-hour Chequepoint branches include 548 Oxford Street and 23 Earls Court Road. Identification is essential when cashing traveler's checks.

POST OFFICES

Stamps can be bought at post offices and some newsstands and shops; Trafalgar Square Post Office, on William IV Street, stays open late. Mail boxes are red.

PUBLIC HOLIDAYS

January 1, Good Friday, Easter Monday, first Monday in May, last Monday in May, last Monday in August, December 25 and 26.

REST ROOMS

Otherwise known as toilets, lavatories, W.C.s (from water closet), conveniences, ladies, and gents. If the public rest rooms are unsavory, slip into the nearest large department store or hotel. In theaters, there are often few rest rooms and long interval lines for them.

TELEPHONES

To make a local call within London, either use coins or buy a BT phonecard from a newsstand or other shop. Omit the code (020) and just dial the 8-digit number. Outside London numbers have a 5-digit code and a 6-figure number. Evenly spaced beeps mean the number is busy; a solid sound means the number is unobtainable.

To make an international call, an international, pre-paid phonecard is the best value, on sale at newsstands and other shops. Dial 00, then the country code, then the number. Before using the phone in your hotel room, check the mark-up charges with the receptionist, including for toll-free phone numbers; they may be substantial.
Directory assistance:
   192 (British numbers)
   153 (international numbers)
Operator help: 100

TIME DIFFERENCES

GMT (Greenwich mean time) is standard time; BST (British summer time) is one hour ahead of GMT and runs from late March to late October. GMT is five hours ahead of eastern U.S. standard time.

TIPPING & LOCAL CUSTOMS

In restaurants, check if the service charge has already been added; if not, the usual tip is ten percent. Smoking cigars is rarely considered polite. In pubs and bars there is no tipping except for table service.

In theaters, cinemas, and concert halls, there is no tipping. Audiences do not usually give standing ovations.
Taxi drivers expect a ten

percent tip, more if they help with luggage, or have to wait.

TOURIST INFO

IN LONDON
Britain & London Visitor Centre (www.visitbritain.com and the excellent www.visit london.com) The walk-in office is at No.1 Regent Street, with information desks, a hotels and reservations desk, a theater reservation service, and a bureau de change.

BRITISH TOURIST AUTHORITY OFFICES ABROAD
In the United States
Chicago 625 N. Michigan Ave., Suite 1010, IL 60611–1977, Tel 312/787-0464, Fax 312/787-9641
Los Angeles 10880 Wilshire Blvd., Suite 570, CA 90024, Tel 310/470-2782, Fax 310/470-8549
New York 551 Fifth Ave., Suite 701, NY 10176–0799, Tel 212/986-2266, Fax 212/986-1188

In Canada
Toronto 5915 Airport Road, Suite 120, Mississauga L4V 1T1 Ontario, Tel 905/405-1720, Fax 905/405-8490.

USEFUL WEBSITES

www.americanexpress.com
www.bbc.co.uk/london
for news, travel, weather, entertainment, and sports
www.firstcalltickets.com
for tickets to shows and events
www.london.gov.uk
the Greater London Authority
www.londonnet.co.uk
information on restaurants, bars, nightlife, and more
www.londontown.com
basic information on top sights, hotels, etc.
www.londontransport.co.uk
for all transport from buses and DLR to river services, plus journey planning help
www.officiallondon theatre.co.uk
the nonprofit organization gives on-the-day information on half-price theater tickets; you must buy them in person

www.pubs.com
www.riverthames.co.uk
places and events along the river
www.s-h-systems.co.uk/ tourism/ london
easy-to-access A-Z London info
www.streetmap.co.uk
plan your day, then print out the street plan
www.thetube.com
London Tube (Underground)
www.ticket-master.co.uk
for tickets to shows and events
www.24hourmuseum.co.uk
includes most London museum information
www.trailfinders.co.uk
for all travel booking
www.timeout.com
for all London events
www.uktravel.com
click on a Tube station to be shown nearby attractions
www.visitbritain.com
the British Tourist Board
www.visitlondon.com
the London Tourist Board

VISITORS WITH DISABILITIES

Facilities are generally good for visitors with disabilities. For extra help, contact Artsline, 54 Charlton Street, NW1 (Tel 7388 2227, www.artsline.org.uk) for advice on access to arts and entertainment venues, and for their publication, *Disability Arts in London.* RADAR (the Royal Society for Disability and Rehabilitation) provides information on tour operators that cater specifically to disabled travelers (Tel 7250 3222, www.radar.org.uk).

EMERGENCIES

POLICE, FIRE, & AMBULANCE

To summon any of these services, dial 999 from any telephone, free of charge. It is important that you tell the emergency services operator the address where the incident has taken place and the nearest landmark, crossroads, or house number; also, precisely where you are. Stay by the telephone until the service arrives.

LOST PROPERTY

Always inform the police, to validate insurance claims. Report a lost passport to your embassy (and always carry a separate photocopy of the information pages so another can be prepared quickly).

On a Tube train: London Transport Lost Property Office, 200 Baker Street, NW1, Tel 7486 2496; fill in a lost property form at any Under-ground station.
On a bus: Tel 7222 1234 and ask for the depot at either end of the bus number's route.
In a taxi: Taxi Lost Property, 15 Penton Street, N1, Tel 7918 2000. Always engaged but the correct number!

Lost credit cards

Report any loss immediately to the credit card company, so credit can be stopped, and to the local police station; also telephone your bank. To find your credit card company's local 24-hour number, dial 192, Directory Enquiries.

HEALTH PRECAUTIONS

If you need a doctor or dentist, ask your hotel reception for advice. If the problem is minor, go to the nearest chemist and speak to the pharmacist. To claim insurance, keep receipts for all treatments and medicines. To call an ambulance, dial 999 (see Emergencies, p. 239).

National Health Service (N.H.S.) hospitals

Hospitals with 24-hour emergency departments include: University College Hospital, Gower Street (entrance in Grafton Way), WC1, Tel 7387 9300.
Chelsea and Westminster Hospital, 369 Fulham Road, SW10, Tel 8746 8000.

Private hospitals (no emergency unit) include the

Cromwell Hospital, Cromwell Road, SW5, Tel 7460 2000.

Other facilities

Great Chapel Street Medical Centre (13 Great Chapel Street, W1, Tel 7437 9360) is an N.H.S. surgery (doctor's office) open to all, but patients without the N.H.S. reciprocal agreement must pay.
For an optician and on-site workshop, try Dolland and Aitchison, 229–31 Regent Street, W1, Tel 7499 8777. Those with more serious eye problems should seek help at Moorfields Eye Hospital, City Road, EC1, Tel 7253 3411.
For homeopathic practitioners and chemists, contact the British Homeopathic Association, 27A Devonshire Street, W1, Tel 7935 2163.

Chemists (Pharmacies)

Many drugs freely available in the U.S. cannot be bought over the counter in the U.K. Be sure to bring sufficient supplies of medicines from home. If more are needed, take the wrapping with full printed description of its contents to the chemist for advice on buying the nearest equivalent.
Chemists open from 9 a.m. until midnight include Bliss Chemist, 5 Marble Arch, W1, Tel 7723 6116.

SENSIBLE PRECAUTIONS

Keep valuables locked in the hotel safe. Note, and preferably photocopy, any important information on passports, tickets, and credit cards, and keep this information in a separate place.
Keep only a small amount of money with you; put the rest in the hotel safe. Keep documents and money in a closed bag when you carry them. Do not leave your bag unattended, or on the floor of a restaurant, theater, or cinema. Do not travel alone at night, unless in a "black cab" or along well-lit streets and in buses with other people. Avoid parks after dark.

Canadian High Commission, Macdonald House, 1 Grosvenor Square, W1, Tel 7258 6600.
Embassy of the United States of America, Grosvenor Square, W1, Tel 7499 9000.

Many films have been set in London, and, in the heyday of the British cinema, London had over 100 film studios. They are often shown on television. Old ones to catch include *The Lady Killers, Passport to Pimlico, My Fair Lady, Oliver,* and *Alfie;* more recent ones include *The Madness of King George* and *Richard III.*
Diaries and letters written in London abound, ranging from well-known ones by Samuel Pepys and Dr. Johnson to James Boswell, Virginia Woolf, Harold Nicolson, Cecil Beaton, and many others. Some are repub-lished in paperback; others are quoted in literary anthologies. Novels, poems, and plays set in London range from the opening of Chaucer's *Canterbury Tales* through Shakespeare's plays, Wordsworth's poems and novels by Thackeray, Dickens, and Conan Doyle (Sherlock Holmes stories) to the more recent poems by Sir John Betjeman, and Peter Ackroyd's historical novels. A wide selection is always in print, and a glance at the plot summary will inform you of the historical period and, sometimes, the area of London where the action is set.
Histories of London have been written at various times during the city's long life. John Stow's is 16th century; Christopher Hibbert's is 20th century. Good bookshops abound in London. Among them, Daunt Books for Travellers, 83 Marylebone High Street, W1, Tel 7224 2295, and Hatchards, 187 Piccadilly, W1, Tel 7439 9921. Both take worldwide telephone orders.

HOTELS & RESTAURANTS

HOTELS

Location is the key to a successful London visit. There are hotels of every level of luxury, from simple to exotic, but their location is paramount: London is very big and hours can be wasted moving around. It is wise to work out where you will be spending your days and evenings, then choose a well placed hotel that suits your lifestyle, dreams, and budget.

London's hotels have undergone a revolution, especially at the top end. The emphasis is on design-led hotels, such as One Aldwych, The Hempel, and the Metropolitan Hotel with its fashionable Met Bar. Myhotel, which opened in late 1998, was Terence Conran's first hotel, planned with a Feng Shui expert as an "oasis of calm." Subsequently, he lavishly transformed the Great Eastern Hotel in the City. Ian Schrager and Phillipe Starck have brought New York panache and success to London with four new hotels, including the Sanderson and St. Martin's Lane.

Boutique hotels have long been established in South Kensington with such successes as Five Sumner Place and the sumptuous Blakes. Now the choice has spread right across central London—to Hazlitt's in Soho, Charlotte Street in Fitzrovia, the Rookery in Clerkenwell, and Threadneedles in the heart of the City.

More traditional luxury hotels, such as the Ritz, Savoy, Berkeley, Claridge's and Dorchester, are now joined by the Mandarin Oriental group's totally over-hauled Hyde Park Hotel and Le Meridien Waldorf. Other Meridien hotels include the Piccadilly and the Grosvenor House. Indeed, lavish refurbishments abound at all levels, while newly built hotels spanning all price brackets open monthly.

It is, nevertheless, important to make reservations well ahead. London hotels are some of the world's most expensive, so when reserving, ask about special deals that are offered. These may include weekends or the quiet month of February—you may find a better deal at a deluxe hotel than at a popular business hotel. New hotels often offer discounts while they deal with teething troubles. Some hotels have economic family rooms; others, such as the new Orion Trafalgar Square, have a kitchen in each room. When reserving you may be asked for a deposit or for your credit card number. Check the room rate carefully: It should include the hefty 17.5 percent VAT, but occasionally prices are given without this.

If anything goes wrong, talk to the duty manager. If the problem is not solved, speak to the manager, then put it in writing.

The London Tourist Board has a hotel information and reservation section on its website (www.visitlondon.com) and publishes the reliable booklet "Where to Stay & What to Do." It also handles serious complaints.

Some of the nicest hotels are in old buildings. If you have particular needs in comfort, services, or anything else, check that your hotel can provide them.

Visitors with disabilities can obtain information on suitable places to stay from the Holiday Care, 2nd floor, Imperial Buildings, Victoria Road, Horley, Surrey, Tel 0845-124 9971, www.holidaycare.org.uk.

APARTMENTS

Those visiting for longer periods may wish to rent a serviced apartment on a weekly basis. Rates can be very competitive even in the city center. Agencies specializing in vacation rentals include **Aston's,** Tel 7590 6000, Fax 7590 6060, www.astons-apartments.com, **The King's Wardrobe,** 6 Wardrobe Place, Center Lance, EC4 (Tel 7792 2222, www.bridgestreet.com) has modest, well-priced apartments right near St. Paul's Cathedral. **No. 5 Maddox Street,** 5 Maddox Street, W1 (Tel 7647 0200, wwwliving-rooms.co.uk) has contemporary suites equipped with workstations, balconies, and minimalist decor. **Orion Trafalgar Square,** 18–21 Northumberland Avenue, WC2 (Tel 7766 3701) has 189 simple studios and one-and two-bedroom apartments in an unbeatable location.

RESTAURANTS

London's food revolution began in the 1980s and continues today. In London, if you know where to go, you can find impressive cooking of almost every cuisine in the world, from Thai to modern Californian, from Indian to north Italian. The result is that the London restaurant world spins fast in an upward spiral. Chefs are the stars, emerging from the shadow of their mentors to open strings of their own restaurants, to write columns for newspapers, publish cookbooks, and star in television series. A sous-chef of a major restaurant in January opens his own restaurant in March, a second, off-beat brasserie in June, and publishes his first book by the autumn. Sommeliers and front-of-house managers can also determine the success of a restaurant. High-fashion restaurants, mentioned in gossip columns and reviewed repeatedly, need to be reserved well in advance; even then, tables will be kept for regular favored clients. Certain tables may be unacceptable, such as ones beside the kitchen, near the rest rooms, or by the drafty door; do not hesitate to refuse these. In summer, it requires luck or an early arrival to win a prized outdoor table on the sidewalk or in restaurant back gardens.

Prices are often high, so it is important to check such details as the existence of a cover charge per person. The service charge may or may not be included—if not, ten percent should be added for a satisfactory meal, slightly more for exceptional service. If in doubt, ask. To eat some of London's finest food at a reasonable price, there is usually a good value set menu at lunchtime. As for the wine lists, if the restaurant is any good, its wine buyer will have chosen a good house wine. Tap water, quite safe to drink in London, is so unfashionable that it must be ordered specifically; otherwise, overpriced bottles of exotic waters are delivered.

Few restaurants have a dress code, but in better restaurants, it is usual to dress up in keeping with glamorous surroundings and skillfully prepared food. Traditional restaurants such as the Savoy expect a jacket and tie. Smoking rules are strictly adhered to: Customers can usually select a smoking or non-smoking table. It is considered rude to smoke a cigar or pipe in a restaurant, or to use a mobile phone at the table.

The increasing number of fashionable bars in central London demand nice dress, too. Some are in the deluxe hotels; others at the front of restaurants. Pubs, on the other hand, tolerate all forms of dress, allow smoking, in some if not all bars, and often serve good food. A handful are included in the following selection.

To help give the maximum idea of the explosion of richness in London's restaurant, bar, and pub scene, remarkable hotel restaurants and bars are noted within the hotel entry. Beware: Some well-known chefs move locations regularly; if you want to enjoy a specific chef's creations, check he is still working on site. To be sure of a table at almost any of the restaurants listed below, a reservation is essential. If you have particular needs in cuisine or comfort, check that your chosen resurant can provide them.

Apart from restaurants within hotels, closures for public holidays, Christmas, New Year's, and Easter may vary from year to year, so it is best to check. It is always best to reserve a table and specify smoking or non-smoking. Hotels and restaurants have been organized by price, then in alphabetical order.

Abbreviations:
L = lunch
D = dinner
AE=American Express,
DC=Diners Club,
MC=MasterCard, V=Visa

THE THAMES

There is a limited number of rooms with good Thames views at these north bank choices, so reservations are essential. (For a wider choice of Thames views, see the South Bank, p. 259.) The riverside pubs are some of the best in London, and many serve excellent food; those listed here are near the main sights to visit.

HOTEL

🏨 THE SAVOY
🍴 $$$$$
STRAND
WC2
TEL 7836 4343
FAX 7240 6040
www.savoygroup.co.uk
Ideal stylish location for mixing City with West End. Bathrooms have thunderstorm showers, and some rooms have river views. American Bar, Pavilion Room teas, and River Room restaurant all top notch.
🛈 228 🛏 150 🚇 Charing Cross 🅿 65 ⊟ ⊡ ⊞
🛗 🐾 All major cards

RESTAURANTS

🍴 PUTNEY BRIDGE
$$$
THE EMBANKMENT
SW15 1LB
TEL 8780 1811
Modern European cooking (outstanding risotto) is served in Trevor Gulliver's second restaurant (his first was the St. John in Clerkenwell). Dramatically modern building where all tables enjoy river views.
🛏 148 🚇 Putney Bridge
🅿 ⊡ 🐾 All major cards

🍴 TATE BRITAIN RESTAURANT
$$$
TATE BRITAIN
MILLBANK
SW1
TEL 7887 8877
www.tate.org.uk
There are no river views in this basement, but Rex Whistler's mural covers the walls, while an exceptionally fine wine list complements British food such as herb-

baked cod.
🚇 Pimlico 🕐 Closed D,
all Sun.

🍴 TATE MODERN, LEVEL 7 CAFÉ
$$$
BANKSIDE
SE1
TEL 7401 5020
www.tate.org.uk
Worth dressing up to enjoy the breathtaking views of the City, the buzzy bar, and the good food; book to avoid standing in line.
🚇 Southwark/London Bridge

🍴 TATE MODERN, LEVEL 2 CAFÉ
$$
BANKSIDE
SE1
TEL 7401 5014
www.tate.org.uk
This sleek but modest and informal ground floor Thameside café is ideal for simple, robust food pre- or post- museum exploration.
🚇 Southwark/
London Bridge 🕐 Closed Sun.–Thurs. dinner

WATERSIDE PUBS
(in order from west to east)

🍴 THE DOVE
$
19 UPPER MALL
W6
TEL 8748 5405
Short walk from Chiswick House along a pretty towpath. Simple, 300-year-old pub, good atmosphere, plenty of rowing to watch while eating traditional bread and cheese or a Thai dish.
🚇 Hammersmith 🚯 All major cards

🍴 THE BULL'S HEAD
$
STRAND-ON-THE-GREEN
KEW
W4
TEL 8994 1204
A variety of beers on a pretty towpath, ideal before or after Kew Gardens. Food served

noon to 10 p.m. daily.
🚇 Kew Gardens/ Gunnersbury Park 🚯 All major cards

🍴 LONDON APPRENTICE
$
CHURCH ST.
ISLEWORTH
TW7
TEL 8560 1915
A few yards from the car entrance to Syon House. Good food and notable beers.
🚇 Hounslow East (then bus H37) 🚯 All major cards

🍴 TOWN OF RAMSGATE
$
62 WAPPING HIGH ST.
E1
TEL 7264 0001
Traditional, possibly smugglers', pub a short walk from the Tower of London.
🚇 Wapping 🚯 All major cards

🍴 THE BARLEY MOW
$
BY LIMEHOUSE BASIN
E14
TEL 8265 8931
Broad views of the widening Thames from the many terrace tables.
🚇 Limehouse (DLR) 🚯 All major cards

🍴 THE CUTTY SARK
$
BALLAST QUAY
LASSELL ST.
SE10
TEL 8858 3146
Delightful old village pub with open fire serving warming soups, whitebait, ribs, and steaks. Outside benches.
🚇 Greenwich (DLR)
🚢 to Greenwich (5-minute walk along towpath) 🚯 All major cards

THE CITY, CLERKENWELL, & ISLINGTON
Restaurants in the City of London are booming, and a 5- to 10-minute taxi ride reaches the impressive restaurants of Clerkenwell and Islington—useful for post-theater meals, too.

HOTELS

🏨 GREAT EASTERN
$$$$$
LIVERPOOL ST.
EC2
TEL 7618 5000
FAX 7618 5001
www.great-eastern-hotel.co.uk
Conran has taken a grand Victorian railway station and stylishly transformed it into a modern City hotel with all appointments. Good bars.
🚇 Liverpool Street

🏨 ROOKERY
$$$$
PETER'S LANE, COWCROSS ST.
EC1
TEL 7336 0931
FAX 7336 0932
www.rookeryhotel.com
Under the same management as the successful Hazlitt's (q.v.), simple but tasteful rooms in Georgian rowhouses, and one stunning suite.
🛏 33 🚇 Farringdon

🏨 THREADNEEDLES
$$$$
5 THREADNEEDLE ST., EC2
TEL 7657 8080
FAX 7657 8100
www.etontownhouse.com
The City's first boutique hotel is inside a fine former Midland Bank building, equipped with plasma TVs and other gadgets.
🚇 Bank

RESTAURANTS

🍴 CITY RHODES
$$$$$
1 NEW STREET SQUARE
EC4
TEL 7583 1313
The capacious dining room, neither romantic nor cozy, is best experienced at lunchtime. But Gary Rhodes's modern British food is consistently almost faultless; try whatever fish is on offer, or new season lamb.
🚇 Chancery Lane
🕐 Closed Sat and Sun D

HOTELS & RESTAURANTS

🍴 CLUB GASCON

$$$$
57 WEST SMITHFIELD
EC1
TEL 7796 0600
Diners select three—four if
appetites are big—
scrupulously prepared
Gascony dishes made with
the best ingredients; fois gras
is almost obligatory.
🚇 Barbican/Farringdon
🕐 Closed Sat L, Sun L & D

🍴 LOLA'S

$$$$
359 UPPER ST.
N1
TEL 7359 1932
Enjoy Hywel Jones's much-
praised classy, modern dishes
with superb wines sourced by
the owner, Morfudd Richards.
🪑 80 🚇 Angel 🔄 All
major cards

🍴 TATSUSO

$$$$
32 BROADGATE CIRCLE
EC1
TEL 7638 5863
One of London's best
Japanese restaurants, with
lunchtime entertainment in
the Circle. Pricey if you are
not careful. Sushi bar and
Teppan-yaki tables recom-
mended, as is the *dobin
mushi soup.*
🪑 140 🚇 Liverpool Street
🕐 Closed Sat. & Sun. 🔄
🔄 All major cards

🍴 CAFÉ DU MARCHÉ

$$$
CHARTERHOUSE MEWS
CHARTERHOUSE SQUARE
EC1
TEL 7608 1609
French brasserie dishes
include *daube de boeuf* and
tarte aux fruits in this very
relaxed, informal escape from
city pressures.
🪑 60 🚇 Barbican
🕐 Closed Sat. L, Sun. 🔄 All
major cards

🍴 FREDERICK'S

$$$
CAMDEN PASSAGE
N1
TEL 7359 2888
www.fredericks.co.uk
One of Islington's oldest
restaurants, serving modern
European food in a double
height conservatory. Confit of
lamb, roast salmon, and beef
wellington are all good, and
plenty of vegetarian dishes.
🪑 130 🚇 Angel 🕐 Closed
Sun. 🔄 🔄 All major cards

🍴 MORO

$$$
34–36 EXMOUTH MARKET
EC1
TEL 7833 8336
Husband and wife Sam and
Sam Clark cook innovative
dishes, many influenced by
Spain. Try *cecina* (dry-cured
beef) with artichokes and
Spanish almond cake.
🪑 75 🚇 Farringdon
🕐 Closed Sat. L & Sun. 🔄
🔄 All major cards

SOMETHING SPECIAL

🍴 ST. JOHN

In his fashionably spare
restaurant beside Smithfield
meat market, Fergus
Henderson has revived British
dishes that most British
people had forgotten about.
The emphasis is on meat:
plenty of offal, venison, pork,
and more usual meats; plus
homemade breads. Wickedly
delicious old-fashioned
puddings and English cheeses.
$$$
26 ST JOHN ST., EC1
TEL 7251 0848
www.stjohnrestaurant. co.uk
🕐 Closed Sat. L, Sun.

🍴 RESTAURANT TWENTYFOUR

$$$
TOWER 42 OLD BROAD ST.
EC2
TEL 7877 7703/2424
www.twenty-four.co.uk

PRICES

HOTELS
An indication of the cost
of a double room without
breakfast is given by **$** signs.
$$$$$ Over $280
$$$$ $200–$280
$$$ $120–$200
$$ $80–$120
$ Under $80

RESTAURANTS
An indication of the cost of a
three-course dinner without
drinks is given by **$** signs.
$$$$$ Over $80
$$$$ $50–$80
$$$ $35–$50
$$ $20–$35
$ Under $20

You can enjoy views of Tower
Bridge and the Millennium
Dome from this modern
restaurant located in the
heart of the city. Try the
breast of cannette duck with
red onion Tatin.
🪑 70 🚇 Bank/Liverpool
Street 🕐 Closed Sat. & Sun.
🔄 🔄 All major cards

🍴 CICADA

$$
132–136 ST JOHN ST.
EC1
TEL 7608 1550
www.cicada.nu
Large, modern interior with
central bar and friendly
atmosphere for enjoying all
kinds of Asian food, including
seared salmon and crab and
ginger dumplings.
🪑 70 🚇 Farringdon
🕐 Closed Sat. L & Sun. 🔄
🔄 All major cards

🍴 THE EAGLE

$$
159 FARRINGDON RD.
EC1
TEL 7837 1353
Jolly atmosphere in this
converted pub with scrubbed
floors. The short menu
written on a blackboard
might include wholesome

Italian sausages with butter beans or grilled swordfish. ⊟ 55 🚇 Farringdon 🅂 All major cards

🍴 SMITHS OF SMITHFIELD
$$
66-77 CHARTERHOUSE S.
EC1
TEL 7251 7950
www.smithsofsmithfield.co.uk
Head up past the noisy dining room to the top (fourth) floor for peace, splendid views across Smithfield to St. Paul's, and good food: tender steaks and desserts such as fruit-filled summer pudding and "British cheese from Neal's Yard with oatcakes."
🚇 Farringdon
🕒 Closed Sat L

🍴 THOMAS'S
$$
13-15 LEADENHALL MARKET
EC3
TEL 7626 3659
City food can be disappointing and pricey; here is good-value food with good service in a relaxed atmosphere
🚇 Monument/Bank
🕒 Closed Sat & Sun L; all D

WESTMINSTER, ST. JAMES'S, MAYFAIR, & MARYLEBONE

At the heart of London, the capital's grandest hotels have exceptional restaurants and jolly bars, which make excellent rendezvous spots.

HOTELS

🏨 ATHENAEUM
$$$$$
116 PICCADILLY, W1
TEL 7499 3464
FAX 7493 1860
www.athenaeumhotel.com
The elegant comfort and high level of service draw guests back to Athenaeum repeatedly, as do Bullochs restaurant, Windsor Lounge teas, and the full spa. Higher rooms have park views.

ⓘ 157 ⊟ 50 🚇 Hyde Park ⊟ 🅂 🇾 🅂 All major cards

🏨 BROWN'S
$$$$$
ALBEMARLE ST.
W1
TEL 7493 6020
FAX 7493 9381
www.brownshotel.com
Traditional English elegance in the heart of old Mayfair, just off Bond Street. Roaring fires, and creaking floorboards; an echo of Mayfair mansions.
ⓘ 118 🚇 Green Park ⊟ 🅂 All major cards

SOMETHING SPECIAL

🏨 CLARIDGE'S
The Queen's state guests move here after Buckingham Palace. Huge corner suites. Glorious art deco public rooms include the grand dining room (Anglo-French), and the tea is the best in town.
$$$$$
BROOK ST., W1
7629 8860
FAX 7499 2210
www.savoy-group.com
ⓘ 197 ⊟ 100 🚇 Bond Street ⊟ 🅂 🇾 🅂 All major cards

🏨 THE CONNAUGHT
$$$$$
CARLOS PLACE
W1
TEL 7499 7070
FAX 7495 3262
www.savoy-group.co.uk
Considered the most discreet of London hotels, where the famous can remain anonymous. Guests and visitors, however, can use the tiny back bar, the paneled restaurant, and the intimate Green Room, offering excellent English and French cuisine.
ⓘ 90 ⊟ 70 restaurant, 30 Green Room 🚇 Bond Street ⊟ 🅂 🅂 All major cards

🏨 THE DORCHESTER
$$$$$
PARK LANE
W1
TEL 7629 8888
FAX 7409 0114
www.dorchesterhotel.com
Lavishly refurbished, including the rooftop Oliver Messel rooms. Guests and visitors can enjoy fine Promenade teas, the zippy bar, and two restaurants: the traditional Grill and opulent Oriental (Cantonese).
ⓘ 248 ⊟ 81 Grill, 51 Oriental Ⓟ 21 🚇 Hyde Park Corner ⊟ 🅂 🇾 🅂 All major cards

🏨 FOUR SEASONS
$$$$$
HAMILTON PLACE
PARK LANE
W1
TEL 7499 0888
FAX 7493 6629
www.fourseasons.com
Modern, intelligently designed hotel with excellently appointed rooms, especially Conservatory rooms; some of London's top chefs have worked in the Four Seasons restaurant (modern European).
ⓘ 220 ⊟ 90 Ⓟ 55 🚇 Hyde Park Corner ⊟ 🅂 🇾 🅂 All major cards

🏨 LANDMARK HOTEL
$$$$$
222 MARYLEBONE RD.
NW1
TEL 7631 8000
FAX 7631 8080
www.landmarklondon.co.uk
The spectacular Winter Garden, a palm court that operates all day, sets the tone for this converted grand late Victorian building. Large bedrooms with good bathrooms.
ⓘ 299 Ⓟ 90 🚇 Marylebone ⊟ 🅂 🇪 🇾 🅂 All major cards

🏨 LE MERIDIEN
🍴 **PICCADILLY**
$$$$$
21 PICCADILLY
W1
TEL 7734 8000

FAX 7437 3574
www.lemeridien.com
Located at the crossroads of St. James's, Mayfair, and theaterland. Guests enjoy fine rooms, a splendid health club and spa, and Robert Reid's stunning food in Marco Pierre White's Oak Room.
[i] 267 [seats] 80 [tube] Piccadilly Circus [elevator] [card] [card] [card]
[card] All major cards

SOMETHING SPECIAL

THE METROPOLITAN
Reopened in February 1997, The Metropolitan instantly became London's hottest modern hotel. Getting a reservation at its Nobu restaurant (Japanese) is hard; gaining entry to its Met Bar harder.
$$$$$
19 OLD PARK LANE, W1
TEL 7447 1000
www.metropolitan.co.uk
[i] 155 [tube] Hyde Park Corner [P] [elevator] [card] [card]
[card] All major cards [seats] 120
[closed] Restaurant closed Sat. L, Sun. L

THE RITZ
$$$$$
150 PICCADILLY
W1V
TEL 7493 8181
FAX 7493 2687
www.theritzhotel.co.uk
Exquisite hotel overlooking Green Park, whose painted and gilded dining room is London's most beautiful. Tea is disappointing but the bar is a promenade for the stylish.
[i] 131 [seats] 120 [tube] Green Park [elevator] [card] [card] [card] All major cards

THE STAFFORD
$$$$$
16–18 ST. JAMES'S PLACE
SW1
TEL 7493 0111
FAX 7493 7121

www.thestaffordhotel.co.uk
One of London's most luxurious small hotels, tucked down an alley off St. James's Street. Delightful dining room, fine wines stored in 350-year-old cellars.
[i] 81 [seats] 42 [tube] Green Park [elevator] [card] Nearby [elevator]
[card] All major cards

TRAFALGAR
$$$$$
2 SPRING GARDENS
W1
TEL 7870 2900
FAX 7870 2911
www.thetrafalgar.hilton.com
Designed to attract younger guests, this life-style hotel has sharp service, good design, and the popular Rockwell Bar and Jago restaurant.
[tube] Charing Cross

DURRANTS
$$$
GEORGE ST.
W1
TEL 7935 8131
www.durrantshotel.co.uk
The hotel opened when its Georgian terrace was quite new, in 1790, and descendants of that family maintain its homely tone today.
[tube] Bond Street

RESTAURANTS

LE GAVROCHE
$$$$$
43 UPPER BROOK ST.
W1Y 1PF
TEL 7408 0881
legavroche.co.uk
Calm decor, perfect service, and an extensive wine list form the backdrop for Michel Roux's theater, which has been running for over 25 years. Perfect French dishes include *darne de boeuf à l'ancienne*.
[seats] 60 [tube] Marble Arch
[closed] Closed Sat. & Sun. [card]
[card] All major cards

PETRUS
$$$$$
33 ST. JAMES'S ST.

SW1
TEL 7930 4272
www.petrus-restaurant.com
For people serious about their French food. Ignore the high prices and the chilly formal atmosphere to indulge in Marcus Wareing's superb creations and a wine list to match.
[tube] Green Park/St. James's Park [closed] Closed Sat. L, Sun. L & D

AL SAN VICENZO
$$$$
30 CONNAUGHT ST.
W2
TEL 7262 9623
Customers return to Elaine and Vincenzo Borgonzolo's well-established restaurant for Vincenzo's goose breast with *mostarda di Cremona*, haunch of venison with quince sauce, and deep-fried eels.
[seats] 24 [tube] Marble Arch
[closed] Closed Sat. L, Sun.
[card] All major cards

BENARES
$$$$
12 BERKELEY HOUSE, BERKELEY SQUARE, W1
TEL 7627 8886
www.benaresrestaurant.com
Atur Kocchar, who made Tamarind (q.v.) to special, focuses on the dishes of his native area of India, the ancient city of Benares and its surrounding area.
[tube] Green Park/Bond Street

LE CAPRICE
$$$$
ARLINGTON ST.
SW1
TEL 7629 2239
This and The Ivy (see p. 248, tables even more of a premium) are run with supreme efficiency by one team. Atmosphere is club like, with chic customers greeting each other over champagne and *risotto nero* or baked fish, all fashionably modern. European.
[seats] 80 [tube] Green Park
[card] All major cards

KEY [hotel] Hotel [restaurant] Restaurant [i] No. of guest rooms [seats] No. of seats [tube] Tube/rail [closed] Closed [elevator] Elevator

🏨 GORING HOTEL
$$$$
15 BEESTON PLACE,
GROSVENOR GARDENS
SW1
TEL 7396 9000
www.goringhotel.co.uk
The place to indulge in British tradition that is now rare enough to make this seem like make-believe: a calm and deeply civilized setting for such treats as impeccable full English breakfast or roast grouse with all the trimmings.
🚇 Victoria

🍴 MATSURI
$$$$
15 BURY ST.
SW1
TEL 7839 1101
www.matsuri-restaurant.com
The title is Japanese for "festival." The food is theatrical but precise. Try the sushi, simple okonomi-yaki, or the full teppan-yaki experience.
🪑 133 🚇 Green Park
🕐 Closed Sun. 🅰 🅲 All major cards

🍴 MIRABELLE
$$$$
56 CURZON ST.
W1
TEL 7499 4636
www.whitestarline.org.uk
Marco Pierre White creates his classic French dishes in a glamorously romantic setting, matching his impeccable food with an impressive wine list; ideal for that very special dinner.
🚇 Hyde Park Corner/ Green Park

🍴 OLD DELHI
$$$$
48 KENDAL ST.
W2
TEL 7723 3335
One of London's finest Indian restaurants, much patronized by discerning north Indians who enjoy the rich, correctly cooked Mughal and Persian dishes such as lamb cooked with whole baby limes.

🪑 56 🚇 Bayswater/Marble Arch 🅰 🅲 All major cards

🍴 LA PORTE DES INDES
$$$$
32 BRYANSTON ST.
W1
TEL 7224 0055
www.la-porte-des-indes.com
Following a success in Brussels (hence the French), this extravagantly decorated, large and beautiful restaurant serves very high quality, if pricey, Indian food.
🪑 350 🚇 Marble Arch
🕐 Closed Sat. L 🅰 🅲 All major cards

🍴 SKETCH
$$$$
9 CONDUIT ST.
W1
TEL 0870 777 4488
www.sketch.uk.com
A dizzy combination of Mourad Mazous, founder of nearby Momo (q.v.), Parisian chef Pierre Gagnaire, and a grand Mayfair mansion decked in uncompromisingly contemporary design. Great café and dining rooms.
🚇 Oxford Circus/Piccadilly Circus 🕐 Closed: café Sun.; dining Sun., Mon.

🍴 THE SQUARE
$$$$
6–10 BRUTON ST.
MAYFAIR
W1
TEL 7495 7100
www.squarerestaurant.com
Philip Howard's modern European dishes, with a French emphasis, served in a high-ceilinged, large-windowed space. The terrine of foie gras and the guinea fowl and artichokes with cured ham are especially good.
🪑 70 🚇 Green Park
🕐 Closed Sat. L, Sun. L 🅰 🅲 All major cards

🍴 TAMARIND
$$$$
20 QUEEN ST.
W1
TEL 7629 3561

www.tamarindrestaurant.com
Serious Indian cooking. Original recipes, often gleaned from traditional Indian homes, are cooked to conserve their distinctive spices and aromas, such as chicken marinated in green chili and mustard.
🪑 95 🚇 Green Park
🕐 Closed Sat. L 🅰 🅲 All major cards

🍴 THE AVENUE
$$$
7–9 ST. JAMES'S ST.
SW1
TEL 7321 2111
www.theavenue.co.uk
David Copperfield's design, plus good value wines thanks to a partnership with Christie's, an ideal combination for modern European dishes such as coq au vin with parsley and garlic mashed potatoes.
🪑 180 🚇 Green Park
🅰 🅲 All major cards

🍴 BLANDFORD STREET
$$$
5–7 BLANDFORD ST.
W1
TEL 7486 9696
www.blandford-street.co.uk
This modern hideaway still pleases serious foodies with its original dishes (for both carnivores and vegetarians) and congenial service despite the loss of its former inspiration, Stephen Bull.
🚇 Baker Street/Bond Street
🕐 Sat. L & D, Sun. L

🍴 CAFÉ BAGATELLE
$$$
WALLACE COLLECTION,
MANCHESTER SQUARE
W1
TEL 7563 9505
www.wallacecollection.com
Laze over late breakfast, a coffee, or lunch in the covered courtyard of one of London's great mansions, now home to the Wallace Collection, which includes the best private collection of French art outside Paris.
🚇 Bond Street/Marble Arch
🕐 Closed D

HOTELS & RESTAURANTS

🍴 **CHOR BIZARRE**

$$$

16 ALBEMARLE ST.

W1

TEL 7629 9802

www.chorbizarrerestaurant.com

Despite the junk-shop setting, the Indian food is extremely controlled and good, particularly interesting home recipes from the Kashmiri owners. Try the *baghare baingan* (eggplant) and *missi roti*.

🪑 85 🚇 Green Park ♿
♿ All major cards

🍴 **THE CINNAMON CLUB**

$$$

THE OLD WESTMINSTER LIBRARY, GREAT SMITH ST.

SW1

TEL 7222 2555

www.cinnamonclub.com

Spacious late-Victorian municipal grandeur sets the tone for a stylish marriage of Western and Indian cuisine—and pricey wines; try the Rajasthani roast saddle of venison, and be adventurous with dessert.

🚇 Westminster/St. James's Park 🕐 Closed Sat. L, Sun. D

🍴 **IL VICOLO**

$$$

3 CROWN PASSAGE, KING ST.

SW1

TEL 7839 3960

Seek out this hideaway to join local St James's art dealers and Christie's experts for good value, home-style Italian food served with speed and a smile.

🚇 St. James's/Green Park
🕐 Closed Sat., Sun.

🍴 **ODIN'S**

$$$

27 DEVONSHIRE ST.

W1

TEL 7935 7296

www.langansrestaurants.co.uk

The late Peter Langan's pictures give this long-established discreet and comfortable Marylebone restaurant a particular charm; enjoy straightforward English dishes.

🚇 Baker Street 🕐 Closed Sat., Sun.

🍴 **UNION CAFÉ**

$$$

96 MARYLEBONE LANE

W1

TEL 7486 4860

www.brinkleys.com

Light, airy café serving modern European dishes that emphasize fresh ingredients gleaned from all over England; for instance, chargrilled royal bream. Breakfast also.

🚇 Bond Street 🕐 Closed Sun.

TRAFALGAR SQUARE & SOHO

HOTELS

SOMETHING SPECIAL

🏨 **HAZLITT'S**

Once the home of writer William Hazlitt (1778-1830), this gracious building is now a town-house hotel in the heart of Soho. There are antiques in the beautifully furnished rooms. Ideal for theater and museum visits. As this is a landmark hotel, there are no elevators. Minimal room service.

$$$$

6 FRITH ST., W1

TEL 7434 1771

FAX 7439 1524

www.hazlittshotel.com

ⓘ 23 🚇 Tottenham Court Road ♿ All major cards

🏨 **ST. MARTIN'S LANE**

$$$$$

45 ST. MARTIN'S LANE

WC2

TEL 0800 634 5500/7300 5500

FAX 7300 5565

www.ianschragerhotels.com

Hovering between West End theaters and Covent Garden restaurants, Philippe Starck's dramatically minimalist rooms and extensive bars attract

design-conscious clients.

🚇 Covent Garden/Leicester Square

RESTAURANTS

SOMETHING SPECIAL

🍴 **THE IVY**

Getting a table is the difficult part. Once achieved, the sharp staff ensures a memorable meal in this old Soho restaurant. Lunchtime clientele eat roast fish and irresistible puddings while enjoying Howard Hodgkins and Alan Jones art hung on the walls.

$$$$

1 WEST ST., COVENT GARDEN, WC2

TEL 7836 4751

🪑 100 🚇 Leicester Square/Covent Garden ♿
♿ All major cards

🍴 **ALASTAIR LITTLE SOHO**

$$$$

49 FRITH ST.

W1

TEL 7734 5183

In a small, bare restaurant, Alastair Little's inventive

modern European dishes include slow-roasted belly-pork and poached skate wing, and follow his "simple, simple, quality, quality" mark. Toby Gush cooks at Alaistair Little's Lancaster Road restaurant (Tel 020-7243 2220).

🔲 35 🔳 Leicester Square/ Tottenham Court Road 🕐 Closed Sat. L, Sun. 🅰 🅰 All major cards

🍴 ELENA'S AT L'ÉTOILE
$$$$
30 CHARLOTTE ST.
W1
TEL 7636 7189
www.trpplc.com
Having made her name at the Soho landmark L'Escargot (48 Greek Street, Tel 020-7437 2679), Elena Salvoni runs this century-old Soho restaurant. French food includes brill with horseradish and parsley crust.

🔲 80 🔳 Goodge Street/Tottenham Court Road 🕐 Closed Sat. L, Sun. 🅰 🅰 All major cards

🍴 PIED À TERRE
$$$$
34 CHARLOTTE ST.
W1
TEL 7636 1178
www.pied.a.terre.co.uk
Shane Osborn maintains the high standards set by Richard Neats. Serious haute-cuisine dishes include the orientally inspired quail consommé with confit quail, and braised pig's head and tongue.

🔲 40 🔳 Goodge Street 🕐 Closed Sat. L, Sun., 2 weeks at Christmas, & 2 weeks in Aug. 🅰 🅰 All major cards

🍴 QUO VADIS
$$$$
26–29 DEAN ST.
W1
TEL 7437 9585
www.whitestarline.org.uk
This Soho restaurant offers excellent service and a smart interior featuring artwork by

Marco Pierre White himself. The European menu includes old fashioned, as well as more modern dishes. Try the delicious salmon and fennel ravioli with Emmenthal glaze, teamed with a tomato sauce; and duck confit matched with pak choi, chargrilled carrots and a bitter-sweet sauce.

🔲 90 🔳 Leicester Square/ Tottenham Court Road 🕐 Closed Sat. L, Sun. L 🅰 🅰 All major cards

🍴 BERTORELLI'S
$$$
19 CHARLOTTE ST.
W1
TEL 7636 4174
www.santeonline.com
A classy, modern Italian restaurant. Maddalena Bonino's cooking for the upstairs room includes grilled squid and smoked chicken risotto.

🔳 Goodge Street/ Tottenham Court Road 🕐 Closed Sat. L, Sun.

🍴 CRIVELLI'S GARDEN
$$$
NATIONAL GALLERY,
TRAFALGAR SQUARE
WC2
TEL 7747 2869
If you need a break from the tip-top art, take a snack or a full-blown lunch overlooking Trafalgar Square; book early for the best views.

🔳 Charing Cross/Leicester Square 🕐 Closed Wed. L, Mon.–Wed. D

🍴 MON PLAISIR
$$$
21 MONMOUTH ST.
WC2
TEL 7836 7243
www.monplaisir.co.uk
A traditional, long-established French bistro. Choose from a good range of reliable main dishes, but end with the crème brûlée.

🔲 96 🔳 Covent Garden/ Leicester Square 🕐 Closed Sat. L, Sun. 🅰 All major cards

🍴 ALPHABET
$$
61–63 BEAK ST.
W1
TEL 7439 2190
www.alphabetbar.com
With an enviable reputation across London, this bar concentrates on drink, not food. The well-made cocktails and impressive, affordable wines make it very popular with Londoners.

🔳 Oxford Circus/Piccadilly 🕐 Closed Sun. 🅰 🅰 All major cards

🍴 BLUES BISTRO
$$
42–43 DEAN ST.
W1
TEL 7494 1966
www.bluesbistro.com
Sophisticated American styling, with chrome bar, friendly staff, and trendy clientele; good salads, rabbit in mustard, plaice on noodles, and key lime pie.

🔲 140 🔳 Leicester Square/Tottenham Court Road 🕐 Closed Sat. & Sun. L 🅰 🅰 All major cards

🍴 CANTON
$$
11 NEWPORT PLACE
WC2
TEL 7437 6220
Discerning Chinese come to this simple diner to pay fair prices for delicious roast duck and its fine sauces; crab and oysters are good here, too.

🔳 Leicester Square

🍴 CHUEN CHENG KU
$$
17 WARDOUR ST.
W1
TEL 7437 1398
One of the last restaurants to serve dim sum from the trolley (11 a.m.–6 p.m.). Arrive early to try fresh steamed dumplings, steamed snails, and about 30 other morsels.

🔲 500 🔳 Leicester Square/Piccadilly Circus 🅰 🅰 All major cards

HOTELS & RESTAURANTS

GOLDEN HARVEST
$$
17 LISLE ST.
WC2
TEL 7287 3822
This innovative Chinese restaurant combines traditional flavors with new ingredients, as in the many seafood dishes—pomfret, squid, carp—and lamb with mint.
120 Leicester Square All major cards

KULU KULU
$$
76 BREWER ST.
W1
TEL 7734 7316
Popular Japanese café-restaurant, patronized for its handmade sushi served on a long, narrow conveyor belt. Non-sushi dishes include *agedofu* and tempura *udon*.
26 Piccadilly Circus Closed Sun. All major cards

PIERRE VICTOIRE
$$
5 DEAN STREET, W1
TEL 7287 4582
Find hearty-sized portions of no-fuss French food and a bottle of wine enjoyed in a calm, unhurried, candlelit room; and do not miss out on the tarte au citron.
Tottenham Court Road

CAFÉ IN THE CRYPT
$
CRYPT OF ST MARTIN-IN-THE-FIELDS, TRAFALGAR SQ., WC2
TEL 7839 4342
Ideal for a cheap, cheery, and peaceful pause. Delicious wholesome food at bargain prices include cassaroles and, among the desserts, apple pie and custard.
Charing Cross/Embankment Open L daily, D Mon.–Wed. 5–7:30 p.m., Thurs. 8:30–10:30 p.m.

COVENT GARDEN TO LUDGATE HILL

A few, rather grand hotels appear in this superb location. There are many restaurants, but fewer of quality than might be expected: The area has been hit by the exit of Fleet Street's newspapers and the simultaneous rise of City restaurants to the east.

HOTELS

COVENT GARDEN
$$$$$
10 MONMOUTH ST.
WC2
TEL 7806 1000
FAX 7806 1100
www.firmdale.com
The wood-paneled drawing room and atmospheric Tiffany library, together with the individual, brightly colored decor, make this seem far from urban London's hub.
50 Covent Garden AE, MC, V

LE MERIDIEN WALDORF
$$$$$ ★★★★★
ALDWYCH
WC2
TEL 0870-400 8484
FAX 7836 7244
www.lemeridien.com
Splendid Edwardian hotel, luxuriously refurbished and maintaining a leather-chaired bar, the grand Palm Court (modern British cuisine), and popular weekend tea dances.
292 Holborn/Covent Garden Nearby All major cards

THE FIELDING HOTEL
$$
4 BROAD COURT, BOW ST.
WC2
TEL 7836 8305
FAX 7497 0064
www.the-fielding-hotel.co.uk
Quiet, simple accommodation in a pedestrian lane across from Covent Garden Opera.
Covent Garden

SOMETHING SPECIAL

ONE ALDWYCH
One of London's most dynamic contemporary renovations. Built in 1907 for the *Morning Post* newspaper, now transformed by Gordon Campbell-Gray and Mary Fox Linton into a state-of-the-art hotel. Serious art on the walls, sumptuous and extensive health spa. Indigo restaurant by restaurant bar; formal adjoining Axis restaurant.
$$$$$
1 ALDWYCH, WC2
TEL 7300 1000
FAX 7300 1001
www.onealdwych.com
105 110 AXIS, 62 INDIGO CHARING CROSS ALL MAJOR CARDSALDWYCH ALL MAJOR CARDS

RESTAURANTS

BANK ALDWYCH
$$$$
1 KINGSWAY, WC2
TEL 7234 3344
www.bankrestaurants.com
Dramatic bar, public kitchen, and buzzy, big restaurant space fill a vacated bank's corner site. Christian Delteil's modern dishes focus on fish such as smoked haddock. Good breakfasts.
200 Holborn/

SOMETHING SPECIAL

BLEEDING HEART
A little off the beaten track, but well worth seeking out. The bar, bistro, and restaurant in a warren of rooms off Holborn offer the perfect combination of good atmosphere, a wide choice of wines, and authentic French food.
$$$$
BLEEDING HEART YARD, GREVILLE ST., EC1

KEY Hotel Restaurant No. of guest rooms No. of seats Tube/rail Closed Elevator

HOTELS & RESTAURANTS

TEL 7823 7383
🚭 Farringdon 🕐 Sat., Sun.

🍴 CHRISTOPHER'S
$$$$
18 WELLINGTON ST.
WC2
TEL 7240 4222
www.christophersgrill.com
A grand former casino houses
Christopher Gilmour's
restaurant, just off Aldwych.
Quality American food in the
basement bar/café and the
beautiful upstairs dining room.
🚭 100 🚇 Covent Garden
🕐 Closed Sun. D 🆒
🆒 All major cards

🍴 J SHEEKEY
$$$$
28-32 ST. MARTIN'S COURT
WC2
TEL 7240 2565
Modern lighting and a fresh
look contrast well with the
original 1890's wood paneling,
creating an individual style.
The menu, with a strong
emphasis on seafood, also
includes a host of other
modern dishes. Try the
salmon fishcake with sautéed
spinach and sorrel sauce.
🚭 105 🚇 Leicester Square
🆒 🆒 All major cards

🍴 JOE ALLEN
$$$
13 EXETER ST.
WC2
TEL 020-7836 0651
www.joeallen.co.uk
Comfortingly American menu
served in a continuously buzzy
basement. Reliable Caesar
salad, clam chowder, ribs, and
pecan pie. American cocktails.
🚭 180 🚇 Covent Garden
🆒 🆒 AE, MC, V

🍴 THE PORTRAIT
$$$
NATIONAL PORTRAIT
GALLERY, WC2
TEL 7312 2490
Perched on top of the
renovated galleries, this is an
ideal place to pause between
portraits. Stunning London

views make up for unspecial
food.
🚇 Leicester Square
🕐 Closed Sat.–Wed. D

🍴 RULES
$$$
35 MAIDEN LANE
WC2
TEL 7836 5314
www.rules.co.uk
Established in 1798, this
traditional English restaurant is
the place to eat such dishes as
potted duck, Highland deer,
and steak, kidney, and oyster
pudding.
🚇 Covent Garden

🍴 SIMPSONS-IN-THE-STRAND
$$$
100 STRAND
WC2
TEL 7836 9112
www.savoygroup.com
Almost a caricature of a
traditional English restaurant,
Simpsons was founded in
1828 as a coffee house. A full
English breakfast is the best
meal to eat here.
🚭 350 🚇 Charing
Cross/Covent Garden
🕐 Closed 9 p.m. Sun. 🆒
🆒 All major cards

🍴 THE SEVEN STARS
$$
53 CAREY STREET, WC2
TEL 7242 8521
The splendid, ever smiling
publican Roxy sets the
atmosphere in her 1604-
foundation pub. To complete
the package, the food is great
as are the real ales.
🚇 Chancery Lane
🕐 Closed Sun.

🍴 WORLD FOOD CAFÉ
$$
1ST FLOOR, 14 NEAL'S YARD
WC2
TEL 7379 0298
www.worldfoodcafe.com
Quality vegetarian food with
the owner's photographs
hung on the walls. Try the
impressive salads, Egyptian
falafels, lemon tart, and

mango-yogurt drink.
🚭 42 🚇 Covent Garden
🕐 Closed 5.00 p.m. Mon.–
Sun. 🆒 All major cards

🍴 ZIZZI
$$
20 BOW ST.
WC2
TEL 7836 6101
www.askcentra.co.uk
In a plum location opposite
the Royal Opera House, this
is a branch of one of the few
London restaurant chains to
try hard and mostly succeed:
straightforward Italian dishes
served with a smile. All the
more unusual in this area.
🚇 Covent Garden

BLOOMSBURY

This area now has a full range of
good hotels, all within walking
distance of the Bloomsbury
museums, and Covent Garden,
and West End theaters.

HOTELS

🏨 CHARLOTTE STREET
🍴 HOTEL
$$$$$
15 CHARLOTTE ST.
WC1
TEL 7806 2000
FAX 7806 2002
www.charlottestreethotel.com
Smart yet friendly and relaxed
hotel inside a period building,
with a small gym and reliable
Oscar restaurant.
🚇 Tottenham Court Road

🏨 THE MONTAGUE ON
THE GARDENS
$$$$$
15 MONTAGUE ST.
WC1
TEL 7637 1001
FAX 7637 2516
www.redcarnationhotels.com
Centrally located, this
stylish hotel is imaginatively
decorated, with attention to
detail. Bedrooms offer bold
decor and quality furnishings.
🛏 104 🚇 Kings Cross/
Holborn 🆒 🆒 🆒 All
major cards

🏨 ACADEMY
$$$$
21 GOWER ST.
WC1
TEL 7631 4115
FAX 7636 3442
www.etontownhouse.com
Set in five Georgian rowhouses, with opulent furnishings and discreet art, this professionally run fairytale view of English interiors works well.
🚇 Goodge Street

🏨 HOTEL RUSSELL
$$$$
RUSSELL SQUARE, WC1
TEL 7837 6470
FAX 7520 1835
www.lemeridien.com
Beautifully lush revival of the late Victorian landmark Bloomsbury hotel by Le Meridien hotels who gave the same lift to the Waldorf (q.v.).
🚇 Russell Square

🏨 MYHOTEL
$$$$
11–13 BAYLEY ST.
BEDFORD SQUARE
WC1
TEL 7667 6000
FAX 7667 6044
www.myhotels.co.uk
Sir Terence Conran's design team, helped by a Feng Shui expert, aim to combine high service with calming spirituality. Library and music room.
🛏 76 🚇 Goodge Street 🔃 🅿 🛎 💳 All major cards

🏨 SANDERSON
$$$$
50 BERNERS ST.
W1
TEL 7300 1400
FAX 7300 1404
www.ianschragerhotels.com
As with its sister hotel, St. Martin's Lane, the Schrager-Starck partnership creates minimalist rooms but crowded public spaces; try the Long Bar and the spa.
🚇 Oxford Circus

🏨 ST. MARGARET'S HOTEL
$$
26 BEDFORD PLACE
EC1
TEL 7636 4277
FAX 7636 3066
www.stmargaretshotel.co.uk
Handsome, spacious townhouse with no-fuss rooms, plenty of common lounge space, and a rarity, a garden.
🚇 Holborn, Russell Square

🏨 GENERATOR
$
37 TAVISTOCK PLACE
WC1
TEL 7388 7666
FAX 7388 7644
www.the-generator.co.uk
Steel, chrome, and exposed pipes plus its huge size, jolly bar, and Internet room keep the setting sleek, the prices low, and the guests hip and happy.
🚇 Russell Square

🏨 MORGAN HOTEL
$
24 BLOOMSBURY SQUARE
WC1
TEL 7636 3735
FAX 7636 3045
Superbly located, this modest and good value family-run hotel by the British Museum has both rooms and small apartments.
🚇 Tottenham Court Road

RESTAURANTS

🍴 ALFRED
$$$
245 SHAFTESBURY AVENUE
WC2
TEL 7240 2566
Uncomplicated British food cooked with fine ingredients and served in fresh surroundings. Sample the ham and pea soup, juniper-cured salmon, steamed gurnard, roast ling, and Sussex pond pudding.
🪑 60 🚇 Tottenham Court Road/Covent Garden 🅿 💳 All major cards

PRICES

HOTELS
An indication of the cost of a double room without breakfast is given by $ signs.

$$$$$	Over $280
$$$$	$200–$280
$$$	$120–$200
$$	$80–$120
$	Under $80

RESTAURANTS
An indication of the cost of a three-course dinner without drinks is given by $ signs.

$$$$$	Over $80
$$$$	$50–$80
$$$	$35–$50
$$	$20–$35
$	Under $20

🍴 BACK TO BASICS
$$
21A FOLEY ST.
W1
TEL 7436 2181
www.backtobasics.uk.com
Local fish restaurant housed in a former corner shop. Try Dover sole with tarragon and mahimahi with lentil vinaigrette, and leave space for bread and butter pudding with whiskey sauce.
🪑 36–40 🚇 Goodge Street/Oxford Circus 🕐 Closed Sat. & Sun. 💳 All major cards

🍴 TABLE CAFÉ
$$
HABITAT
TOTTENHAM COURT RD.
W1
TEL 7636 8330
Conran's in-house Italian café enables shoppers to shop, drop, revive, and shop again. Breakfast; lunches of pasta, salads, and ciabattas; and cakes for tea.
🪑 80 🚇 Goodge Street 🅿 💳 All major cards

🍴 WAGAMAMA
$
4A STREATHAM ST.
WC1
TEL 7323 9223
www.wagamama.com
Japanese noodle bar a skip from the British Museum. No reservations, possibly some waiting for the chicken ramen, *gyoza* (stuffed dumplings), and *edamame* (green soybeans). Success has given birth to almost a dozen branches throughout town.
🔁 104 🚇 Tottenham Court Road 🏧 All major cards

REGENCY LONDON: PICCADILLY CIRCUS TO HAMPSTEAD

For ease of use, restaurants covering this long strip are listed south to north.

HOTELS

🏨 DORSET SQUARE
$$$
39 DORSET SQUARE
NW1
TEL 7723 7874
FAX 7724 3328
www.firmdale.com
Tim and Kit Kemp's first hotel—Charlotte Street and Covent Garden are also theirs—with their trademark professionalism, individual attention, and British relaxed atmosphere.
🚇 Marylebone

🏨 30 KING HENRY'S ROAD
$$
30 KING HENRY'S ROAD,
PRIMROSE HILL
NW3
TEL 7483 2871
FAX 7209 9739
www.30kinghenrysroad.co.uk
A delightful and welcoming bed-and-breakfast home, well-located in a lovely Victorian house near Primrose Hill.
🚇 Chalk Farm

🏨 HAMPSTEAD VILLAGE GUESTHOUSE
$
2 KEMPLAY ROAD, HAMPSTEAD
NW3
TEL 7435 8679
FAX 7794 0254
www.hampsteadguesthouse.com
Very pretty setting for an ideal bed-and-breakfast home, with good breakfasts and the Heath for morning walks. There is also a cottage.
🚇 Hampstead

RESTAURANTS

PICCADILLY

🍴 THE RITZ
$$$$
150 PICCADILLY
W1
TEL 7493 8181
www.theritzlondon.com
Dress up (men need a jacket and tie) to enjoy not tea but lunch in London's most beautiful dining room, preferably at a window table amid extravagant Louis XVI decoration and attentive waiters.
🚇 Green Park

🍴 THE CRITERION
$$$
224 PICCADILLY
W1
TEL 7930 0488
www.whitestarline.org.uk
Standing right beside the Eros statue at Piccadilly Circus, marble walls and mosaic ceiling are the attractive setting where Marco Pierre White oversees modern French food such as roast French chicken.
🔁 175 🚇 Piccadilly Circus 🕐 Closed Sun. L ❄️ 🏧 All major cards

🍴 DOVER STREET
$$$
8–10 DOVER ST.
W1
TEL 7629 9813
www.doverst.co.uk
Good value lunchtime food.

Even better at night when diners in the bars and restaurant enjoy some of London's best live jazz, blues, Latin, and soul music.
🚇 Piccadilly
🕐 Closed Sat. L, Sun.

SOMETHING SPECIAL

🍴 THE SUGAR CLUB
Almost everything on Peter Gordon's menu is imaginative and innovative and, where possible, uses organic and wild produce. It is also beautifully presented. Inspired by Australian, Pacific, and other cuisines, dishes range from roast quail with coriander-flavored yogurt to mint tea granita with papaya and dragon fruit. Good value, too.
$$$
21 WARWICK ST., W1
TEL 7437 7776
www.thesugarclub.co.uk
🚇 Piccadilly Circus/ Oxford Circus

REGENT STREET

🍴 VEERASWAMY
$$$
99–101 REGENT ST
W1
TEL 7734 1401
www.realindianfood.com
Take the entrance on Swallow Street, then upstairs to a dramatic room where traditional Indian dishes have been made fashionably modern.
🔁 121 🚇 Piccadilly Circus ❄️ 🏧 All major cards

🍴 VILLANDRY
$$$
170 GREAT PORTLAND ST.
W1
TEL 7631 3131
Having feasted on an impeccable snack or full lunch rounded off with some of Villandry's superbly sourced cheeses, there is the irresistible adjoining food

HOTELS & RESTAURANTS

store for buying more of their tip-top ingredients.
🚇 Great Portland Street
🕐 Closed Sun. D

🍴 RIBA CAFÉ
$
ROYAL INSTITUTION OF BRITISH ARCHITECTS, 66 PORTLAND PLACE
W1
TEL 7631 0467
Find the sleek 1930s building among Adam's grand mansions, check out the events program, and then head upstairs for a stylish breakfast or light lunch—on the roof terrace in summer.
🚇 Great Portland Street
🕐 Closed D, Sun. L & D

PRIMROSE HILL

🍴 LEMONIA
$$$
89 REGENT'S PARK RD.
NW1
TEL 7586 7454
Near Primrose Hill, this local favorite serves Greek Cypriot dishes such as louvia (black-eyed beans and spinach), squid, and pudding of Greek yogurt, honey, and nuts.
🪑 160 🚇 Chalk Farm
🕐 Closed Sat. L, Sun. D
🗓 All major cards

HAMPSTEAD

🍴 CUCINA
$$$
45A SOUTH END RD.
NW3
TEL 7435 7814
Very good modern European dishes make up for the dull setting. Try the squid ink blini with salmon caviar, roast chicken with thyme, and smoked plum tomatoes.
🪑 96 🚇 Hampstead (10-minute walk) 🕐 Closed Sun. D 🎦 🗓 All major cards

🍴 LA CAGE IMAGINAIRE
$$
16 FLASK WALK
NW3
TEL 7794 6674

Follow locals to this intimate dining room serving French food with charm in the heart of atmospheric Hampstead village.
🚇 Hampstead 🕐 Closed Mon. L

🍴 LOUIS PATISSERIE
$
32 HEATH ST.
NW3
TEL 7435 9908
Ideal stop during a Hampstead visit or after a walk on the Heath. Good apple danish pastries and interesting Hungarian ones such as cinnamon pretzels.
🚇 Hampstead 🕐 Closed 6 p.m. 🗓 All major cards

KENSINGTON & SOUTH KENSINGTON

There are several town-house hotels in this residential area on the west side of central London, plus good restaurants much patronized for dinner by local residents.

HOTELS

🏨 BLAKES
$$$$$
33 ROLAND GARDENS
SW7
TEL 7370 6701
FAX 7373 0442
www.blakeshotels.com
Anouska Hempel's first hotel: two Victorian mansions luxuriating in lavish fabrics and dramatic color, attracting a range of famous people with promises of privacy. There is a delightful garden. See also the latest version—The Hempel, p. 258.
ⓘ 50 🚇 Gloucester Road/South Kensington
🛏 Some suites 🗓 All major cards

🏨 FIVE SUMNER PLACE
$$$$
5 SUMNER PLACE
SW7
TEL 7584 7586
FAX 7823 9962

www.sumnerplace.com
This stucco terrace perfectly located for museum visits and shopping pleases guests with traditional English interiors, conservatory breakfast room, and charming staff.
ⓘ 13 🚇 South Kensington
🗓 All major cards

🏨 THE GORE
$$$$
189 QUEEN'S GATE
SW7
TEL 7584 6601
FAX 7589 8127
www.gorehotel.com
Opened over a century ago, the Gore carefully preserves its Victorian details with paneled rooms, potted ferns, rugs, and glorious stained-glass windows. The same building houses the fine quality restaurants, Downstairs at 190 and Bistro 190 (Tel 020-7581 5666).
ⓘ 54 🚇 South Kensington
🗓 All major cards

🏨 GALLERY HOTEL
$$$
8–10 QUEENSBERRY PLACE
SW7
TEL 7915 0000
FAX 7915 4400
www.eeh.co.uk
Flagship hotel of the Elegant English Hotels chain (which includes the Gainsborough and Willett in London), good value in well-furnished period buildings.
🚇 South Kensington

🏨 HOTEL 167
$$$
167 OLD BROMPTON RD.
SW5
TEL 7373 0672
FAX 7373 3360
www.hotel167.com
Good value, individually decorated rooms have drama and style, and there is a fine show of modern art in the breakfast room of this town-house hotel.
ⓘ 19 (18 with private bath)
🚇 Gloucester Road 🗓 AE, MC, V

ABBEY HOUSE
$$
11 VICARAGE GATE
W8
TEL 7727 2594
www.abbeyhousekensington.com
Good value and reliable quality
bed-and-breakfast in a charming
Victorian house. In the heart of
Kensington, near antiques shops
and Undergrounds.
16 High Street
Kensington/Notting Hill Gate
No credit cards

MAYFLOWER
$$
26–28 TREBOVIR ROAD
SW5
TEL 7370 0991
FAX 7370 0994
www.mayflowerhotel.co.uk
Modern, well-appointed rooms
of character with a touch of the
exotic, such as colonial ceiling
fans; plus adjoining apartments.
Earl's Court

VANCOUVER STUDIOS
$$
30 PRINCE'S SQUARE
W2
TEL 7243 1270
FAX 7221 8678
www.vienna-group.co.uk
A well-furnished Victorian
building, with winter fires and
modern bedrooms.
Bayswater

RUSHMORE
$
11 TREBOVIR ROAD
SW5
TEL 7370 3839
FAX 7370 0274
www.rushmorehotel.co.uk
Frescoed wall, draped beds, an
elegant breakfast room, and good
service make this a bargain deal.
Earl's Court

RESTAURANTS

ABINGDON
$$$
54 ABINGDON RD.
W8
TEL 7937 3339
Modern bistro in a converted
corner pub. Try loin of tuna,
grilled steak with pommes
frites, or duck leg confit.
45 High Street
Kensington MC, V

BRASSERIE ST. QUENTIN
$$$
243 BROMPTON RD.
SW3
TEL 7589 8005
www.brasseriestquentin.co.uk
Between Harrods and the
Victoria & Albert Museum, this
perfect French brasserie has
frozen in time. Local French
diplomats enjoy the French
onion soup, *boudin blanc*, and
tarte Tatin; good wines.
75–80 South
Kensington All
major cards

CLARKE'S
$$$
124 KENSINGTON
CHURCH ST.
W8
TEL 7221 9225
www.sallyclarke.com
In the late 1970s, Sally Clarke's
Cal-Ital food introduced new
ideas to many young chefs.
Fresh juices, home-baked
breads, chargrilled duck, and
perfect cheeses are all part of
a good meal here.
90 Notting Hill Gate
Closed Sat. L, Sun.,
Christmas week & 2 weeks
in Aug. All major
cards

KENSINGTON PLACE
$$$
201–205 KENSINGTON
CHURCH ST.
W8
TEL 7727 3184
Plate glass public eating in a
buzzy, loud, big room. Equally
designer modern food includes
grilled scallops with pea puree
and mint vinaigrette—and
don't miss the breads.
140 Notting Hill Gate
All major cards

Chains & Gangs
The great overexpansion of restaurant chains, from low market up to Marco Pierre White, Sir Terence Conran, and other high fliers, has evened out thanks to the public voting with their feet, refusing to pay for overpriced goods at any level. Only the better restaurants have survived. Thus, the Belgo Group's The Ivy, Le Caprice, and J Sheekey's are shining on. At a more modest level, Zizzi, Ask!, Express (all Italian), Wagamama (Japanese), and Livebait (fish) are reliable. If in doubt, go to an owner-run restaurant.

LAUNCESTON PLACE
$$$
1A LAUNCESTON PLACE
W8 5RL
TEL 7937 6912
www.launcestonplace.co.uk
Sophisticated setting, modern
dishes. Try the crab risotto
with poached egg and the
strawberry and chocolate
roulade.
85 Gloucester
Road/High Street Kensington
Closed Sat. L, Sun. D
AE, MC, V

LUNDUM'S
$$$
119 OLD BROMPTON ROAD
SW7
TEL 7373 7774
Of the few Scandinavian
restaurants in London, this is
not just the best: The
traditional Danish dishes are
served with a smile in a
charming and pretty room.
South Kensington
Closed: Sun.

HOTELS & RESTAURANTS

❚❚ STAR OF INDIA
$$$
154 OLD BROMPTON RD., SW5
TEL 7373 2901
Once a favorite for homesick Indians; now revamped by Reza Mohammed with extravagant decor and food such as "sealed in the pot" dishes or scallops with coriander.
🛏 95   🚇 Gloucester Road
🕒   💳 All major cards

CHELSEA, BELGRAVIA, & KNIGHTSBRIDGE

Smart Londoners and foreign diplomats set the tone for elegant, discreet hotels and up-market eating, even in shops.

HOTELS

🏨 BASIL STREET
$$$$$
BASIL ST., SW3
TEL 7581 3311
FAX 7581 3693
www.the basil.com
Regular guests enjoy what they see as the Englishness of this hotel: an Edwardian building with restful public rooms, and helpful staff.
🛏 80   🚇 Knightsbridge 🛗
🕒 Some   💳 All major cards

🏨 THE BERKELEY
❚❚ **$$$$$**
WILTON PLACE, SW1
TEL 7235 6000
FAX 7235 4330
www.savoy-group.co.uk
Modern hotel run on tradi-tional lines: open fire in the lobby, lavish flower arrange-ments, spacious rooms, valet service. Excellent top-floor health club and swimming pool, equalled by the bar and restaurants. La Tante Claire (French) with Pierre Koffmann as chef, and Vong (Southeast Asian) are both superb.
🛏 168   🅿 50   🚇 Hyde Park Corner 🛗 🕒 💳
🏊   💳 All major cards

🏨 THE HALKIN
The innovator: London's first design-aware hotel. Inspired by classic Italian style; notably the good air-conditioning and lighting control, staff dressed in Armani, and consistently impressive modern Italian food cooked by Stefano Cavallini.
$$$$$
HALKIN STREET, SW1
TEL 7333 1000
FAX 7333 1100
www.halkin.co.uk
🛈 41   🛏 45   🚇 Hyde Park Corner 🛗 🕒 🍷
💳 All major cards

🏨 THE CAPITAL
❚❚ **$$$$$**
BASIL ST.
KNIGHTSBRIDGE
SW3
TEL 7589 5171
FAX 7225 0011
www.capitalhotel.co.uk
Egyptian cotton sheets cover the beds in this immaculate, design-aware hotel. Eric Chavot cooks notably in The Capital restaurant.
🛈 48   🛏 35   🅿 15
🚇 Knightsbridge 🛗 🕒
💳 All major cards

🏨 GORING
❚❚ **$$$$$**
BEESTON PLACE
GROSVENOR GARDENS
SW1
TEL 7396 9000
FAX 7834 4393
www.goringhotel.co.uk
Run by the Goring family since 1910, this hotel promises excellent hospitality and service. The restaurant serves both traditional and contemporary British cuisine.
🛈 74   🅿 8   🚇 Victoria 🛗
🕒   💳 All major cards

🏨 HYATT CARLTON
❚❚ **TOWER**
$$$$$

CADOGAN PLACE
SW1
TEL 7235 1234
FAX 7235 9129
www.carltontower.com
Impressive modern hotel, whose sky-high swimming pool and health club indicate top quality services at all levels; Chinoiserie Lounge for tea, Rib Room (traditional food) and Grissini (modern Italian) restaurants.
🛈 220   🅿 80
🚇 Knightsbridge 🛗
🕒 🏊 🍷   💳 All major cards

🏨 THE LANESBOROUGH
❚❚ **$$$$$**
HYDE PARK CORNER
SW1
TEL 7259 5599
FAX 7259 5606
www.lanesborough.com
Located on Hyde Park Corner, this hotel offers lavish furnishings, splendid flower arrangements, and extremely comfortable bedrooms. The Conservatory restaurant, with its palms and fountains, serves International cuisine.
🛈 95   🛏 104   🅿 38
🚇 Hyde Park Corner 🛗
🕒 🍷   💳 All major cards

🏨 MANDARIN ORIENTAL
🍴 HYDE PARK
$$$$$
66 KNIGHTSBRIDGE
SW1
TEL 7235 2000
FAX 7235 4552
www.mandarinoriental.com/
london
A splendid Edwardian
landmark, which has been
extravagantly refurbished.
Large rooms, lavish
bathrooms, and many fine
Hyde Park views. The Park
Restaurant has subtle food,
stunningly presented.
ℹ️ 200 🔌 80
🚇 Knightsbridge 〰️ ❄️
🏋️ 🅾️ All major cards

🏨 THE KNIGHTSBRIDGE
$$$$
10 BEAUFORT GARDENS
SW3
TEL 7584 6300
FAX 7584 6355
www.firmdale.com
Good location for
Knightsbridge shopping, and
smart rooms to match; but no
bar, restaurant, or gym.
🚇 Knightsbridge

🏨 MORGAN HOUSE
$$
120 EBURY ST, SW1
TEL 7730 2384
www.morganhouse.co.uk
The same couple run this
and the Woodville bed-and-
breakfast home in pretty,
well-located Pimlico; good
breakfasts; some rooms share
bathrooms.
🚇 Victoria

🏨 WOODVILLE HOUSE
$$
107 EBURY ST.
SW1
TEL 7730 1048
www.woodevillehouse.co.uk
See Morgan House; here the
breakfasts are equally good,
but some bathrooms are
shared.
🚇 Victoria

RESTAURANTS

🍴 AUBERGINE
$$$$
11 PARK WALK, SW10
TEL 7352 3449
Highly respected chef
William Drabble creates his
imaginative French dishes in
this small Chelsea street. Try
the germiny of lobster with
new potatoes and mint, or the
organic fillet of beef with
celeriac purée and Madeira jus.
🔌 50 🚇 Fulham Road
🕐 Closed Sat. L & Sun. ❄️
🅾️ All major cards

🍴 FOLIAGE
$$$$
MANDARIN ORIENTAL HOTEL,
66 KNIGHTSBRIDGE
SW1
TEL 7201 3723
www.mandarinoriental.com
Remarkable contemporary
French dishes (including a
good prix fixe lunch) eaten in
a beautiful, two-tiered
modern dining room
overlooking Hyde Park that
could equal The Ritz's allure.
🚇 Knightsbridge

🍴 GORDON RAMSAY
$$$$
68 ROYAL HOSPITAL RD.
SW3
TEL 7352 4441
Celebrated chef Gordon
Ramsay creates his modern
French dishes in this small,
intimate restaurant. Try the
frogs' legs in a curry batter
and Jerusalem artichoke sauce
or the red mullet on
caramelised endive with
langoustine beignets and red
pepper vinaigrette.
🔌 44 🚇 Sloane Square
(10-minute walk) 🕐 Closed
Sat. & Sun., 2 weeks at
Christmas ❄️ 🅾️ All major
cards

🍴 KEN LO'S MEMORIES
OF CHINA
$$$$
67-69 EBURY ST., SW1
TEL 7730 7734
Top-quality cooking in a top

residential area means this
ever popular, refurbished,
elegant Belgravia dining room
has a classy buzz. Discerning
regulars go for the good value
set menus that have well-
chosen dishes.
🚇 Sloane Square/Victoria

🍴 SALLOOS
$$$
62-64 KINNERTON ST.
SW1
TEL 7235 4444
Mr. Salahuddin's classy Pakistani
restaurant, founded in 1979,
serves his family recipes. The
focus is meat: marinated lamb
chops, chicken shish kebab,
and quails, eaten with warm
nan breads.
🔌 65 🚇 Knightsbridge
🕐 Closed Sun. ❄️ 🅾️ All
major cards

🍴 ZAFFERANO
$$$
15 LOWNDES ST.
TEL 7235 5800
This Belgravia establishment
is said by many to be the
finest Italian in town from
the prawn ravioli to the
home-made amaretti and
chocolatte truffles.
🚇 Knightsbridge

WEST LONDON
(HOLLAND PARK
WESTWARD)

**Some special hotels and some
good restaurants to combine
with sightseeing**

SOMETHING
SPECIAL

🍴 FIFTH FLOOR
RESTAURANT

The ultimate shopping
dream: four floors of
Harvey Nichols fashion
sandwiched between chic
restaurants. This one is the
smartest, serving dishes such as
quail with pumpkin ravioli.
Popularity sometimes affects
the quality of the service and
the food, but there is a trendy
bar next door, a simpler café,
and a sublime food store

HOTELS & RESTAURANTS

nearby. In the basement, Foundation is just as chic but less expensive. .
$$$
HARVEY NICHOLS, KNIGHTSBRIDGE, SW1
TEL 7235 5250
www.harveynichols.com
🏨 110 🚇 Knightsbridge
🕐 Closed Sun. D 🕐
🔲 All major cards

HOTELS

🏨 HALCYON
🍴 $$$$$
81 HOLLAND PARK
W1
TEL 7727 7288
FAX 7229 8516
Grand town house transformed into an elegant, impressive small hotel furnished by a fine aesthetic eye. Spacious bedrooms and bathrooms.
① 43 🚇 Holland Park ⬍
🕐 🔲 All major cards

🏨 THE HEMPEL
$$$$$
31–35 CRAVEN HILL GARDENS
W2
TEL 7298 9000
FAX 7402 4666
www.the-hempel.co.uk
Anouska Hempel's second hotel is in absolute contrast to her first, Blakes (see p. 254). Here she pushes minimalism farther than any other hotelier would dare—natural fabrics, slate, sand-blasted glass, a Zen garden, Shadows Bar, and I-Thai restaurant (Italian/Thai).
① 41 + 6 apartments
🚇 Lancaster Gate/ Queensway 🕐 🔲 All major cards

🏨 ABBEY COURT
$$$$
20 PEMBRIDGE GARDENS
W2
TEL 7221 7518
FAX 7792 0858
www.abbeycourthotel.co.uk
Designers Guild fabrics are used in the individually decorated rooms of this

friendly town-house hotel. All rooms have plenty of books and a relaxing Jacuzzi bath.
① 22 🚇 Notting Hill Gate
📺 Nearby 🔲 All major cards

🏨 THE PORTOBELLO HOTEL
$$$$
22 STANLEY GARDENS
W1
TEL 7727 2777
FAX 7792 9641
www.portobello-hotel.co.uk
Town-house hotel whose stuccoed Victorian facade belies a delightfully idiosyncratic interior much loved by guests.
① 22 🚇 Holland Park/ Notting Hill Gate 🔲 All major cards

🏨 COLONNADE
$$$
2 WARRINGTON CRESCENT, LITTLE VENICE
W9
TEL 7286 1052
FAX 7286 1057
www.etontownhouse.co.uk
Leafy, romantic Little Venice is the rural setting for the sumptuous Victorian hotel with classically decorated rooms; worth the edge-of-town location.
🚇 Warwick Avenue

SOMETHING SPECIAL

🍴 THE BELVEDERE
To date, London's only quality restaurant in the city's many parks, The Belvedere was formerly the summer ballroom of Holland House. Now one of London's most romantic settings, run by Marco Pierre White and serving reliable, not exceptional, French cuisine.
$$$
ABBOTSBURY ROAD, HOLLAND PARK, W8
TEL 7602 1238
www.whitestarline.org.uk
🏨 132 🚇 HOLLAND PARK
🕐 🔲 All major cards

🏨 PEMBRIDGE COURT
$$$
34 PEMBRIDGE GARDENS, NOTTING HILL
W2
TEL 7229 9977
FAX 7727 4982
www.pemct.co.uk
Furnished with Victorian and Edwardian pieces, this tastefully restored townhouse is classy, relaxed, and ideal for Portobello Road antique hunting.
🚇 Notting Hill Gate

RESTAURANTS

🍴 JASON'S
$$$$
OPPOSITE 60 BLOMFIELD RD.
W9
TEL 020-7286 6752
www.jasons.co.uk
Mauritian fish dishes eaten in a brick-walled room on a sunny terrace in Little Venice; soupe de poissons is especially good, as are the soft-shell crab and Creole sauce and parrot fish with ginger.
🏨 40 🚇 Warwick Road
🕐 Closed Sun. 🔲 All major cards

🍴 LA TROMPETTE
$$$$
5–7 DEVONSHIRE ROAD
W4
TEL 8747 1836
Worth the journey out (combine with Kew, Chiswick, or Syon, perhaps) to enjoy the impressive French dishes of Nigel Platts-Martin, together with his well-chosen wines and charming staff; a memorable and good value treat.
🚇 Turnham Green

🍴 CHINON
$$$
23 RICHMOND WAY
W14
TEL 7602 5968
Jonathon Hayes and Barbara Deane run this neighborhood restaurant, using the freshest ingredients to create French-inspired food with impressive

presentation. Try the crab ravioli or the calves' liver with mustard sauce and fondant potatoes.

🔢 30 🚇 Shepherd's Bush/Olympia 🕐 Closed L, & Sun. 🅿 🃏 All major cards

🍴 RIVA
$$$
169 CHURCH RD.
SW13
TEL 8748 0434
Enjoy Francesco Zanchetta's almost perfect rustic Italian food. Classic regional dishes include fritelle, *osso buco alla milanese* with saffron risotto.
🔢 50 🚇 Hammersmith (then bus 33, 72, 209, or 283) 🕐 Closed Sat. L, 2 weeks at Christmas, Easter, & 2 weeks in Aug. 🃏 All major cards

EAST LONDON

Outside the traditional Thistle Tower Hotel, this area retains something of its multicultural (immigrant) character. For the adventurous, this is the place to try a lesser known Indian restaurant: Enter Brick Lane from Whitechapel Road and choose one of the restaurants lining it, all run by local Bangladeshis.

HOTEL

🏨 FOUR SEASONS CANARY WHARF
$$$$$
46 WESTFERRY CIRCUS
E14
TEL 7510 1999
www.fourseasons.com
Canary Wharf's first deluxe hotel, a stunning building and setting run by the reliable Four Seasons chain that pampers guests with all mod cons including pool and tennis courts.
🚇 Canary Warf

RESTAURANTS

🍴 UBON
$$$$
FOUR SEASONS HOTEL,
34 WESTFERRY CIRCUS
E14
TEL 7719 7800
A stunning river view setting, with food that more than equals that of its big sister, Park Lane's Nobu. Sushi experts claim this has the best in town; sashimi impresses, too.
🚇 Canary Wharf/Westferry 🕐 Closed Sat. L, Sun.

🍴 CAFÉ SPICE NAMASTE
$$$
16 PRESCOT ST.
E1
TEL 020-7488 9242
Modern, highly inventive Indian cooking by Cyrus Todiwala. Try the tandoori duck, Goan seafood pilau, and whichever new dish he has created.
🔢 115–120 🚇 Tower Hill 🕐 Closed Sat. L, Sun. 🅿 🃏 All major cards

🍴 BRICK LANE BEIGEL BAKE
$
159 BRICK LANE, E1
TEL 7729 0616
The fact than more than 7,000 bagels leave Sammy's tiny, unremarkable café on a Saturday night confirms its status as the best in town. Quality smoked salmon, cream cheese, and breads, too.
🚇 Liverpool Street 🕐 Open 24 hours

🍴 SOUP OPERA
$
CONCOURSE LEVEL, CABOT PLACE EAST
E14
TEL 7513 0880
www.soupopera.co.uk
Delicious, robust, original soups from this efficient carryout chain. When London's weather is off-color, this makes a hearty and good

value alternative to sitting in a stuffy restaurant.
🚇 Canary Wharf/Westferry 🕐 Closed Sat., Sun.

SOUTH BANK

The strip along the south bank of the Thames is now reviving to be one of the city's most exciting and innovative areas.

HOTELS

🏨 LONDON MARRIOTT COUNTY HALL
$$$$$
COUNTY HALL
SE1
TEL 7928 5200
FAX 7928 5300
www.marriott.com
Hotel in part of the London administrators' 1930s building. Some rooms have river views and the leisure facilities are first class.
🛏 200 🅿 120 🚇 Westminster/Waterloo 😊 😊 🏋 🏊 🃏 All major cards

🏨 LONDON BRIDGE
$$$$
8–18 LONDON BRIDGE ST.
SE1
TEL 7855 2200
FAX 7855 2233
www.london-bridge-hotel.co.uk
This well-equipped modern hotel is just south of London Bridge, a short walk from the City. No river views.
🛏 138 🚇 London Bridge 😊 😊 🏋 🃏 All major cards

🏨 MAD HATTER
$$$
3–7 STANFORD ST.
SE1
TEL 7401 9222
FAX 7401 7111
www.fullershotels.co.uk
A welcome new arrival located behind South Bank theaters, near Blackfriars Bridge, a short walk to the City or taxi to the West End. No river views.
🛏 30 🚇 Blackfriars 😊 🃏 All major cards

HOTELS & RESTAURANTS

🏨 LONDON COUNTY HALL TRAVEL INN
$$
COUNTY HALL
SE1
TEL 7902 1600
FAX 7902 1619
www.travelinn.co.uk
Excellent location for this no-frills, good value hotel tucked behind the deluxe London Marriott. No river views.
🛏 312 🚇 Westminster/Waterloo 🛗 🅰 All major cards

RESTAURANTS

🍴 BLUE PRINT CAFÉ
$$$$
THE DESIGN MUSEUM
SHAD THAMES ST., SE1
TEL 7378 7031
www.conran.com
Of the clutch of Conran-owned restaurants, this has the best views of Tower Bridge and the nicest service; riverview tables a premium. Try the bourride of cod. Conran's other restaurants are Le Pont de la Tour (Tel 020-7403 8403), Butler's Wharf Chop House (Tel 020-7403 3403), and Cantina del Ponte (Tel 020-7403 5403).
🍽 120 🚇 Tower Hill 🕐 Closed Sun. D 🅿 🅰 All major cards

🍴 FOUR REGIONS
$$$
COUNTY HALL, RIVERSIDE BUILDING
SE1
TEL 7928 0988
Location is everything: Book a window seat in this mezzanine dining room and you will gaze across to the Houses of Parliament as you enjoy reasonably good Chinese dishes.
🚇 Westminster/Waterloo

🍴 LIVEBAIT
$$$
43 THE CUT
SR1
TEL 7928 7211
A favorite fish restaurant,

among Londoners, who sit at closely packed tables to eat worldwide fish dishes—monkfish fajitas, teriyaki-glazed halibut, palourde clams, and cod with couscous.
🍽 76 🚇 Waterloo 🕐 Closed Sun. 🅰 All major cards

🍴 THE PEOPLE'S PALACE
$$$
ROYAL FESTIVAL HALL
BELVEDERE RD.
SE1
TEL 7928 9999
www.capitalgrp.co.uk
There are splendid views of the Thames matched by a relaxed atmosphere and interesting food, including knuckle of ham, lamb steak over Roquefort butter, and steamed chocolate pudding.
🍽 200 🚇 Waterloo/Charing Cross 🅿 🅰 All major cards

🍴 RANSOME'S DOCK
$$$
RANSOME'S DOCK
BATTERSEA
SW1
TEL 7223 1611
www.ransomesdock.co.uk
It merits a taxi ride to this former ice factory, where Martin and Vanessa Lam's excellent modern European dishes include Loch Fyne scallops, Trelough duck breast, and hot prune and Armagnac souffle.
🍽 60 🚇 Sloane Square (20-minute walk) 🕐 Closed Sun. D 🅿 🅰 All major cards

🍴 RIVIERA
$$$
GABRIELS WHARF
SE1
TEL 7401 7314
Rises above the many inadequate bistros on the South Bank thanks to its outside tables and some softly Mediterranean food. And the view counts for a lot.
🚇 Southwark

🍴 FILM CAFÉ
$
RIVERSIDE, NATIONAL FILM THEATRE
SE1
TEL 7928 5362
Good salads and desserts at this canteen style café found among the second-hand bookstalls beneath Hunderfood Bridge, ideal for a pause in the South Bank walk.
🚇 Waterloo

SHOPPING

There are various ways of shopping in London. You may come with a specific shopping list, you may want to see the latest fashions, or you may simply wish to window shop with the possibility of a purchase. Whichever it is, London has several shopping centers and offers several ways of shopping.

Shopping facts:
Although shops are traditionally open between 9 a.m. and 5 p.m., opening hours are no longer fixed times. Many Oxford Street, Regent Street, and High Street Kensington shops remain open until 7 or 8 p.m. on Thursday; most Knightsbridge and Chelsea shops do the same on Friday; and many shops, including those on Tottenham Court Road, are open on Sunday. Seasonal sales take place in January, extending into February, and July, extending into August.

Most shops accept the major credit cards. There is often a fee for using travelers' checks.

The VAT, currently 17.5 percent, is payable on almost everything (exceptions include books, food, children's clothes). All non-U.K. passport holders are exempt from the VAT if they are taking the goods out of the U.K. within three months. The tax must be paid, then reclaimed. There is one system for those living in EC countries, another for those living outside the EC. Shopkeepers are usually good at helping customers complete the necessary forms.

London shoppers are well protected by the law. For instance, a shopkeeper displaying a credit card sign is obliged to accept that card; goods in sales should be perfect unless they are labeled otherwise; and if an object fails to perform its job, there should be a full refund.

SOUVENIRS

Museum and gallery shops have quality goods ranging from desk diaries featuring their treasures to full sets of tableware and related toys. Examples of these can be found at:
British Museum, Great Russell Street, Tel 7636 1555. Three shops plus a children's shop.
Natural History Museum, Cromwell Road, Tel 7942 5000. Thousands of dinosaur souvenirs.
Queen's Gallery, Buckingham Palace Road, Tel 7321 2233. Quality goods, often bearing the royal stamp of authenticity.
Science Museum, Exhibition Road, Tel 7942 4000. Projects for budding scientists.
Tate Britain, Millbank, Tel 7887 8000. **Tate Modern,** Bankside, Tel 7887 8000. Both Tates have excellent stocks of books and designer gifts.
Victoria & Albert Museum, Cromwell Road, Tel 7938 8500.

Collection-inspired goods.
The BBC Shop, Broadcasting House, Portland Place, Tel 7765 0025. A wide range of BBC-based gifts, including books and videos.

STREET MARKETS

Market goods range from antiques to fruits and vegetables, to cheap hardware and imitation goods (beware of the perfumes that only look like the real thing), to junk (see pp. 154–5).
Portobello Market, Portobello Road. Over a mile long, selling quality antiques and fruits and vegetables.
Petticoat Lane Market, Middlesex Street. Bargain hunt for fashion, leather, household goods, and knickknacks at London's best known market.

DEPARTMENT STORES

The one-stop shopping that department stores offer has several advantages.
Harrods, Knightsbridge, Tel 020-7730 1234. The epitome of these grand, multi-floored shops. It is often derided by Londoners who then admit they go there for one department— (see pp. 172-73).
Selfridges, 400 Oxford Street, Tel 7629 1234. Vast store with notable food and cosmetics. Currently considered by shopaholics to rival Harrods.
Fortnum & Mason, 181 Piccadilly, Tel 7734 8040. High prices, but the own-brand goods make perfect presents.
Harvey Nichols, 109-25 Knightsbridge, Tel 7235 5000. Classy clothes for women.
Fenwick, 63 New Bond Street, Tel 7629 9161. Fashion, cosmetics, and fabrics.
Liberty, Regent Street, Tel 7734 1234. Goods range from sumptuous fabrics to the best china and glass.
Dickens & Jones, Regent Street, Tel 7734 7070. A fiesta of clothes, smells, accessories, and fabrics.
John Lewis, Oxford Street, Tel 7629 7711. Good for reasonably priced, sensible homeware.
Peter Jones, Sloane Square, Tel 7730 3434. John Lewis's slightly more stylish sister.
Marks & Spencer, 458 Marble Arch, Tel 7935 7954. An obligatory visit to M&S for underwear the world wears.

SPECIALTY SHOPS

This is where the fun lies, although some homework with the map may be needed to avoid crisscrossing London. Certain kinds of shops tend to group together, such as in Bond Street or Sloane Street for fashion, Brompton Cross, Soho, and Clerkenwell for contemporary design and jewelers, and St. James's and Mayfair for upscale art. Here are some ideas:

ACCESSORIES
Herbert Johnson, Bennett House, Bond Street, Tel 7408 1174. For classic hats.

Tiffany & Co., Bond Street, Tel 7409 2790. For chic jewelry.
James Smith & Sons, 53 New Oxford Street, Tel 7836 4731. Every kind of umbrella and walking stick.

ART AT AUCTION
The two top auction houses are:
Christie's, 8 King Street, St. James's, Tel 7839 9060.
Sotheby's, 34 New Bond Street, Mayfair, Tel 7493 8080.

It is also well worth visiting:
Phillips, New Bond Street, Tel 7629 6602.
Bonhams, Montpelier Galleries, Montpelier Street, Tel 7584 9161.

SPECIALTY BOOKSTORES
Books for Cooks, 4 Blenheim Crescent, Tel 7221 1992. Possibly the world's best for cookery and cuisine.
Henry Sotheran, 2 Sackville Street, Tel 7439 6151.
Murder One, 71 Charing Cross Road, Tel 7734 3483. Every type of crime.
Maggs Brothers, 50 Berkeley Square, Tel 7493 7160. Locate that out-of-print, first edition, or rare antiquarian book.

DECOR AND DESIGNS
Designers Guild, 277 King's Road, Tel 7351 5775.
Divertimenti, 33–34 Marylebone High Street, Tel 7935 0689.
Heal's, 196 Tottenham Court Road, Tel 7636 1666.
Monkwell, 227 King's Road, Tel 7823 3294. This and **Design Archives** (18th- and 19th-century designs), **Hills & Knowles,** and **Crowson** fill two floors with more than 12,000 top-quality fabrics, wallpapers, and trimmings, plus furniture and furnishing accessories.

DESIGNER FASHION
Many top designers have their flagship store in or near Bond Street, in Mayfair. Branches are usually in Knightsbridge (Sloane Street, Brompton Road), Kensington, and/or Covent Garden. Large department stores such as Harvey Nicholas and Selfridges also house top designer lines.
Donna Karan, Tel 7495 3100.
Gucci, Tel 7629 2716.
Joseph, Tel 7629 3713.
Emporio Armani, Tel 7491 8080.
Jigsaw, Tel 7491 4244.
Nichole Farhi, Tel 7499 8368.
Prada, Tel 7647 5000.
Dolce & Gabbana, Tel 7659 9000.
MaxMara, Tel 491 4748.
Browns, South Molton Street, Tel 7514 0000.
Whistles, 12 St Christopher's Place, Tel 7487 4484.
Vivienne Westwood, 6 Davies Street, Tel 7629 3757.
Comme des Garçons, 59 Brook Street, Tel 7493 1258.
Mulberry Company, 12 Gees Court, Tel 7491 3900.
Karen Millen, Tel 7287 6158.
Emanuel Ungaro, Tel 7629 0550.
Burberry, Tel 7839 5222.
Moschino, Tel 7318 0555.
Pleats Please, Tel 7495 2306.
Pringle, Tel 0800 360 200.
Ronit Zilkha, Tel 7499 3707.
Yohji Yamamota, Tel 7491 4129.

Other well-known names to seek out include:
Louis Vuitton, Tel 7399 4050.
Paul Smith, 122 Kensington Park Road, Tel 7727 3553.
Agnes B, Floral Street, Tel 7379 1992.
Betty Jackson, 311 Brompton Road, Tel 7589 7884.
Issey Miyake, 270 Brompton Road, Tel 7581 3760.
Gallery Gaultier, 171 Draycott Avenue, Tel 7584 4648.
Egg, 36 Kinnerton Street, Tel 7235 9315.
Joseph, 315 Brompton Road, Tel 7225 3335.
Zandra Rhodes, 81 Bermondsey Street, Tel 7403 0222.

It is also worth checking out the department stores, which house many designer lines.
GIFTS

Paxton & Whitfield, 93 Jermyn Street, Tel 7930 0259. Cheeses.
Carluccio's, 30 Neal Street, Tel 7240 1487. Designer delicatessen with cheeses, herbs, and cosmetics.
Alessi Oggetti, 143 Fulham Road, Tel 7584 9808. For chic designer objects.
Waterford Wedgwood, 173–74 Piccadilly, Tel 7629 2614. The largest selection of Waterford glass, Wedgwood china.
Bibendum, 113 Regent's Park Road, Tel 7722 5577. Fine selection of wines.
Falkiner Fine Papers, 76 Southampton Row, Tel 7831 1151. Beautiful paper.
Asprey, 167 New Bond Street, Tel 7493 6767. Ultimate deluxe gifts, but for most people just ultimate window shopping.

SHOES
Specialty shoe shops include:
Natural Shoe Store, 21 Neal Street, Tel 7836 5254.
Emma Hope, 53 Sloane Square, Tel 7259 9566.
Shellys, 266 Regent Street, Tel 7287 0939.
Manolo Blahnik, 49 Old Church Street, Chelsea, Tel 7352 3863.

SPORTS EQUIPMENT
Lillywhites, Lower Regent Street, Tel 0870 3339 6000. Whatever the sport, this shop has the equipment and outfit.

TOYS & GAMES
Hamleys, 188 Regent Street, Tel 7734 3161. A seven-floor wonderland for kids and adults alike rivaled only by the fourth floor of Harrods, whose bonus is that they take orders.

UNUSUAL SIZES
Evans, 36–8 Great Castle Street, Tel 7927 0202. Stocks fashionable clothes in sizes 14 to 32, plus the French & Teague 1647 range, plus clothes for petite women.
Base, 55 Monmouth Street, Tel 7240 8914. Similar to 1647.

ENTERTAINMENT

One of the most exciting, if frustrating, things about London is that there is so much theater, music, cinema, and other entertainment that it is impossible to see everything you would like to see. The range is wide, too, from serious opera, cinema, and sacred music to jazz restaurants, spectator sports, and extravagant musicals. And that does not include the plays, often the biggest draw for visitors. It would be impossible to list every entertainment venue in London— *Time Out* magazine needs more than 200 pages to do that. But here are some tips and essential information to help you find the right entertainment for your taste.

INFORMATION

Time Out, published every Tuesday, has impressively comprehensive entertainment listings. Their often acerbic reviews should not be taken too seriously. The *Evening Standard,* published daily Monday through Friday, is London's monopoly evening newspaper, featuring day-after reviews of new plays and shows, plus plenty of listings.
Reliable reviews can be found in *The Times,* the *Financial Times,* and other broadsheet newspapers. See also websites p. 239.

THEATER

STATE-SUPPORTED THEATER

The state supports the Royal National Theatre, which has three stages, each of a different size and shape. Each stage has several plays in production concurrently, so there may be up to ten plays in repertory on any one week. Plays range from Greek to contemporary first runs, and there is usually a Shakespeare play on the list.
Note: The Royal Shakespeare Company currently does not have a London venue (see p. 230 for its home in Stratford-upon-Avon).
Royal National Theatre, South Bank Tel 7452 3400, tickets 7452 3000. Three theaters under one roof.

COMMERCIAL THEATERS

The commercial theaters of the West End stage plays and musicals with broad appeal.

OFF-WEST END THEATER

Here is where some of London's most exciting theater can be seen:
Royal Court, St. Martins Lane, Strand, Tel 7565 5000. Known for new writing.
The Old Vic, Waterloo Road, Tel 7928 7616. Recently saved from closure.
Almeida, Almeida Street, Tel 7359 4404. Lures top actors to perform highbrow plays.
Donmar Warehouse, Earlham Street, Tel 7369 1732.
Hampstead Theatre, Swiss Cottage Centre, Tel 7722 9301.
The Gate, 11 Pembridge Road, Tel 7229 0706.
The Kings Head, 115 Upper Street, Tel 7226 1916.
Theatre Royal Stratford East, Tel 8534 0310.
Young Vic, The Cut, Tel 7928 6363.

"THE FRINGE"

The Fringe consists of little theaters scattered across London, the venues often small and basic, many of them in pubs, often promoting young people and new ideas. Try these:
Etcetera Theatre, Oxford Arms Pub, Tel 7482 4857.
The Finborough, Hen & Chickens, 109 St. Paul's Road, Tel 7373 3842.

OTHER THEATER

Shakespeare's Globe (p. 215)
Regent's Park (see p. 135)

THEATER INFORMATION AND TICKETS

Tickets for almost any show can be bought legally. It is extremely unwise to buy from a ticket tout. Ticketmaster (Tel 7344 4444) and First Call (Tel 0870 840 1111) are two good agencies, both with reservation fees. Harrods (direct line 7225 6666) has amazingly good allocations and can supply hot tickets at the last moment, for a hefty fee of 25 percent. Beware: Theaters taking reservations direct by phone may also charge a fee.
Artsline (Tel 7388 2227) gives free advice on London arts for visitors with disabilities.
At the half-price ticket booth, called tks (Leicester Square, WC2, no tel, *www.officallondon theatre.co.uk*), you can save up to 50 percent on seat prices. It is open Monday through Saturday from 10 a.m. to 7 p.m., Sunday noon to 3 p.m., selling tickets for that day's performance only. One person may buy up to four tickets (credit cards accepted; £2.50 service charge per ticket).

DANCE

Sadler's Wells Theatre, Rosebery Avenue, Tel 7863 8000.
The Coliseum, St. Martin's Lane, Tel 7632 8300. Major world dance companies in summer and at Christmas; otherwise, opera.
Royal Opera House, Covent Garden, tel 7304 4000. Home to the Royal Ballet, sharing time with the Royal Opera.
Barbican Centre (see Music venues). Now a major dance venue.
The Place, Dukes Road, Tel 7387 0031.
Bhavan Centre, 4A Castletown Road, Tel 7381 3086. Quality, traditional Indian dance.
The **South Bank** and **Barbican Centre** (see Theater section) are also major dance venues.
Dance Umbrella (Tel 8741 5881) is the late autumn dance festival held throughout London.

MUSIC

CLASSICAL

It is said that there are a thousand concerts given across London each week. The capital has four world-class orchestras,

many small ensembles, and countless venues, from the huge concert halls to small churches and museum rooms. Major venues include:
Royal Festival Hall, Queen Elizabeth Hall, and **Purcell Room** on the South Bank, Tel 7960 4242.
Royal Albert Hall, Kensington Gore, Tel 020-7589 3203 and 020-7589 8912 (reservations). London's circular concert hall and venue for the Proms.
Wigmore Hall, 36 Wigmore Street, Tel 020-7935 2141.
Barbican Centre, Silk Street, EC2, Tel nos.: information 7638 4141, box office 7638 8891

Churches
St. Paul's Cathedral, Westminster Abbey, St. James's Piccadilly, St. John's Smith Square, and St. Martin-in-the-Fields are a handful of the many churches regularly filled with music, often at lunchtime. Summer waterside concerts at Kenwood and Marble Hill can be bliss.

Festivals
Major festivals include the Hampton Court Palace Festival, the City of London Festival, the Henry Wood Promenade Concerts, the Spitalfields Festival, and the Almeida Festival.

CONTEMPORARY
Big stars play major venues such as:
Wembley Arena, Tel 8902 8833.
London Arena, 36 Limeharbour, Tel 7538 1212.
Earl's Court Exhibition Centre, Tel 7373 8141.
Brixton Academy, 211 Stockwell Road, Tel 7771 2000. The lesser, or newer, ones play here.
Astoria, 157 Charing Cross Road, Tel 7434 0404.
Hackney Empire, 291 Mare Street, Tel 8985 2424.

OPERA
The Coliseum (see Dance). English National Opera performs

in English for seasons alternating with dance.
Royal Opera House (see Dance). The controversially renovated theater is home to the Royal Opera and the Royal Ballet.
Sadler's Wells (see Dance) and **Holland Park Theatre** (tel 7602 7856) also host opera.

JAZZ
Find some of the best jazz in town at:
Ronnie Scott's, 47 Frith Street, Tel 7439 0747. Run by jazz musicians for jazz lovers.
PizzaExpress, 10 Dean Street, Tel 7439 8722. Quality pizzas and great mainsteam jazz.
Bull's Head, 373 Lonsdale Road, Barnes, Tel 8876 5241. Good jazz in a friendly riverside pub.
Dover Street Wine Bar, 8–9 Dover Street, Tel 7629 9813. Popular basement bar.
Jazz Café, 5 Parkway, Tel 7916 6060. Favorite among the young.

Jazz Festivals
The Soho Jazz Festival and **Oris** London Jazz Festival both take place in the autumn.

MUSIC & DANCE WITH FOOD
London is less good at upscale restaurants with dancing—the **Savoy's River Room** (see p. 242) is an exception—than it is at more modest places with more funky music. Pubs and bars with good music include:
Bull & Gate, 389 Kentish Town Road, Tel 7485 5358.
Dublin Castle, 94 Parkway, Tel 7485 1773.

NIGHTCLUBS

Annabel's, 44 Hays Mews, Tel 7629 1096. Upscale and thoroughly international.

London's many large, friendly clubs with DJs, dancing, and showcase bands are always lots of fun:
Borderline, Orange Yard, off Manette Street, Tel 7734 2095.
Dingwalls, 35 Camden Lock Place, Tel 7267 1577.

100 Club, 100 Oxford Street, Tel 7636 0933.
Spitz, 109 Commercial Street, Tel 7392 9032.

Any Saturday night there may be a myriad of clubs throbbing the night away. Many clubs operate one night a week and have complicated dress codes. *Time Out* will steer you through.

CINEMA
London's cinema is not as good as some other European cities such as Paris. That said, there is a good mix of Hollywood, independent, European (subtitled, not dubbed), and oldies.

Large-screen theaters
The best places to see commercial first runs include:
Empire, Leicester Square, Tel 7734 7123. Tickets: 0870 010 2030.
Warner Village West End, West End, Tel 7437 3484. Tickets: 7437 4343.
Odeon West End, Leicester Square, Tel 0870 505 0007.

Other theaters
National Film Theatre, South Bank, Tel 7928 3232. Independent theater with two cinemas showing a mixed program.
Everyman, Hampstead, Tel 7435 1777. Shows fine films, old and new in repertory.
BFI London IMAX Cinema, 1 Charlie Chaplin Walk, South Bank, SE1, Tel 7902 1234.
Museum films. Some museums, such as the Imperial War Museum, the National Gallery, the Tate Britain and Tate Modern, and the V&A, include film in their programs.

COMEDY

The Comedy Store, 1 Oxendon Street, Tel 7344 0234. Great test for a budding comic, with a fierce, unforgiving audience.
Comedy Café, 66 Rivington Street, Tel 7739 5706.

ILLUSTRATIONS CREDITS

One of the world's largest non-profit scientific and educational organizations, the National Geographic Society was founded in 1888 "for the increase and diffusion of geographic knowledge." Fulfilling this mission, the Society educates and inspires millions every day through its magazines, books, television programs, videos, maps and atlases, research grants, the National Geographic Bee, teacher workshops, and innovative classroom materials. The Society is supported through membership dues, charitable gifts, and income from the sale of its educational products. This support is vital to National Geographic's mission to increase global understanding and promote conservation of our planet through exploration, research, and education.

For more information, please call 1-800-NGS LINE (647-5463) or write to the following address:

National Geographic Society
1145 17th Street N.W.
Washington, D.C. 20036-4688
U.S.A.

Visit the Society's Web site at
www.nationalgeographic.com.

Published by the National Geographic Society
John M. Fahey, Jr., *President and Chief Executive Officer*
Gilbert M. Grosvenor, *Chairman of the Board*
Nina D. Hoffman, *Executive Vice President,*
    President, Books and School Publishing
Kevin Mulroy, *Vice President and Editor-in-Chief*
Marianne Koszorus, *Design Director*
Charles Kogod, *Director of Photography*
Elizabeth L. Newhouse, *Director of Travel Publishing*
Barbara A. Noe, *Senior Editor and Series Editor*
Cinda Rose, *Art Director*
Carl Mehler, *Director of Maps*
Joseph F. Ochlak, *Map Coordinator*
R. Gary Colbert, *Production Director*
Richard S. Wain, *Production Project Manager*
Sharon Berry, Lawrence Porges, Kay Kobor Hankins, Judith Klein,
    Contributors

Edited and designed by AA Publishing (a trading name of Automobile Association Developments Limited, whose registered office is Norfolk House, Priestley Road, Basingstoke, Hampshire, England RG24 9NY. Registered number: 1878835).

Betty Sheldrick, *Project Manager*
David Austin, *Senior Art Editor*
Josephine Perry, *Editor*
Bob Johnson, *Designer*
Simon Mumford, *Senior Cartographic Editor*
Nicky Barker-Dix, Helen Beever, *Cartographers*
Richard Firth, *Production Director*
Picture Research by Kathy Lockley
Area maps drawn by Chris Orr Associates, Southampton, England
Cutaway illustrations drawn by Maltings Partnership, Derby, England

Reprinted with updates 2001, 2004.

Library of Congress Cataloging-in-Publication Data
The National Geographic traveler. London.
        p.   cm.
        Includes index.
        ISBN 0-7922-7428-8 (alk. paper)
        1. London (England)—Guidebooks.   I. National Geographic Society
    (U.S.) II. Title: London
    DA679.N28   1999
    914.2104'859—dc21   99-12613
                                                              CIP

Printed and bound by Mondadori Printing, Verona, Italy.
Color separations by Leo Reprographic Ltd., Hong Kong
Cover separations by L.C. Repro, Aldermaston, U.K.

Visit the society's Web site at http:/www.nationalgeographic.com

NATIONAL GEOGRAPHIC
TRAVELER

A Century of Travel Expertise in Every Guide

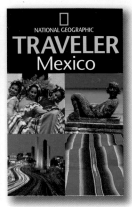

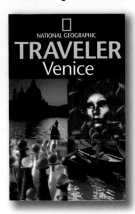

AVAILABLE WHEREVER BOOKS ARE SOLD